Women and the bush

for my mother

Women and the bush

FORCES OF DESIRE IN THE AUSTRALIAN CULTURAL TRADITION

Kay Schaffer

South Australian College of Advanced Education

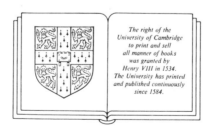

The right of the
University of Cambridge
to print and sell
all manner of books
was granted by
Henry VIII in 1534.
The University has printed
and published continuously
since 1584.

CAMBRIDGE UNIVERSITY PRESS

Cambridge

New York   New Rochelle   Melbourne   Sydney

Promotion of this title has been assisted by the South Australian Government through the Department for the Arts

Published by the Press Syndicate of the University of Cambridge

The Pitt Building, Trumpington Street, Cambridge CB2 1RP, England
32 East 57th Street, New York, NY 10022, USA
10 Stamford Road, Oakleigh, Melbourne 3166, Australia

Printed in Australia by Southwood Press

National Library of Australia cataloguing in publication data
Schaffer, Kay, 1945-
    Women and the bush: forces of desire in the Australian cultural tradition.

    Bibliography.
    Includes index.
    1. Australian literature — History and criticism. 2. Women in literature. 3. Women and
    literature — Australia. 4. National characteristics, Australian. 5. Australia — Civilization.
    6. Frontier and pioneer life in literature. 7. Frontier and pioneer life — Australia. 8. Sex role
    in literature. 9. Sex role — Australia. I. Title.

A820'.9

British Library cataloguing in publication data
Schaffer, Kay
    Women and the bush: forces of desire in the Australian cultural tradition. 1. Australia. Sex
    roles. Cultural aspects, 1788-1988
    I. Title
    305.3'0994

Library of Congress cataloguing in publication data
Schaffer, Kay, 1945-
    Women and the bush: forces of desire in the Australian cultural tradition/Kay Schaffer.
        p.   cm.
    Bibliography: p.
    ISBN 0-521-36244-X. ISBN 0-521-36816-2 (pbk.)
    1. Australian literature—History and criticism. 2. Women in literature. 3. Women and
    literature—Australia. 4. National characteristics, Australian. 5. Australia—Civilization.
    6. Frontier and pioneer life in literature. 7. Frontier and pioneer life—Australia. 8. Sex role
    in literature. 9. Sex role—Australia. 10. Arts, Australian. I. Title.
    PR9605.6.W6S34 1989
    820'.9—dc19

ISBN 0 521 36244 X (hard cover)
ISBN 0 521 36816 2 (paperback)

CONTENTS

CONTENTS

ACKNOWLEDGEMENTS

For reading and offering advice on various aspects of the manuscript I would like to thank Phil Barker, Lenore Coltheart, Bob Iseman, Trish Kelly, Bronwen Levy, Helen Menzies, Meaghan Morris and Judith Stitzel. I am grateful to Suzanne Callinan, Janet Gloria, Miriel Lenore and Sandy Taylor for sharing stories which I have incorporated into the book. I am also indebted to my students and Women's Studies colleagues for their encouragement. Their questions about my work and enthusiastic responses helped me to sound out the connections between post-structuralist perspectives, cultural theory and feminist practice and to write in an accessible fashion.

My thanks to Jyanni Steffensen for providing quick and efficient research assistance; to Jill Golden, Miriel Lenore and Wendy Seymour for proofreading; and to Gail Patrick and Zebbie Johnstone for typing various parts of the manuscript; to Janet Mackenzie for copy editing it; and to Carole Bowser-Nott for help with the index.

Finally, for offering widsom, love and support through my times of elation and depression, fatigue and exhilaration, confidence and self-doubts I deeply thank my fond friends Margaret Allen, Myra Betschild, Jill Golden and my family Bob, Laura and Juliet.

Some of the material in this book has been published in earlier versions. Portions of Chapter 4 appeared in the *Australian Journal of Cultural Studies* 4, 2 (May 1987). Portions of Chapter 6 appeared in *Australian Literary Studies* 11, 1 (May 1983) under my previous name as Kay Iseman.

INTRODUCTION

What does it mean to be an Australian? How has the idea of Australia functioned as a force of desire for white Western explorers, settlers and adventurers from European discovery to the present? How has Australian culture, and more specifically cultural attitudes concerning women, been shaped by the dominant myths of the bush, mateship, and man's relation to the land—all of which contribute to Australia's and the world's sense of an Australian national identity?

This study provides a new approach to these questions. It explores cultural myths of masculine identity to determine not so much what they say about men and women but how they construct ideas about masculinity and femininity and how these ideas circulate in Australian culture. The approach is interdisciplinary. The questions are posed with reference to a diverse body of materials which can be said to contribute to an understanding of the Australian cultural tradition. They include: the narratives of early exploration and settlement; the nationalistic literature of the 1890s and its critical reception; major twentieth-century historical studies of Australia; modes of landscape representation in Australian writing, film and popular culture; contemporary cultural studies of national identity, including feminist approaches; recent Australian films, including *Picnic at Hanging Rock* and *Crocodile Dundee*; and the continued vitality of myths about Australian identity as evidenced in current newspaper articles and television news reports, popular programs and advertisements, as well as attitudes about Australia and Australians which are asserted in everday life.

The questions have particular relevance today for a variety of reasons. In the first place, Australia celebrates its bicentennial in 1988. The theme of the event is 'to find a national identity'. Many books, television programs, historical recreations, articles and reports are being generated which attempt to define a national culture. There is also widespread opposition to the bicentennial and its jingoistic features by many members of the Australian population. Many women, migrants and especially Aborigines—whose history is not and cannot be represented in the national event—resist the celebration which does not speak for them. Much national as well as international interest in 'things Australian' is currently in evidence. This book acknowledges the importance of the historical endeavour while at the same time it offers a critique of the project from positions of difference within the culture. It provides an overview and insight into the dominant modes of cultural representation for readers interested in Australian culture. At the same time, it provides access to evolving modes of analysis which attend questions of difference within an Australian cultural context.

Secondly, Australia has a local and an international reputation for being both an effective socialist democracy and a deeply misogynistic society. Feminist historians have attempted to find explanations for this. Political activists continue their attempts to rectify the relatively low social, political, and economic status held by women in Australia. No prior study has attempted to link the personal and social manifestations of women's position within Australian culture to language. Yet constructions of sexuality and gender-based identity are embedded in the discourses which inform an Australian cultural tradition. Women have been considered to be absent in the bush and the nationalistic bush tradition. Yet they are constantly represented through the metaphors of landscape. Women carry the burden of metaphor. The book registers possible social and political significance of woman-as-sign within the discourses on national identity. It offers a new point of departure for feminist cultural analysis.

Thirdly, the dominant discourses on cultural identity tend to mask a recognition of difference, of cultural plurality, not only for women but also for other marginalized groups within the culture. They disguise the existence of open and endless possibilities for meaning, subjectivity and cultural representation. This study attempts to speak differently. It offers a critique of cultural representations and patriarchal practices which might contribute towards a pluralist cultural discourse evolving from multiple positions of difference. In this sense, the text forms a part of a new debate which includes but is not encompassed by feminist challenges to notions of cultural identity.

The book takes up these ideas and examines the continuity and transformations of cultural beliefs and practices. It explores how cultural practices arise out of assumptions about the national character; how the discourses on national identity construct specifically Australian concepts of masculinity and femininity and how these constructions continue to influence contemporary values, attitudes and beliefs. The study concludes with some speculations about the possibilities of going beyond the representations of women, men and the land in the Australian tradition.

OVERVIEW OF THE STUDY

In Chapter One, 'Culture, Language and the Self', I locate myself and this study within Australia in a bicentennial decade. The chapter questions assumptions which underlie the concept of national identity and assumptions about women's place in cultural, social and political life. It suggests that people in Australia come to understand themselves, and others outside of Australia come to identify Australians, by the myths of national identity which circulate both within and beyond the culture. The chapter focuses not on the content of the myths but on how they are structured, received and made meaningful through their frequent representations. It introduces a number of current perspectives from feminist theory and cultural theory which suggest that who and what we think we are occurs at the intersection between the self, social institutions and language. Language as discourse, or the cultural production of meaning, is the main object of investigation in this study. The myths which inform the Australian tradition will be analysed as sign systems, or linguistic structures, which embody codes of meaning existing in a field of other meanings which have value within the culture. These sign systems are read and understood by readers who become inscribed as 'Australians' or not-Australians within them. The way the myths operate to construct ideas about Australian identity influences the tone and character of subjectivity and social life.

Chapter Two, 'In Search of a National Identity', begins with an investigation of the Australian tradition as discourse, examining its evolving structure and its codes of meaning through the major and most popular texts of the twentieth century. It examines the search for national identity by attending to the importance of Henry Lawson and the literature of the 1890s in the search for national origins. Lawson becomes the cultural embodiment of the nationalist codes, at least for modern readers. The chapter follows the search for origins through mainstream nationalist, modernist and New Left histories. It explores instances of the many ways Australian commentators have attempted to locate an indigenous culture before Lawson and have continued to reproduce the code with reference to Lawson, Lawson surrogates and the bush legend. Henry Lawson is a central figure in the study. His name and its representations have assumed the position as founder and origin of the Australian tradition. It is not Lawson nor his stories which ground the tradition but rather the stories about Lawson and how they have functioned in the evolution of a discourse on national identity which crystallize the idea of a nation for later readers and critics. The focus here will be the reception and interpretation of ideas about Lawson. The study will also examine the transformation of the idea of Lawson-as-a-cultural-object in the twentieth century in relation to changing social, political and institutional contexts.

Chapter Three, 'The Bush and Women', begins with a discussion of the centrality of the bush as the terrain on which national identity is constructed.

It examines the ways in which the bush becomes the place of the feminine (as a category of meaning) through metaphoric representation with reference to a variety of cultural materials. It includes a discussion of the bush as represented in nineteenth-century travel guides, historical narratives of exploration and newspaper reports of people lost in the bush. It also considers imaginary constructions of landscape embedded in the 1970s film *Picnic at Hanging Rock* and apparent in the media treatment of Lindy Chamberlain after the disappearance of her baby, Azaria, at Ayers Rock. It then discusses how the relationship of man to the bush is established through the displacement of women. Having located 'woman' in the landscape as an object of representation, it then takes up instances where women are the subjects of representation: feminist perspectives on women in Australia. The chapter concludes with a brief account of recent feminist research which is related to the interests of this study as well as current developments in feminist historiography and the recognition of new critical perspectives within the fields of semiotics, feminism and Australian cultural studies.

Chapter Four, 'Landscape Representation and National Identity', traces the forces of desire evident in man's battle with the land from the colonial discovery of Australia to the present. It provides a semiotic analysis of myths of identity and difference which are framed by man's relationship to the land as an object to be mastered and controlled. With specific reference to narratives of exploration and discovery, settlement tracts and emigration guides, as well as cultural commentaries on Australia, it follows the transformations in colonial and nationalist ideologies and the place of women-as-sign within them. The chapter includes a comparative analysis of divergent approaches to the gold rush of the 1850s in relation to the formation of masculinity/femininity and national identity. It explores the many representations of the land as "other" (the feminine within masculine culture) and discusses marginality with reference to race, class and gender constructions. Finally, it explores dominant cultural norms and dissident perspectives through a comparison of the ways in which texts by male and female writers have represented man's battle with the land.

Chapters Five and Six consider two major writers of significance from the nationalistic decade of the 1890s, Henry Lawson and Barbara Baynton — the honorary father of the Australian tradition and one of its most strident dissidents. The chapters treat the dominant writings of the two authors, their critical reception over time, the studies of personality which attend the writers' places within the Australian tradition, and the ways in which critical commentary has continued to reproduce masculine and feminine divisions. The writers and their reception provide two case studies which extend the earlier arguments as to how culture comes to be represented through the various interlocking discourses. The chapter on Lawson contains a close reading and discussion of the importance of his classic short story 'The Drover's Wife' in locating the place of woman in the bush. The chapter on Baynton concludes with a deconstructive reading of her story 'The Chosen Vessel' to demonstrate how the identity of woman is effaced through masculine cultural appropriation of the family, the church, the law, mateship and the bush tradition.

Chapter Seven considers the ways in which cultural codes continue to affect cultural life in the 1980s. It examines current media representations of the bush, women and national identity in the light of earlier discussions. The text comes to a close (or perhaps a new opening) with an imagined dialogue between the author and Luce Irigaray concerning *Crocodile Dundee*, myths of national identity, women's place within them, and the possibilities for imagining feminine difference beyond the constraints of masculine representation.

A veil hung over Central Australia that could neither be pierced
or raised. Girt round by deserts, it almost appeared as if
Nature had intentionally closed itself upon civilized man, that
she might have one domain on earth's wide field over which the
savage might roam in freedom.

Charles Sturt, *Narrative of an Exploration into Central Australia*
(London, 1849), vol. 2, p. 2.

CHAPTER 1

CULTURE, LANGUAGE AND THE SELF

Australia is a country of contradictions. The earliest historical records attest that this has been so since the first narratives of exploration reached the eyes and ears of an eager European audience. At least two opposing views prevailed. One held that this phantom continent, known only as *Terra Australis Incognita*, was a land of teeming richness abounding with 'Gold, Silver, Pearls, Nutmegs, Mace, Ginger, and Sugar-canes of an extraordinary Size'. Another described the place as an arid, fly-blown, barren land, unlikely to sustain or nourish human habitation. The first view, reported by de Quirós for the Spanish early in the sixteenth century, referred in fact to an island in the New Hebrides, mistakenly thought to be the southern continent which he called *Austrialia del Espiritu Santo*. The second and more familiar description was penned by Dampier for the Dutch in his report of his 1688 explorations, *New Voyage around the World*, which described the north-west coast of the continent in depressingly flat tones. The early writings and the varied experiences of European explorers and settlers in the antipodes gave rise to a Western European conception (which survives today) of Australia as a land of fantastic hopes and harsh realities; a land of ancient secrets and modern discoveries; a land of crude, closed settlements and complex, expanding freedoms. But more than this, the idea of Australia has a long history as a land of desire, traversed in the imaginations of explorers, settlers and visitors alike. The idea of the land as a place of desire against which Australians, at least white, male, European Australians, measure their identity is one of the themes I will trace in this book.

TO FIND A NATIONAL IDENTITY

In 1988 as Australians celebrate 200 years of white European settlement the country is more conscious than ever of the contradictory images and myths which have emerged to define the land. There is, as well, a common awareness of another strange historical juxtaposition—that the youngest Western industrial democracy sits on the remains of what may be the most ancient of all human cultures. The knowledge and significance of what

1

anthropologists call Aboriginal prehistory jostle uncomfortably with the historical demands and desires of contemporary white inhabitants. At a time when the Bicentennial Authority has contributed handsomely to historical research, events and activities to commemorate the Australian Bicentennial, Aborigines still battle in a grossly unequal struggle for land rights. In addition, significant archaeological work which challenges the whole conception of the history and evolution of the human race lies dormant for lack of funding. Recent discoveries include the oldest known examples of completely modern men and women, who lived some 35 000 to 40 000 years ago, as well as evidence of what may be the oldest surviving cave paintings and burial rites. These discoveries demand a thorough revision of what was previously known about human evolution on earth. Textual evidence for what is already known may not emerge for another fifty years, however, while a spate of books will surface to fill in the gaps and spaces of a narrow band of history known as white Australian culture. Clearly, in a bicentennial decade, the more dominant historical interests take precedence over and remain separated from the Australian Aboriginal concerns as well as Anglo academic desires to investigate the origins and evolution of the human race. Critics of culture, witnessing these consolidations of the dominant culture, have begun to ask: who decides what the dominant images of Australia are, whose interests are served by the various representations and how do these meanings function in everyday life?

The impulse to record and know the nation's history, whether it be directed toward Aboriginal prehistory or to the European presence, must be acknowledged as a white, Western and predominantly male activity. The desire to detail and document historical origins, to determine stages of progress and name the features of human development are the preoccupations of a Western historical consciousness. The detailing of evolutionary firsts will hardly excite the imagination of an Aboriginal population. Aborigines may welcome and utilize the knowledge that their ancestors date back far into the past as some small element in their struggle to claim land rights. Nonetheless, anthropological diggings and displacement of ancient burial remains violate the spiritual affinity of the self to the earth and sever the connections between the ancestral spirit life of the people. Western studies of Aboriginal culture, whether for anthropological or historical purposes, are seen now as an intellectual appropriation of black tribal culture and traditions. The anthropological search for origins, the historical sense of human evolution, of white settlement and of Australian history all emerge through Western modes of knowledge and forms of representation.

Nonetheless, questions of who and what Australians think they are absorb

2

the national interest and attract world-wide attention. The Bicentenary encourages an international impulse to know and celebrate the historical past. In 1980, when the Australian Bicentennial Authority was established, its first director announced that in his view the aim of the celebration was 'to find a national identity'. Even in these words we are confronted with paradox: to find, rather than to celebrate, a national identity. The phrase suggests two things at once. On the one hand, the words signal to a desire to come to some understanding of what it means to be an Australian, to posit an identity. On the other hand, the phrase suggests that this is a time to attend to the process of discovery, to live with questions about an unsettled entity in process. The bicentennial celebrations come at a time of epistemological crisis, a time when a growing number of historians and cultural commentators acknowledge that all perspectives are partial. It is a time to begin to explore the ways in which modes of representation, once thought to be objective and factual, are actually tied to assumptions about race and class, ethnicity and gender.

Some of the questions I want to address in regard to the Australian tradition in a bicentennial decade are: How has the imaginative place which has come to be called Australia functioned as a site of desire for those who arrived on her shores from other lands, other places? By what textual processes has the landscape taken form, definition and texture, giving the continent a Western structure, shape and meaning? What dominant and muted images of the Australian character have emerged? Whose interests do they serve? How do these dominant images affect everyday life, consciousness and culture in Australia today? How has an Australian tradition been formulated and why is it so resolutely blind to women? And, finally, what does it mean 'to find a national identity'?

I do not expect to find, nor am I looking for, the answer to these queries. There is a plethora of possible responses and perspectives. My intention is not to rewrite history, but to follow the traces of ideas and representations which appear in the guise of history. I want to register the various ways in which the history of Australia, its land and its people, have been constructed—to play with the ideas, discover the codes of meaning through which we understand the histories and begin to question them. Further, I want to analyse the constant calls for 'national identity' and their relationship to the masculinization of a national culture.

A few weeks ago my mother wrote to say that she was pleased to know that I was working on a book for publication. Then she asked: 'Will ordinary people be able to read it, or will it be like your thesis?' I hope the answer to her query is 'yes . . . and yes'. The study grows out of work for a doctoral thesis which I completed in 1983. At that time few people within Australia were working as I was within cultural studies at the intersection between feminism, post-structuralism and semiotics. The theoretical positions were reputed to be unnecessarily complex and exceedingly dense. Since that time, however, a growing number of commentators have taken up one or several of these perspectives and demonstrated the rewards and pleasures to be gained from reading culture differently. This investigation partakes of that more general critical impulse.

It begins with and foregrounds questions of national identity, questions which have occurred to me and occupied my attention since my arrival as an outsider. It virtually goes without saying that national identity and the Australian character are masculine constructions. But this is not to say that women, or ideas about the feminine aspects of culture, are absent. The myth of the typical Australian exudes a style of masculinity which excludes but also defines the Australian woman who stands in relation to him. In addition, the relationship of man to the land, central to the legend of the 1890s, for example, pits the native son against the bush. The bush is typically imagined as a *feminine* landscape—one that is imagined as particularly harsh and unforgiving. 'Woman' carries the burden of this metaphor. Ideas about masculinity and femininity circulate in the culture and contribute to its specificity as 'Australian'. I hope that this study will extend awareness of the processes through which national identity is produced and reproduced. It may, in addition, broaden the analysis of the connections between ideas about masculinity and femininity as they are represented in language, and how these assumptions about gender affect the attitudes and beliefs of actual men and women in society.

THE AUSTRALIAN TRADITION

There is now a fairly well-established set of ideas about national identity, a code of meanings which are recognized as 'typically Australian'. After 200 years on the track, a few writers and critics occasionally have the nerve to refer to it as an Australian Tradition. There is also a lot of resistance to this development, perhaps because in a post-modernist world we know that meanings are suspect. The Australian tradition is a kind of ghost tradition . . . one that is easily recognized, sometimes seriously and with a sense of pride, but more often with a gamut of emotions which run from amusement, to embarrassment, to hostile rejection. Still, a nationalist code exists, echoed in the catch-cry phrases of mateship and the bush and egalitarian democracy, even if the evidence is slim, even if it does not speak for 'us'. The representations of nationalist tradition in Australia are tangible entities, even if they are, as Richard White has suggested, inventions artificially imposed on

4

a diverse landscape and its people.[1] Traces which inform the tradition can be found in the narratives of early explorers and settlers, in the texts of historians, fiction writers, cultural critics and commentators on the critics. The outlines are visible in the speeches of civic leaders and politicians, embedded in the celluloid of the Australian film industry and in the pages of the press. They are crudely transparent in the most successful of television commercials and visible in the reactions of local audiences. The representations of national identity may be constructions which disguise more dimensions of cultural life than they bring to light, but they are constantly reproduced. And at least some of us, both within and outside Australia, have begun to take them seriously.

WOMEN IN THE NATIONAL TRADITION

Taking seriously representations of national identity can be a very difficult enterprise. This is especially true if one is a woman. When I first came to Australia in 1974 from the United States, I came to an imagined place, a site of desire. The country had a reputation, yes—for sports, open spaces, heat, drought, male chauvinism and misogyny. It also had a new gloss during the heady days of the Whitlam era as the last place in the Western world where it might be possible to establish an effective Western socialist democracy. It was the test of socialism which pulled me toward the shores of Sydney. Upon arrival I set about trying to come to terms with this new environment. I talked with new friends and acquaintances, absorbing attitudes and beliefs with my daily dose of sunshine. I sat in on a course in Australian literature, surprised to find it less popular and less well regarded than the English or even American literature courses on offer at the local College of Advanced Education. And I began scouring the shelves of the library for texts on Australian history, literature, politics, sociology and the like. I was interested to find out how white Australians, both men and women, defined themselves and their culture. There were not as many texts as I had expected. I devoured them all within a month, keeping an annotated bibliography on a stack of guide cards. A number of new sociological studies on Australian culture emerged at the time. It surprised me to find how many of them addressed the culture negatively in hostile, defensive or self-mocking tones. I found it curious that few made mention of women. The only text I came across which specifically addressed the question of women was Norman MacKenzie's pioneering study *Women in Australia* (1962). MacKenzie makes the comment in the Introduction that 'Australia is more a "man's country" than other industrial democracies'.[2] His argument was borne out by a host of other social critics at the time. Discussions about the notion of a national character may have differed, but they all agreed that (whatever else it might or might not be) it was decidedly, if somewhat defensively, masculine.

That was over ten years ago. The Whitlam era put many Australians in touch with the knowledge of partial perspectives and fired them with a desire to be more inclusive in their definitions of Australia and Australians— women, migrants, workers, Aborigines and other deviants from the white, male, Western European and largely middle-class norm were permitted entrance on the great stage of history. In the last decade more serious attention has been paid to questions of Australian identity and to the marginal status and position of those 'others' listed above. Despite this, one gets the feeling that not much has changed. There is a dominant tradition, which remains strong. One possible difference is that it now occasionally knows and acknowledges its boundaries which are marked by texts which address the tradition from perspectives of dissidence. But the radical texts have not yet altered nor eclipsed the tradition.

In the 1980s it was still possible for G. A. Wilkes, Professor of English Literature at the University of Sydney, to have written a book studying the 'literary evidence for Australia's cultural development', which includes a chapter on 'alternative traditions' beyond the narrowly defined stereotypes of republican nationalism, and not mention women in or outside the tradition, nor allude to the fact of this omission, nor cite even one text which studies women in literature, or women in history, or treats Australian culture from a feminist perspective.[3] His text has a familiar blind spot, which is the place of woman and sexual difference and the relevance this absence has in the posing of questions of literary or cultural traditions. It is not my intention to contest Wilkes' perspective. He attempts to challenge and move beyond an Australian tradition founded on 'the antithesis of the genteel and the robust, the refined and the crude, the old world and the new, and the contest between them for mastery'.[4] It is a challenge with which on another level I engage as well. His text, however, attempts to posit a new truth. Mine assumes the impossibility of such a project.

In 1986 it was still possible for Marian Aveling, feminist historian, to present a paper to the Australian Historical Association conference entitled 'Taking Women's History out of the Ghetto', in which she called attention to the extensive work in the area of women's history and feminist history which has had 'very little impact on the writing of a general Australian history'.[5] The same could be said of the apparent impact of feminist research in other fields, including philosophy, literary studies, politics, psychology, sociology, art history and the like.

When I shifted my attention from texts on Australian culture to empirical data on the social, political, economic and cultural position of women in Australia I confronted a similar dilemma. In 1975, the beginning of the United Nations' International Decade of Women, preliminary research detailed women's diminished social and economic status. Historians, sociologists, political scientists, economists, literary historians and cultural commentators had acknowledged the masculine bias in Australian culture as one causal factor.[6] Countless conferences and research projects produced reports and recommendations about women's health, economic position, political rights, educational standards, as well as problems related to racial, class and ethnic differences between women. Anti-discrimination laws and affirmative action legislation have been introduced. Still, despite the changes in laws, attitudes, rights and opportunities—all of which have broadened the horizons for women—masculine bias has maintained its stranglehold. I found this strange in a 'fair go' country which supports other radical social legislation designed to improve the situation of those less advantaged.

Since International Women's Year a great deal of feminist research has emerged. Empirical measures and diverse political theories have been used to define, explain and interpret women's inferior social and economic status. Feminist writers have explored the marginalization of women's lives and experiences in Australian cultural studies and the muting of women's voices and writings within the national tradition. Feminist texts have examined women's position from a variety of perspectives, including Marxist, socialist and psychoanalytic theories and methods of analysis. In addition, a great deal of feminist historical research has occurred which brings the lives and experiences of Australian women to light and makes possible the reconstruction of the writing of Australian history, politics, art history, literary and cultural studies. Unlike the situation in Canada, the United States and Great Britain, this valuable and challenging work has had little noticeable impact on the general outlines of mainstream writing in Australia.

Miriam Dixson introduced the discussion of the position of women in Australian culture in her 1975 study, *The Real Matilda*. She wrote of 'a profound unconscious contempt for women that pervades the Australian ethos.'[7] She traced this cultural contempt for women through historical studies, which exclude any consideration of women; in a literary tradition, which produces no love stories or poems, but, rather, a profound sense of sexual loneliness and an awkwardness or fear about the flesh of women; in social life, where women have little power or status, low self-esteem, and virtually no representation in the unions, professional life or politics. Dixson concluded that the Australian woman's only acceptable domain is that of the family—one from which men are curiously absent.[8] Anne Summers, in

Damned Whores and God's Police, analysed woman's position in Australian society as a colonized sex.[9] The androcentric bias which appears to be rigidly resistant to women and the widespread denial of value to that which is designated 'feminine' in Australian culture has led Delys Bird recently to conclude that the whole idea 'Australian woman', as a cultural construct, is 'a national joke'.[10]

The masculine bias which we encounter in the texts on Australia and see reproduced in films and the media and hear on the television and in the criticisms of overseas visitors about Australian attitudes to masculinity and femininity, bears little resemblance to the diverse and rich experiences of strong and colourful women encountered daily in interaction with friends, neighbours, workmates and students. There is a sense of a country struggling with contradictory impulses: a desire to accept and deny the diverse nature of Australian culture; to ignore and uphold its masculine bias; to come to terms with and reinvent a national identity.

The fact that nothing could satisfy my curiosity as to why attitudes toward women were so slow to change led me to this study and the desire to approach questions of national identity from another perspective. I decided to re-read the mainstream literature which takes 'Australia' as its theme, looking again at the processes of its production and attending to its masculine bias.

CULTURE, LANGUAGE AND THE SELF

National identity is a cultural construction. What we think we know about men and women, or the Australian character and the woman who stands in relation to him, comes to us through codes of meaning embedded in language and other forms of representation. Codes of meaning are ideas which operate together within a particular culture. There is an agreement that certain meanings go together—like man, mateship and the bush as aspects of an Australian nationalist tradition in literature and history, or 'football, meatpies, kangaroos and Holden cars' as icons for Australia within popular culture. These meanings are reproduced together so often that they become taken for granted. The notion of national identity projects a set of ideas which coalesce into an ideal self—the 'real' Australian. The 'real' Australian is a national type. He does not exist. Nonetheless, the idea of his existence is given status and value within culture. According to Australian cultural codes which have become common-sense knowledge, if he did exist he would come from and preferably live in the bush, of poor but honest Anglo-Irish stock. He would be unpretentious, shy of women, a good mate and a battler. He is what advertisers seem to believe all of 'us' who live in Australia want to be and the way we define ourselves and 'Australia' to the rest of the world. The

Australian character and the attributes which are ascribed to him exist within a symbolic system of cultural meanings which are both Western and specifically Australian. As a type he represents the self and the nation in a way which is imaginary. Yet, his existence is made to seem real through its representation in films, advertisements, political speeches, news reports, historical reconstructions and the like. The imaginary construction which is taken to be real is given social meaning through the symbolic order of language.

The terms real, imaginary and symbolic (used as nouns) may be unfamiliar to some readers. Since they are terms which I will refer in this study, a brief explanation is necessary. They are derived from the work of Jacques Lacan, a French psychoanalyst whose investigations into the interrelationship between the self, subjectivity and language have been employed in various ways by feminists, semioticians and post-modernist writers. These writers would agree on a few propositions which defy 'common-sense' notions concerning the nature of reality, consciousness, culture and the self. Put simply, the concepts offer new ways of investigating who and what we are as individuals with sexed identities living within specific cultures. They insist that identity is not immanent in oneself, one's consciousness or personality but is constituted through language and the social order. Initially, the concepts may seem difficult but they should become clearer and their relevance more obvious as I apply them to aspects of Australian cultural identity and the place of woman within it as this study proceeds.

Within a Lacanian schema, there is no real world. The Real does not exist. It is what might be if existence were not mediated by language. It is what lies beyond language and cannot be grasped within it. The Imaginary refers to two phases in the formation of the self within culture. It refers to a state of being which is imagined as real but actually arises through fantasies, memories, illusory images of the self and the like. The first phase is connected with early infancy before the child enters language when it imagines itself as an undifferentiated being with no sense of separation or boundaries between itself, its mother and the world. The second imaginary phase is connected with the child's sense of itself as autonomous from the mother as a distinct social being. The Symbolic is the order of language and network of meanings through which the social self and social values are constructed, communicated and maintained.

The child's entrance into culture and the symbolic order occurs in what Lacan calls the mirror phase.[11] At this time, between six and eighteen months of age, the child sees a reflection of itself in the mirror and attaches its sense of identity to the image. The image is not the self but a social or external reflection of the self. This image, nonetheless, is associated with the 'I' which begins to take on social meaning. Further, the image is reflected back to the child and mediated though the gaze of the mother. The Imaginary (or fantasies, memories, images of the self arising out of illusion but thought to be real) coexists with and is given meaning within the symbolic order of language. Language paradoxically divides the child from itself while it places the child in a symbolic order which promises us the illusion of coherent identity. What the child recognizes as the 'I' or self or ego in the mirror or in the mirror of another's eyes is an illusion of a unfied body, a unified ego. It sees an other (the image in the mirror) as the self. The image is perceived and understood as both different from 'me' and the same as 'me'. The mirror image is reflection of difference imagined as the same. The self is already at one remove from the image. The child paradoxically recognizes itself as what it is not but what it also wishes to be.

At the same time the child takes on a cultural identity as a male or female and a proper name, a patronym—what Lacan calls the name of the Father. This places the child at a second remove from the self. It also places the child in a network of social and symbolic meanings through which sexual differences and subjectivity are organized. The pre-linguistic imaginary unity with the mother must be repressed. It is replaced by an identity formed through language which takes the masculine as the norm for the self. In a phallocentric culture the masculine is valued, the feminine exists in an inferior relation to the masculine. The ideal self to which the subject (whether male or female) in culture attaches desire is an impossible masculine subject. As soon as the child speaks it assumes a subjective place in language as either male or not-male.

This means that you and I are constituted through a linguistic system of meanings. We are not the makers of that meaning. Within language, women exist in the category 'not-men' and then are produced as wives, mothers, lovers, daughters and sisters rather than subjects in their own right. The self as a cultural category is imagined as a masculine self. Women as subjects in culture can be subsumed into this category, but as not-men. They lack the wholeness imagined as belonging to men. Man and the self are overlapping categories. Woman exists in the space of the other, what man is not. Thus, the position of women as a subject in culture is always problematic. But subjectivity and social meaning is never fixed once and for all. It is negotiated as individuals experience themselves through relations of similarity with and difference from others. The mirror phase of identification and the acquisition of language together inscribe the self, whether male or female, as a split-subject, a subject in process, within a phallocentric symbolic cultural order.

National identity can be understood within the terms of the imaginary and symbolic. Like an ideal mirror image of the self, the idea of the national character is imaginary. It represents a construction of the self arising out of fantasies, memory and desire, and is given value within a particular culture through the symbolic order of language. It does not exist. But it is what Australians may want to believe is true. It signifies a cultural identity as a nation and a people similar to and different from others. The Australian character is a construction which has taken a variety of forms through the national history. One of his latest manifestations is in the character of Paul Hogan, hero of the film *Crocodile Dundee*, actor, comedian and spokesperson for the Australian tourist industry. Hoges (the image or popular representation and not necessarily the man himself, although the two are often collapsed into one entity) represents the national type, beloved by Australians and friends of Australia throughout the world. What is revered is not inherent in the man himself but in his image as the matey, egalitarian, blonde boy from the bush. What we like is the witty, unpretentious, laid-back roustabout popularized through TV and the film industry. In *Crocodile Dundee* Hogan plays the role of a 'real' Australian who fits the national type. He is a remarkable character: a cunning yet innocent boy from the bush who can befriend Aborigines and live with them in harmony on their own terrain; woo and win the heart of a desirable, well-educated, female journalist from a privileged, urban American background; and defeat both bourgeois middle-class rivals and Black street gangs at their own games in New York city.

This character coalesces with our knowledge of 'Hoges' the film star, actor, comedian and publicist for Australia who is known not only through his acting roles but also through frequent interviews and news stories about him. The man is not the same as his publicized image, although many Australians and people in other parts of the world believe in him. There are other dimensions to Paul Hogan which sometimes surface in the news. They convey the impression of a very clever and successful businessman and entrepreneur who can be difficult indeed in his business dealings with other capitalists, Aborigines and women. The popular media images form a coherent whole, although they contradict other knowledge about Paul Hogan, the sometimes sighted businessman/entrepreneur. We both know and do not want to know about the contradictions. They destroy the illusion of an authentic national type.

Who is this 'we' who desire a recognition of the national type in the popular image of Paul Hogan? In one sense, it is all of us. The desire to believe in national identity and a national type which can be located in history and real life is a belief which circulates in the dominant culture, not only in Australia but in all nationalistic countries. The impulse to identify specific cultural attributes is perhaps stronger among so-called new world nations since the new nations share in common a need to separate themselves off from the neo-colonial parent culture and also establish identifiable differences between themselves. People living in Australia and those receiving news about Australia in the rest of the world are all within the ambit of this 'we'. All of us are subject to the desire for a unique identity for ourselves as attractive individuals and an attachment to a specific cultural identity as Australians (or Americans, or Canadians, or New Zealanders) as *different from* people living, in this case, in other new world, neo-colonial British nations. Identity is established through a system of differences.

There are problems, however. In Australia, all native-born or naturalized citizens, including Aborigines, may be 'Australians' by law but some people can identify more closely with the category of the 'real' Australian than others. At least some women, Aborigines and immigrant Australians from non-Anglo-Irish backgrounds resist identification with the national type, although they no doubt recognize its existence as a dominant cultural norm. The way the category is constructed within a dominant order of power relations deserves our attention. As the above discussion should make clear, the national type does not emanate from specific individuals. It exists, however, within a system of related meanings through which individuals are defined and define themselves. Depending on the context, the category 'real' Australian could include:

all Australian-born men (as long as they are heterosexual)

Anglo-Irish Australian-born men and women

Australian bush dwellers (but never the Chinese)

'mates' involved together at important moments of national life (diggers, Anzacs, union comrades, etc.)

naturalized English-speaking migrants (without 'foreign' accents)

other naturalized citizens (as long as they are white)

rarely, naturalized citizens from Southern European or South-East Asian backgrounds, and Aborigines

As the listing suggests, the dominant norms of Australian culture are masculine, White, Anglo-Irish and heterosexual. There is also a hierarchy of differences informed by ideology. Who and what has value in a particular instance or context is based on overlapping considerations of gender, sexual preference, race, class, age and ethnicity. The high-status attributes identify the 'self' (the national type as well as living Australians) as a norm against which each of us is measured, defined, desired, included or excluded as subjects in culture. Meanings are not inherent in individuals. Rather, they are embedded in networks of other arbitrary but related meanings. The Australian is defined in relation to what is deemed to be non-Australian, the non-Australian by his difference from that norm. Each of us negotiates our position in culture with reference to these networks of dominant or preferred meanings. Our identity is inscribed by and through them. If we are located on the margins, as women, or migrants, or Aborigines, for example, we are defined in relation to the dominant norms. Meaning is made possible through reference to a system of differences (of relations between things) within an order of sameness (a white, masculine, heterosexual, middle-class culture).

French feminist writer Hélène Cixous refers to this network of meanings which circulate within the symbolic order as an economy—a masculine economy of sameness.[12] Some meanings within the economy (or the system of meanings which is both political and libidinal) have more value than others. Binary thinking structures the masculine economy. That which is masculine has more value than that which is feminine. The masculine/feminine dichotomy extends to other hierarchies of meaning, such as culture/nature, self/other, subject/object, activity/passivity. Social life, subjectivity and desire in men and women are all organized with reference to this order of masculine sameness. As we live within Western culture we receive, accept and reproduce these meanings and the values ascribed to them. We attach desire to them. In terms of national identity, the oppositions white/black, men/women, Australian/non-Australian, English speaking/non-English-speaking and the like operate to construct and express the dominant values. Those people whose identities overlap with the category of the white Australian male may find it easier to identify with the Paul Hogan type as a cultural projection of an ideal self than those who stand outside the dominant norms. Australian women, migrants and homosexuals as well as Aborigines are likely to take up a variety of oppositional stances in relation to these received cultural codes of meaning. None of these 'others' will escape, however, being implicated in their relationship to the dominant Australian masculine economy. Nor will they escape the desire to be identified with the attitudes and values of the dominant culture.

The differences between men and women, 'real' Australians and others, at the most fundamental level, are not those marked by biology or politics, history, country of origin or socialization, but by systems of meaning embedded in language and social practices. Further, the meanings ascribed to men and women through the categories of masculinity and femininity also operate symbolically in language to establish the 'place' of the feminine as juxtaposed to the masculine in culture. For example, I mentioned earlier that man's relation to the land is commonly represented in terms of masculine and feminine categories. Man's relation to the land, or the relation masculine to feminine, is a self–other relationship. The bushman who is the native son of the nationalist tradition exists within a masculine category. The position of 'native son' could, however, in an exceptional circumstance, be filled by a woman. That is, the bush woman can stand in place of her husband, lover or brother and take on masculine attributes of strength, fortitude, courage and the like in her battle with the environment. She could be called and have the status of a pioneering hero, even though she is a woman. But the land as an object virtually always is represented as feminine. It functions as a metaphor for woman—as in father sky to mother earth, colonial master to the plains of promise, native son to the barren bush, contemporary Australians to the red/dead centre. All of these equations reproduce the 'perfect' couple: masculine activity/feminine passivity. These are common-sense, taken for granted, everyday meanings. They reproduce the idea that man/masculinity is the universal norm for culture (which can include both men and woman but in different ways) and woman/femininity is the other, the adjunct, an object of desire for man.

Actual men and women are defined and define themselves within and across these masculine and feminine categories. They can shift positions, men taking on feminine attributes and vice versa, although not without difficulty. Women can be afforded status when they act in ways deemed masculine, but their behaviour will be acceptable within a total social network of meanings only if they remain true to what is believed to be their feminine nature. For this reason, the drover's wife of Henry Lawson's classic short story must cry; Margaret Thatcher must have a perfectly feminine coiffure; Ripley of the film *Aliens* must save the child at any cost. These attributes (being emotional, looking feminine, acting as if motivated by maternal instinct) are marks of femininity within a masculine economy. Actual men and women may resist or oppose these meanings, but they are also inscribed within them.

All of this leads to a reconsideration of the interrelationship between language, culture and the self. What can it tell us about the persistent misogyny exhibited by and accepted of Australian men, and about the ways women are regarded in Australian social, political and cultural life? How do Australian women fare as compared to the position of women in other Western countries? Tracing the network of meanings for the feminine within the Australian tradition may give us some clues. There are some general characteristics, behaviours and positions understood as feminine within a Western economy and there are some specifically Australian meanings which have accrued through representations of the feminine within Australian culture. The particularly harsh depictions of the land in the Australian

14

tradition, for example, may take on new importance when we realize that these depictions help to constitute the category of the feminine in Australia through which Australian women secure a sense of themselves.

If the representation of women in culture, and on a symbolic register of the feminine in discourse, is particularly negative, or marked by inferiority in culturally specific ways which are quite different from say, notions of the feminine in the cultural discourses on American national identity, or those of Canada, or New Zealand, might this in itself be significant? Language may indeed be a dominant force acting within the culture generally and within all of us specifically in unconscious ways to subvert overt measures which attempt to promote equality. Perhaps 'equality' itself is an ideological concept which is impossible to achieve. I referred earlier to the data which details woman's oppression in the concrete organization of social, political and economic structures and practices of Australian culture. But the position of women—how they are regarded and how they regard themselves—is also, and perhaps more significantly, embedded in the politics of language.

The identity of the self and the construction of an ideal self said to represent the national character can be understood as the effects of language. But there is more to be considered. It is language employed by particular individuals who work within a range of institutions, as well as the establishment of institutional practices, which give these meanings a force of authority. The categories masculine and feminine inform the Australian tradition. The Australian tradition takes shape through a history of texual representations within the fields of Australian history, literature and other academic disciplines. The meanings thus produced and transmitted through the culture are taken up in different but related ways by publicists for Australian culture. These representations set up a range of possibilities for understanding actual men and women within cultural and political life.

CULTURAL CONSTRUCTIONS

This study traces the Australian tradition as a discourse and the myths of the land and its people which inform that tradition. The Australian tradition will be taken here to mean a construction of the nation's idea(s) of itself. They are constituted not solely but significantly by that body of texts which attempt to define the unique qualities of Australian life by reference to events which privilege the Australian man in relation to his specific environment. These texts form a discourse, in Michel Foucault's notion of the term—a corporate body of historical, literary and cultural texts and materials which make statements about the nature of the Australian character.[13] The codes of meaning found in the texts and read through them by readers through time form a system of relations which already exist prior to and external to the texts. In fact, there are many discourses (of history, literature, politics, economics, and the like) and discursive practices (found in the operations of institutions, cultural productions, political events and the like) which interpenetrate and fuse to form a conceptual schema which make possible the discussion and articulation of an Australian tradition.

A. A. Phillips, a prominent Australian literary critic writing in the 1950s, first dignified the term 'the Australian Tradition' by using it as the title for his study of Australian literature. He tied the tradition to 'the fervent celebration of a robust nationalism', grounded in the literature of the 1890s.[14] Many scholars and critics deferred, claiming the term to be an embarrassment, a literary formulation of the national character without social or political foundation. Phillips responded that the hostile reaction to the idea of an Australian tradition gave evidence of a 'cultural cringe', a term and an attitude which has currency today. Nonetheless, there exists a diverse and ever expanding body of texts which purport to define real or imagined qualities of Australian culture, literature, history, politics and social life. Their existence has contributed significantly to a general taken-for-granted understanding of 'the Australian character'. The codes of meaning recognized by readers of the texts on national identity provide a starting point, a centre and a ground for the discourse which makes possible a wide range of critiques of culture.

In the past few years several monographs have appeared which treat the concept of national identity not as a fact of history to be revealed but as a social and ideological construction. Although they are not overtly concerned with feminist questions, these texts form a background to the present study in several important ways. Richard White introduces the shift in perspective regarding national identity in his book *Inventing Australia*.[15] He traces the changing images of Australia and the ways in which they have been manipulated through time to suit the needs and interests of dominant power groups within the society. White reminds us that concepts of nationalism are framed by Western European ideas about science, nature, race, society and nation. Australian nationalism arises out of a fusion of ideologies of Empire and colonialism. The changing images of the nation have been moulded by writers, artists, journalists, critics and the like who are themselves aligned to powerful but competing interest groups. White details changing attitudes to the land and a national heritage through an examination of the convict era, the gold rush of the 1850s, immigration, unionism, the rise of an Australian type signified in the phrase 'the Coming Man', the bushman of the 1890s and the Anzac soldier of World War I. The diverse images of the nation and the national character serve social and ideological functions which promote ruling-class interests. Ultimately, there is no 'real' Australia, no essence behind the images. Rather, the images themselves produce and reproduce meaning which endlessly circulates to represent the real.

John Docker has delineated what he sees as ruling-class interests at work in the production of Australian literary studies in his book *In a Critical Condition*.[16] Docker contrasts a radical nationalist tradition in literary studies with what he calls the metaphysical ascendancy of the modernist New Critics. Docker defines the radical nationalist tradition as that fostered through such critics as Vance and Nettie Palmer, A. A. Phillips, Russel Ward, Geoffrey Searle and Ian Turner. These critics promoted the social realist writers of the *Bulletin* school of the 1890s, Henry Lawson, Joseph Furphy and Miles Franklin, as well as those writers who identified with what was seen as the robust and optimistic democratic spirit of the nation. In the twentieth century they include Eleanor Dark, Barnard Eldershaw, Kylie Tennant, Dymphna Cusack, Xavier Herbert, Katharine Susannah Prichard and Frank Hardy. The metaphysical ascendancy is represented by the modernist New Critics of the 1950s (with whom Docker also identifies the Leavisites) such as G. A. Wilkes, Vincent Buckley, Harry Heseltine, and more recently Leonie Kramer and Leon Cantrell. These critics promoted a new canon of writers who represented the more metaphysical and pessimistic undertones of the culture. Poets such as Christopher Brennan, Kenneth Slessor, A. D. Hope, Douglas Stewart and James McAuley as well as the novelists Henry Handel Richardson, Patrick White and Martin Boyd come to replace the democratic nationalist canon of Australian works. *In a Critical Condition* outlines how, in Docker's view, the debate on what constitutes Australian literature has been regulated and contained by the orthodox New Critics who worked within the limiting and conservative domains of the nation's academic institutions, particularly the Universities of Melbourne and Sydney.

Graeme Turner's *National Fictions* further extends the debate on national identity. He focuses on Australian culture and its construction through a study of the dominant forms and patterns of meaning which constitute an Australian tradition in literature and film, which produce a specifically 'Australian' way of seeing.[17] Turner sets out to demonstrate how narratives produce meaning, thus creating imaginary relationships between Australians and the actual situations in which they live. The dominant pattern he identifies for the Australian character is that of the battler from the bush surviving against the odds of a hostile and indifferent nature. He finds this pattern—of the individual brought down by his environment—in texts from both the Democratic Nationalist and the metaphysical traditions. The myths of a national culture, structured through the opposition of man against nature, articulate several national traits which Turner identifies as an ambivalence to nature, a sense of individual defeat or, at best, accommodation to the environment and a limited faith in social action. In the end a pessimism prevails in Turner's text, which serves to parallel what Docker calls the 'gloom thesis' of the modernist New Critics. Turner identifies common patterns to be found within a wide range of films and fictional works. The study calls attention to articulations of dominant themes in literature and film through which we come to understand the national culture.

As Barthes points out, myths provide a vehicle through which cultural concepts and values are transmitted, disrupted and transformed.[18] Turner deciphers the common patterns in a number of dominant cultural myths. He traces the continuity and constancy of the myths. But they can also be understood as shifting and indeterminate in their final meanings. They give access to received common values and a plurality of possibilities beyond their ideological structures. Further, his study, which focuses on the plight of the individual in his particular context, excludes analysis of how that individual and his environment are constructed textually.

Although I would take issue with some aspects of these studies by White, Docker and Turner, they all contribute to new directions in Australian cultural studies which I would applaud. In their use of Marxist, structuralist and semiotic modes of analysis they offer new points of departure for understanding the complex relations between language, culture, politics and representation. Like Raymond Williams they recognize culture not as a given entity but as 'a signifying system through which a social order is communicated, reproduced, experienced and explored'.[19] The studies demonstrate that meaning is not derived from actual historical events or immanent in the authentic voices of Australian authors, but produced through the ideologies of culture. Further, they maintain that what we know about Australia does not emanate from the scholarship of historians, literary critics, sociologists, nor from the original creative vision of artists, film-makers and writers, but through discourse as a system of meanings, regulated by ideologies and power relations within the society.

A network of diverse interests have been at work in the construction of an Australian tradition. What we take to be common-sense knowledge about Australia and Australians is the effect of relations and strategies of power produced by the various discourses. Certain meanings are dominant, others muted. Regardless of the speaker's relation to the knowledge/power nexus the positions of certain groups and interests within the culture have been marginalized. The recent studies cited above analyse dominant traditions

18

within the culture. They do not deal with marginalization nor the ways in which cultural norms are created with reference to their margins, although these issues have been a central concern for feminist commentators on the tradition.

THE MYTH OF THE TYPICAL AUSTRALIAN

What is the dominant myth of the typical Australian? The profile of the typical Australian which opens Russel Ward's study, *The Australian Legend*, brings the subject to life. He is the hero of the Democratic Nationalist tradition as delineated by Docker. He serves as an abstract mythic construct analogous to those presented by Turner. And his image has been transformed to suit the ideological desires and demands of diverse power groups within the culture as analysed by White. The text reads:

> According to the myth the 'Typical Australian' is a practical man, rough and ready in his manners and quick to decry any appearance of affectation in others. He is a great improviser, ever willing to 'have a go' at anything, but willing too to be content with a task done in a way that is 'near enough'. Though capable of great exertion in an emergency, he normally feels no impulse to work hard without good cause. He is a 'hard case', sceptical about the value of religion and of intellectual and cultural pursuits generally. He believes that Jack is not only as good as his master but, at least in principle, probably a good deal better . . . He is a fiercely independent person who hates officiousness and authority . . . yet he is very hospitable and above all will stick to his mates through thick and thin . . . He swears hard and consistently, gambles heavily and often, and drinks deeply on occasion.[20]

The typical Australian, then, stands for certain identifiable values, attitudes and behaviours. He is defined, however, not only in terms of what he is but also by what he is not, that is, in terms of an other. There are two sets of terms implicit in Ward's description. Both gain meaning through the contrast between them. The binary oppositions which are brought into service, both explicit and implied, in the myth of the typical Australian look something like this:

Typical Australian ('me')	*Other* (not-me)
practical	theoretical
rough and ready manners	polished manners
natural/common man	affected/civilised man
improvisor/original	planner/derivative
'near enough' standards	exacting standards

laid back	hard working
skeptical of:	believer in:
religion	religion
intellectual/cultural pursuits	intellectual/cultural pursuits
Jack/egalitarian	master/elitist
fiercely independent	officious authority
a mate	an individual
swears/gambles/drinks	controls swearing, gambling, drinking
freedom	containment

We can begin to register a relationship of differences within this system of meanings. It could be said to represent the digger on the goldfields, the bushman of the legend of the 1890s or the Anzac soldier of World War I. 'Jack' in Ward's description refers to the Australian digger of the Eureka stockade. He asserts his independence within a British colonial context. He is the native son. The (absent) other is the colonial father. At Eureka the paternal position was occupied by the Crown police. In the 1890s the typical Australian becomes the bushman. The paternal position is replaced by the squatter, with his pretensions to the gentry. In World War I the Anzac soldier stands in the mould of the typical Australian, while the British command at Gallipoli became his other. This model pits the bush underdog as hero against an urbanized authoritarian foe. This myth of identity is a sign within a specifically Australian system of cultural signification for the common man, whose values of mateship and egalitarian principles of democracy are said to shape the national character. But the national character takes on shape and definition in opposition to what it is not. And in this dichotomy, *both* the self (as the male, Western, neo-colonial, Australian hero of the bush) and its other (as the British parental authority representing an old-world bourgeois culture) are defined in relation to each other.[21] As a cultural hero of archetypal status, the character generally comes from the bush, of poor but honest Anglo-Irish stock. Elements encoded in and by the myth combine to produce and reproduce widely disparate 'typical' Australians. The model functions to produce the cricket champion Don Bradman of the television series *Bodyline*, the condemned soldier in the film *Breaker Morant*, the 'real' Henry Lawson of whom Colin Roderick writes, Supreme Court Justice Lionel Murphy as eulogized at his funeral by the Premier of New South Wales, as well as Paul Hogan as the latest icon of Australian identity. The myth of the typical Australian has wide and valued cultural currency.

It was a system of meanings employed with some considerable force by

Gough Whitlam on the day of his sacking by the Governor-General, Sir John Kerr. The day was 11 November—Remembrance Day, the day which commemorates the fallen Anzac soldiers at Flanders Field. When Whitlam called it 'infamous' in 1975 all Australians knew why. The sacking had overturned the traditional relationship between the Australian native son and the British parent culture against which he struggles. Whitlam referred to Malcolm Fraser, the newly appointed Prime Minister, as 'Kerr's cur'—lower than the lowest drover's dog. In so doing he made meaningful in specifically Australian terms the relationship between British authority and Australian independence. In the speech Whitlam employed a self-other dichotomy in which the self, represented by the deposed prime minister, confronted the other as British authority and also reduced Fraser, his successor and Kerr's appointee, to an otherness of a despised non-human realm.

In most cases male figures occupy the paternal position of the Father or British authority within a nationalist tradition but this is not necessarily the case. Those who attempt to control the native son on behalf of the Father— through religion, manners, morals, etc. — can also be so named. And they are often women. This is the space of Henry Lawson's drover's wife; the role ascribed to 'ladies' on the goldfields; and the responsibility cast on the shoulders of emigrant women in the 1850s who have come to be known as 'God's police'. In addition, since the construction opposes the natural to the cultural, aspects of culture inherited from the parent culture (religion, intellectual and cultural pursuits generally, and also class divisions and the authority of members of the ruling class) are given negative value. Within discourse, in relation to masculine–feminine dichotomies, that which is demeaned in value is also feminized. So, the city, urban life, morals, intellectual and cultural pursuits come to be represented as derivative, inauthentic, unnatural and thus 'feminine'.

Within the narratives of national identity, Australian native sons confront the British parent culture to determine who will have authority, power and presence in the land. National identity, constructed as a battle between fathers and sons, is a battle for mastery over physical and ideological barriers and boundaries. Sometimes the prize is woman, but more often it is the land itself which is desired and possessed. What is assumed in the constructions of the masculine character is an otherness at their borders against which identity is measured. As should be obvious from the previous discussion, this otherness works in several contradictory directions. On the one hand, Australia is largely the 'other' of England. In metaphoric terms which have reference to Lacan's 'mirror phase', the child directs his gaze back to the parent whose authority he challenges, but whose recognition he desires. His difference is but a repetition of the same. On the other hand, the Australian character asserts an independent identity through an assumed relation not to the parent culture but to the land as other. This is a representation of difference within the order of the same. Man's relation to the land establishes his unique difference from England and from all other neo-colonial types as Australian. The land takes on the characteristics of feminine otherness in opposition to the masculine sameness of national self-identity. The land is not mentioned in Ward's description. But it would be safe to say that it is the context for the 'typical' Australian. These symbolic associations present in the discourse on Australian identity are endemic to Western capitalist culture, but they take on an Australian specificity which deserves our attention.

LANDSCAPE REPRESENTATION: WOMAN AS OTHER

In order to understand woman's inscription in the national mythology we need to analyse instances of man's struggle for identity. But as we investigate this Australian character who comes to represent the nation, we see that it is founded on particular notions of femininity or 'the feminine'. Actual figures of women do not appear with regularity in the discourse on national identity, which critics often (and sometimes gleefully) concede as being 'masculinist', even 'misogynist', but this does not mean that the idea of woman is absent. In the relationship between the native son and the old-world father, she can stand in the place of parental authority. In the relationship of the Australian character to the bush, her presence is registered through metaphors of landscape. The concept of a feminine landscape, even if repressed or censored, makes possible the specific constructions of the bushman-as-hero. Its content helps us to locate another 'place' for woman in the Australian tradition.

Landscape looms large in the Australian imaginary, although its infinite variety has been reduced to a rather singular vision—the Interior, the outback, the red centre, the dead heart, the desert, a wasteland. It is against this land that the Australian character measures his identity. It can be a place of vision and inspiration but most often it is represented as a hostile, barren environment.[22] Turner comments that through its 'callous indifference to man's hopes' the Australian environment is the great leveller of man's aspirations, status, intelligence and destiny.[23] Vance Palmer refers to the bush as a cruel mother—'an enemy to be fought'.[24] It is a familiar depiction. The metaphor calls to our attention a common construction of the land as mother earth within a Western European discourse. But in Australia the fantasy of the land as mother is one which is particularly harsh, relentless and unforgiving. Although desired within a framework of imperial and colonial

22

ideologies as an object to be possessed, conquered and tamed, the Australian landscape in the nationalist tradition is also a loathed and feared plain of exile which threatens madness and defeat. And Woman, metaphorically, resides here.

The place of woman in the discourse is a linguistic signification, dependent on notions of masculinity and femininity which circulate through language in culture. But if one takes seriously the theoretical position that individuals are the *effects* of language, and not fundamentally its producers or simply users, then the place of the feminine in discourse sets up possibilities for women's subjective life. Lacan posits that 'the images and symbols in the woman can never be separated from the images and symbols of the woman'.[25] This may not be an altogether accurate statement since, as deconstructive critics point out, meaning is never secure. But to open up the possibilities for plural perspectives and the slippages of signification which might create new possibilities for women, we need to be aware of the normative elements within discourses which produce the meaning of 'woman' in culture and operate to constrain actual women as subjects in culture. These particular constructions of masculinity and femininity within the Australian tradition may help to explain why negative attitudes towards women, and to that which is designated 'feminine', are so entrenched within the society.

It is not always women who occupy the imaginary and symbolic space of Other. Objects which stand in a desired or despised relation to man—the land, the Chinese, migrants and Aborigines—can also be so marked. Within the male imaginary they mirror masculine identity by posing a threat to the wholeness of the self. Cultural objects placed in the position of otherness take on the properties of inferiority in relation to Man. Women speak and locate themselves through and within the metaphors of femininity. Australians view the land through the imaginary constructions set up in the discourse. It could be otherwise. This analysis proceeds not in order to reconstruct and reinforce the tradition but to question it, and the questioning forms a first stage toward the evolution of a new epistemology, a new space of articulation, and possibilities of meaning new for the land, women (and men).

A QUESTION OF ORIGINS

For the native son there is also a question of origins. The desire to know one's origins marks the beginning of first paradigm for the desire for identity. Under nationalist codes, the origins of identity, which are never in fact discoverable, are posited in the decade of the 1890s. Vance Palmer registers the force of this desire in his study, *Legend of the Nineties*. He suggests that in the 1890s 'a scattered people . . . had a vision of themselves as a nation'. The vision provides the nation, as the mirror provides the child, with an illusion of coherent identity which protects it from disintegration. Palmer provides a birth metaphor for the decade of the 1890s, asserting that literature of the period 'showed this quickening' when the 'dumb continent . . . began to find a voice'. Before exploring the idea of identity posited in the 1890s, and more specifically in the voice of Henry Lawson, Palmer asks 'Is it just one of the myths we have invented . . . to fill the empty spaces of our social history?'[26] The answer, of course, is 'yes' to the myth and 'no' to the qualifying 'just'. The whole concept of identity is a myth, but a significant myth which fills in the empty spaces, the intolerable void of prehistory. The myths of a national culture become the accepted modes of representation for the meaning of the nation.

ON DESIRE

Desire motivates the need to define, to classify, to identify, to know the 'I', the nation, the self as a whole entity, a fullness of being. Desire is insatiable. It can never be satisfied. The more man desires—an object, the land, a woman . . . the more he wants. What he wants is forever beyond his grasp. Desire supplements lack. It arises not from the presence of desirable objects but from the absence of a sense of wholeness. The objects, ideas, definitions partially fill this lack. But they are never enough. This is so because desire is focused on an impossible state of being, rather than an object.

The impulse 'to find a national identity' arises out of man's desire, a desire to know origins, beginnings and endings. It proceeds through an assertion of a national character which has a history, a presence, a voice, a landscape, values, and an evolving tradition. This construction functions as a principle of national unity which protects the national character from a complete identification with England, on the one hand, and a complete fragmentation into a culture without distinction, on the other. Language substitutes for the absence of wholeness by constituting the self through an endless play of sameness and difference. Both men and women are locked into this force of masculine desire although they are positioned differently. Women, and other groups who are assigned to the margins, negotiate their place in culture as both Man and not-man at the same time. Woman is included in Man as a universal; she is also not-man and specifically feminine, that is, different and inferior in relation to the universal category. Women have no access to feminine desire. Our identity and subjectivity are formed within the definitions of masculine desire which encircle us.[27] We live in a space of contradiction. It is the need to explore this contradiction, rather than a desire for unity, which motivates this study.

METHODS AND INTENTIONS

My intention is to provide a different approach to questions of national identity. I analyse the discourse with particular attention to the representation of 'the feminine'. Following the lead of cultural commentaries which preceded this text, I have selected a range of representative studies which enable me to follow the dominant discourses on Australia and Australian nationalism.[28] They were written by explorers, pioneers, settlers, early government officials, their commentators, followers, detractors and the new authorities from settlement to the present. The selection, in itself, presents a problem in that it might create an illusion of a continuity transformed by the shifting interests, ideas and doctrines of the writers, which is not my intention. I do not want to follow the history of ideas about Australian nationalism but to analyse how the discourses have been constructed. The analysis will attend to the rules governing the production, regulation and exchange of ideas. It will trace transformations of the concept of national identity, including the transformations made possible by feminist commentators. And it will re-read the codes of national identity, unravelling the structures and discovering contradictions within them.

In addition, I am not suggesting that individual authors or texts are the source of ideas about the tradition or the origin of meanings they contain. Meaning within a text is an effect of signification produced historically and reproduced through various forms of representation, in relation to particular social practices and institutional settings. Individuals are the effects of discourse. Texts generate meaning in so far as they are read through the cultural codes and social experiences of their readers. Although I may identify a text with reference to the name of its author, my analysis concerns the discourse, not the author nor his or her presumed intention.

The study adopts a semiotic mode of inquiry. Semiotics is the study of the way things mean in culture and the ways in which speakers and readers are inscribed into systems of signification. Its primary focus is on language or textuality. Semiotic modes analysis proceed to discover not what things mean but how they mean. The focus of this study then is not to sort through the evidence to interpret the 'true' meaning of national identity. Rather it examines the evidence to discover how ideas about Australia have been produced. It studies systems of signification. The distinction between interpretation and semiotic analysis does not depend on a distinction between the analysis of form as opposed to content, but an understanding that the form, or the way meaning is organized, itself conveys meaning. Content is not determined by a reader's interpretation of the words as they are organized in a text but how those words are signs within a network of other signs which have value within a particular culture.

A frequent starting point of analysis is to look for binary codes within a linguistic structure and to decode them. A binary code is a set of two oppositional terms, like man/woman, self/other, culture/nature, subject/ object, Australian/non-Australian, bush/city, in which one term is defined in relation to the other and in which one term carries more value than the other. The structures of binary logic and rules of inclusion/exclusion inform the discourses on national identity. Critics take up positions for or against the dominant modes of representation which give Australian culture an apparent substance, a material form which takes shape through language. The values may shift in different contexts but the overall sense of dominant meanings within a culture is preserved. I will re-read the texts which inform the Australian tradition to highlight these linguistic features which allow us to register a way of thinking about Australian identity.

At times this study adopts a deconstructive strategy in analysing a text. Deconstruction attempts to unsettle the apparent logical unity of argument and detect contradiction within a text. Feminist deconstructive techniques attempt to dismantle the masculine framework of knowledge, highlighting contradictions in masculine logic which locates the feminine inside its order (as the opposite of man, his mirror opposite) and allows no place for woman as she might be located outside the logic of the phallus. Deconstructive readings enable us to unravel the contradiction in which woman/the feminine is dispersed across texts and to unearth a plurality of meanings which co-exist in language, literature and critical practice. Australia, read deconstructively, like the signifiers for 'women' and the 'land' can be regarded not as a stable entity but as a site of constantly shifting representation.

A reader produces meaning in her or his interaction with the text. Readers already have a sense of these dominant cultural meanings through which they read and make sense of texts (or any other cultural object—a film, photo-graph, body posture, costume, etc). But readers also know that the tissue of rhetoric through which meaning is organized contains multiple contradictions. As in the Paul Hogan example cited above, Australians may want to identify with and at the same time want to resist accepting 'Hoges' as a sign of the national character. How meaning is produced, received and transmitted depends on many elements—who speaks, what authority they have, how the discourse is organized through its linguistic structure, how it fits within given frameworks of knowledge, who listens, how both the speaker and listener are positioned in culture—to name a few. At different times, these aspects of the Australian tradition will be taken up in this study in order to examine processes which animate the idea of 'Australia' and how the discourse on Australian identity contributes to ideas about men/masculinity, women/ femininity and the relations between them.

In respect to methods and intentions I might be seen as a dissident critic, not in the sense in which Phillips applies the term to Barbara Baynton, as a writer from the 1890s who poses a threat to the Australian tradition, but in the sense presented by Julia Kristeva, as one who would make way for an articulation of a variety of cultural forms as well as a new sense of the feminine, beyond the forms and structures of masculine discourse. In *Polylogues* Kristeva writes:

> A woman is a perpetual dissident as regards the social and political concensus; she is an exile from power and thus always singular, divided, devilish, a witch . . . Woman is here to shake up, to disturb, to deflate masculine values, and not to espouse them. Her role is to maintain differences by pointing to them, by giving them life, by putting them into play against one another.[29]

What woman-as-sign might mean outside the phallocentric operations of discourse remains an open question. But I hope to demonstrate how the feminine has been located in the discourse in ways that establish and maintain masculine identity, authority and presence. An elaboration of the repetition of ideas about women becomes a site of resistance to the dominant cultural order, not only for women but also for other marginalized groups within a diverse culture. In addition, in registering the ways in which the land has functioned as a metaphor for woman within the Australian tradition we can begin to challenge notions that the Australian landscape is an alien and threatening terrain. By displacing the narratives of mastery we can reinscribe the harsh representations of the land and woman's place in relation to it. These representations arise out of man's impossible desire for unity and self-presence. But they also have a political force. Registering the character of cultural representations is a necessary step in the transformation of the social order, a transformation which may lead to a recognition, and beyond that a celebration, of cultural plurality and difference. The received traditions produce an order which alienates man from the land. These traditions also produce an order in which women, migrants, Aborigines and other marginalized groups exist, while at the same time 'they also remain elsewhere'.[30]

CHAPTER 2

IN SEARCH OF A NATIONAL IDENTITY

When critics and commentators set out to define Australian culture and construct a national mythology which would mark the country's distinctive difference from England, they scarcely registered the presence of women—as historical figures whose presence helped to shape and alter perceptions of the landscape; as settlers and citizens with roles to play in social and political life; as writers who contributed significantly to the literary and cultural heritage; or as contributors to a cultural discourse which shaped the distinctive battles between fathers and sons. The 'definitive' texts of the twentieth century, beginning with Nettie Palmer's *Modern Australian Literature* (1924) and W. K. Hancock's history, *Australia* (1930), and continuing through cultural studies like Vance Palmer's *Legend of the Nineties* (1954), A. A. Phillips' *The Australian Tradition* (1958), and Russel Ward's *The Australian Legend* (1958), constitute the makings of a nascent discourse on national identity.[1] They posit an image of the bushman-as-hero, as 'ideal type' who represents the national ethos of mateship. These texts and others which follow purport to construct the history of Australia from the inside, by writers who identify themselves with the cause of Australian nationalism. The selective ordering of the facts of national life encodes a history of the nation from early settlement, through Federation, to the present in terms of unique characteristics which are said to define an Australian identity.

When feminist historians challenged the absence of women from the definitive texts, as did Anne Summers in *Damned Whores and God's Police* (1975) and Miriam Dixson in *The Real Matilda* (1976), they wrote from within the framework of the Australian tradition which the earlier texts had set out to define.[2] The tradition had a materiality and a structure which came into being through the discourse. A critique of its masculine bias and an insistence on the recognition and inclusion of women—as historical actors, as writers, as characters in texts—without an analysis of the dynamics of sexuality and the construction of sexual difference through language, did little to alter that tradition. As Meaghan Morris has explained, woman is never simply that which is excluded. That is, the operations of inclusion and exclusion create an identity of that which remains and that which is excluded.[3] If the concept of the national character assumes a masculine norm, and masculinity is made meaningful in terms of its opposition to femininity, then woman (who is excluded) is represented through the category of the feminine (e.g.: what man is not; an object of desire for man). When writers attempt to include actual women in the discourse they invoke characteristics of femininity which have already been established. There is no separate, autonomous position for women.

NAMING A NATIONAL TRADITION

In the popular imagination, the Australian tradition finds its origin in the writings of the democratic nationalists of the 1890s, 'Lawson, Furphy and the *Bulletin* school', according to a stock phrase. Commentators on the tradition tell us that in these writings we find an image of the bushman-as-hero with his egalitarian values and his ethos of mateship. He represents a unique and original Australian creation, 'the voice of the Bush',[4] which comes to be somehow equated with the voice of Australia. This voice asserts the nation's sense of its difference from the parent culture. It waxes and wanes intermittently through the decades of the twentieth century. It should be remembered, as Graeme Davison and others have pointed out, that the bush myth was a construction of urban writers, artists and critics and the *Bulletin*, in fact, a mouthpiece for the liberal urban bourgeois against the interests of the rural pastoralists.[5] Nonetheless, the legend has endured as the representation of an authentic Australian identity. The strength with which it is asserted, into a national chauvinism, for example, or in the rhetoric of the Democratic Nationalists or the New Right, may depend on the degree of threat felt by those who seek to define the country. That a tradition of radical nationalism, rooted in the literature of the 1890s, should forcefully reassert itself during the decades of the 1930s and 1950s, both periods of conservative political retreat after involvement in international wars on the side of Great Britain, is not insignificant. During these periods the returned soldier came to embody the ethos of mateship and the bush, that is, the ethos of Australian manhood.

David Walker studies 'the getting of manhood' in his review of war novels of the 1950s. He explains that the novels, though differing in quality and political perspective, 'manage to relate the performance of the Australian soldier to an Australian tradition of physical prowess and manly bravado extending back through several generations'.[6] The novels link the World War II returned soldier with the Anzac of World War I and his pioneering predecessors, the bushman and the gold-rush digger. The bush and the battlefield, as opposed to the trivial and fragmenting life of the city, become the testing ground for Australian manhood. On both fronts, women are conspicuously absent. Walker comments that 'the idea was deeply embedded in the culture that the male was destined to enlarge the nation and its history, whereas women would frustrate that end'.[7] Walker remarks that this idea appears not only in imaginative constructions of popular literature: it is a convention of 'high culture' as well.

We need not hold to the distinctions between 'high culture' and 'popular literature'. The distinctions themselves are conventions of a bourgeois culture which maintain class divisions through categories of taste, style, readership and the like. We can register the masculine bias highlighted by Walker and attend to the exclusion of women and the repression of the feminine as linguistic features in the discourse which construct a specifically masculinist Australian cultural identity across class divisions and academic disciplines. Wherever one looks—in the *Bulletin* of the 1890s, in the stories of Henry Lawson, in the commentaries on the *Bulletin* and Henry Lawson, in the cultural studies by Palmer, Hancock, Ward and Phillips, in the writings of literary critics, historians and sociologists throughout the twentieth century— the texts are notable for the absence of reference to women. This attribute within the texts on Australian nationalism is so pronounced that Humphrey McQueen, in his history *A New Britannia?* which debunks the republican nationalist perspective, facetiously includes in his Index the item: 'Women, ignored, page 13'.[8] The neglect of women in nationalist histories may be an attribute of scholarship throughout the Western world. It is particularly pronounced in Australian cultural studies.

There is an assumption within Western philosophy that man is the arbiter of identity and the founding subject of culture. Derrida calls this assumption phallocentrism.[9] It functions to exclude women from the discourse even as they stand within it. Further it allows other groups which also stand at the margins to be identified with women, the metaphorical others. And it presumes that the universal norm for the culture is male. Returning to Walker's statement, that the dominant discourse on the Australian tradition sees men as enlarging and women as frustrating the nation and its history, we can register the ways in which this idea is conveyed through linguistic processes of inclusion *and* exclusion. The texts assert that men forge a national identity with reference to the authority of an English parent culture. But not all men. Some types, like women in general, are excluded. There are many character types on the Australian landscape vying for the title of true native son. In the bush the battle for supremacy is fought out by at least three major character types: the squatter, who has pretensions to the gentry and is associated with English ruling-class values; the selector, who is often represented as an ignorant peasant and associated with the Irish migrants or ex-convicts; and the native bushman, who stands out as original in his difference from squatter and selector types. The bushman has a freedom which is defined in part through his opposition to squatters and selectors and in part through his relation to the land. Through these processes of inclusion and exclusion men are determined by the discourse.

Women, according to Anne Summers' analysis, have been stereotyped into the frustrating roles of 'damned whores' or 'God's police'. These categories, like those of bushman, squatter and selector, also function to uphold a consistent schema of national identity. As God's police, the women, like the squatters, are identified with England, the law, Christianity and ruling-class respectability—that is, the absent Father. As damned whores, they, like the selectors, are identified with the Irish, the ex-convicts, the uncivilized, the feared despised others—that is, the unregenerate feminine. God's police, when personified as the drover's wife or Mrs Spicer of Lawson's stories, become symbols of endurance in a bush which can drive men to madness or defeat. The bush becomes the space in which the native son plays out his primal fear of and love for the mother. In the literature he lives an independent life in the bush, leaving his wife and family behind. Thus the bushman with his ethos of mateship becomes codified in the discourse on national identity.

The code is not without its detractors, however. It evolves into a conceptual schema with social, political and literary manifestations in the texts of Hancock, Palmer, Phillips, Ward and others whose writings establish a school of Democratic Nationalism. There are many forms of resistance to it, both within and beyond the confines of the academy. There have always been feminist challenges to the masculine myth of Australian culture. Women, however, have by and large been denied access to the fellowship of discourse and positions of authority within the closed community of the academy which sponsors and supports the tradition. The feminist challenges to the tradition will be taken up in the next chapter. Here we will remain with the dominant discourses which range across academic disciplines. The challenges which circulate in academic life have come in the main from literary critics and historians.

In literary studies, the modernist New Critics like A. D. Hope, Vincent Buckley, and Harry Heseltine challenge the social, political and literary origins of the myth.[10] Contemporary historians as divergent as the Marxist Humphrey McQueen and the eclectic Manning Clark test its ideological assumptions.[11] All of these commentators occupy respected, scholarly positions within Australian academic life. They have a right, conferred by their positions and the institutions they inhabit, to interpret the tradition. Their words carry significance, their opinions take on the validity of truth, even, ironically, in relation to a national identity which maintains a distinctive anti-intellectual flavour.

Most recently G. A. Wilkes has entered the discourse from a slightly new perspective. He explains:

> It has normally been assumed that Australian cultural identity was first achieved in the 1890's, in such figures as the shearer and the bullock-driver, and that the typically egalitarian spirit of the day is reflected in the writing of such men as Henry Lawson, Joseph Furphy and A. B. Paterson. As a model of cultural development, this has had unfortunate consequences.

Up to this point Wilkes' comments simply reiterate an encoded formula of Australian nationalism. The reader awaits further information to determine how this text will represent the unfortunate consequences to which it refers. The paragraph continues: 'Nationalistic impulses in the earlier nineteenth century, in Harpur or Kendall, have *naturally* been seen as strivings towards the Lawsonian ideal, and their *true nature* has passed unnoticed' (emphases mine). Wilkes' study, like those of the humanist historians writing before him, assumes that there is a truth which can be found behind the misrepresentations of history. His text reinterprets the tradition on the basis of neglected literary evidence from the nineteenth century. His desire is to uncover the 'true nature' of these cultural artifacts. He is motivated by a will to truth.

The problem is that there is no truth beyond its diverse representations, no pure state of 'nature' to which we have access outside language. Nature, whether referring to human nature, the nature of things or mother nature, is a concept within language and the symbolic order. The symbolic representations of nature are inextricably bound to culture and are always present in the discourse, even though nature may be represented differently in historical, scientific and literary texts. Further, Wilkes' idea of a true Australian nationalism assumes that Australia is an entity free to be defined through human thought and action. What does occur, as Wilkes' text amply demonstrates, is that dominant interests are always brought to bear on and are involved in the construction of the idea of Australia. It goes without saying that Wilkes' text refers to and is made possible through the existence of a nationalistic tradition which assumes white, neo-colonial, English prerogatives. Further, his reinterpretation falls within a field of discourse on national identity which, itself, imposes controls and limitations. He does not believe in the efficacy of the Democratic Nationalist tradition, for example. Nonetheless, he uses the received schema of a Democratic Nationalist tradition, modified by the modernist New Critics, as an established framework against and into which he writes. The schema and its code of mateship needs to be there to make his discourse possible. His text must reiterate the prior schema as a pre-text for writing.

Wilkes intends to produce different evidence to put forward a case for another interpretation, one which he suggests is more in keeping with the 'true nature' of nationalistic strivings in the nineteenth century. He assumes that the distortions of history will disappear when the truth is told. This assumption rests on a belief in a centre or core of essential truth that will be discovered when all the evidence is in. It never is, of course. The belief in a centre, and in truth, is a supplement or a disguise for an historical process which endlessly defers meaning while it purports to promise fulfillment. Critics believe that their interpretations can establish the truth. The word (or 'logos' from the Greek) stands in the place of the reality which words attempt to define. The word is not the thing represented although there is a tendency to believe that the two (word and thing, sign and its referent) can be collapsed into a unity. Derrida calls this tendency within Western metaphysics logocentrism. Its operations can be seen across a field of texts written by arbiters of the republican code of nationalism.

There is a schema for representing national identity, and several codes of meaning that are invoked by writers depending on their perspective. Of these codes, the republican code of nationalism is the dominant one within popular culture. Modernist writers establish different codes of meaning (they put ideas together in different ways) to present their case. The differences are ideological. But both perspectives are part of an overall schema for representing national identity. Each side believes that its argument can establish the true schema, but they invoke established codes or networks of meaning to advance their case.

Critics who disagree with the republican code of nationalism argue about its value on political, aesthetic and philosophical grounds. They attempt to alter its truth with reference to literary and historical evidence. They challenge its structure with reference to changing political, economic, and social modes of understanding. They reinterpret it in the light of changing currents in modern social thought. But they do not say 'The Legend does not exist'. They say rather, 'That is not it' and 'That is not it either'. They argue not about the concept of a national identity, but about definitions concerning its nature and constitution. Defenders, detractors and resisters alike would seek to affirm a national identity established and maintained through processes of exclusion and inclusion. Those processes determine who has a right to speak, and be spoken about; what data will be received and what repressed; what categories of meaning will be invoked in order to place the new data within a controlled field of discourse. The arguments, in their continuities and contradictions, give substance to a national history. They establish a domain (or proper place—the academy, the disciplines of history and literature) within which the discourse on national identity is legitimated. Within the domain transformation and change are always possible. When new evidence and interpretative frameworks are introduced into the debate of historians or literary scholars, they may be incompatible or coexistent with what came before. Meaning is never fixed. The truth cannot be established. But historical discourse tends to reduce differences, often by attributing contradictory positions to different authors, rather than recognize that differences are regulated by and through the discourse itself.

The nature of these debates will be analysed with specific reference to the texts and their textual and sexual politics later in this study. But before turning more directly to those issues, it is necessary to fill out another area where there is a common ground for agreement and dispute: the importance of Henry Lawson. Critics commonly cite the 1890s as the central decade of nationalism and credit Lawson, Furphy and *Bulletin* school writers for its promulgation. If one examines the discourse, however, it soon becomes clear that Henry Lawson has a pride of place. His reputation is that of a founding father, the author of the Australian tradition. The bush, bushmen and mateship as they are set out in his short stories in the decade of the 1890s and beyond constitute the core material of the debate. His writings have become a touchstone for the discourse on the Australian tradition. The history of critical responses to Lawson, the social distribution and dispersement of Lawson-as-a-cultural-object and the political and aesthetic uses to which the writer and his works are put, form a large part of the material through which the tradition evolves.

HENRY LAWSON AS FOUNDING FATHER

There is not a word in all his work which is not instantly recognised by his readers as honest Australian . . . He is the first articulate voice of the real Australian.

Statements like this one by David McKee Wright, a poet, writer and literary critic for the *Bulletin* in the 1920s, can be culled with ease by the casual reader of Colin Roderick's edited volume of *Henry Lawson Criticism*.[12] This reiteration of the statement (which appeared without the attribution of author or source) was taken, however, not from the annals of literary criticism, but from the publisher's dust jacket of a recent critical biography of Lawson, Manning Clark's *In Search of Henry Lawson* (1978). The dust jacket also states that the text has significance because it was written by 'Australia's foremost historian, Professor Manning Clark'. Thus readers are assured that they are dealing with a cultural object of high status, 'Henry Lawson', treated by a prestigious historical scholar and author, 'Professor' Manning Clark. The leading statement by David McKee Wright continues the circulation of a discourse on Henry Lawson-as-cultural-object which is at least fifty years old.

Returning to the passage itself, it asserts that Lawson is the 'first articulate voice of the real Australian'. We are in the realm, once again, of the essential, the real. In this instance it is not Lawson but his voice which is evoked, previously called 'the voice of the Bush'. Just as it is usually assumed that nature exists prior to culture, so it is also assumed that speech exists prior to writing. Further, Western metaphysics valorizes the voice as a more authentic and immediate representation of the self and the origin of thought than writing. Derrida deconstructs this idea. He calls it phonocentrism or the primacy of voice-consciousness.[13] Derrida claims that speech is a species of writing. Writing supplements and takes the place of speech because speech is always already written. There is no 'original' voice just as there is no 'original' nature. Language always already exists before it can be spoken. The valorization of nature over culture, of speech over writing and of events over history preserves the myth of presence. Within the Australian tradition voice and more specifically the voice of the Bush, which becomes the voice of Henry Lawson, is posited as the origin of a national culture. In this way Lawson becomes the founding father, the imagined site of origin. Lawson stands in the place of origin. He marks the beginning as the living source that animates the reality of Australian nationalism through his presence.

The arguments which place Henry Lawson at the centre of the debate about national identity proceed through certain assumptions within Western metaphysics which deserve our attention. As Derrida points out, the notion of a structure (for national identity, for example) presupposes a centre of meaning of some sort. The centre cannot be analysed. To do so would be to set up another centre. People desire a centre as a guarantee of being as presence. For example, in terms of the self, our notion of the 'I' presupposes a centre for our mental, emotional and physical life. The 'I' operates as the principle of unity which underlies the structure of personality. We know that the idea of a coherent personality has been undermined by Freud who detailed the division of the self into the conscious and unconscious. It received further challenge from post-structural theorists who attend to the decentred self (the split subject or subject in process) as it is constituted in language through discourse. Nonetheless, the idea of a centre is recouperated in Western thought by innumerable terms which establish centring principles. The belief in origin, essence, truth, reality, being, consciousness and man, for example, have been implicit in Western philosophy since Plato. These are centring principles which underlie and make possible structures of meaning. Lawson's imagined presence as the founding father of the Australian tradition creates a centre through which a tradition evolves. The logocentric assumption of Western metaphysics that structure has a centre, that a play of elements can only take place within a total form, effectively limits and closes off the play of differences. This assumption, according to Derrida, rests on a concept which he claims is 'contradictorily coherent . . . the centre is not a centre.'[14] The concept represents the force of a desire, a desire for certitude and immobility. It allows anxiety to be mastered. We desire a centre as a guarantor of being as presence. For post-structuralist writers, the desire to establish a centre, origins and truth coexists with the knowledge of the impossibility of the project. It coexists with the desire to affirm the endless play of difference which tries to pass beyond man and humanism.

In addition to the desire for a centre, for truth and for knowledge of origin which can be detected in the literature, there exist principles of discursive formation which are relevant to our concern with Lawson as founding father. Foucault analyses several principles which operate to control the possibilities of discourses. These principles govern thinking and writing in a particular field or academic discipline. He refers to three principles: the author as founding subject; the commentary on the author; and the disciplines which support, reinforce and validate the field in which the author is an object. For Foucault, the author is not an individual but a function of criticism. The author function is a construction of the critics which establishes 'a unifying principle in a particular group of writings or statements, lying at the origins of their significance, as the seat of their coherence'.[15] Henry Lawson has been constructed with just this author function.

Academic commentary, according to Foucault, operates in two contrary ways: it 'creates an open possibility for discussion' of the primary texts, while it also effects closure through an interpretative repetition by the critic of the original text's final or deepest truth. Traditional academic disciplines enable us to construct new meanings but within a narrow framework which constrains discourse by 'determining the conditions under which it may be employed, of imposing a certain number of rules upon those individuals who employ it, thus denying access to everyone else'.[16] Henry Lawson is an object within the fields of literature, history, psychology, sociology, politics and cultural studies—all of which invoke his name and reiterate knowledge about him through their methods and practices.

Foucault's analysis of author function, commentary and discipline helps us to locate elements at work within the discourses on national identity; within dominant and muted approaches. For Foucault, there is no truth to be found, only more or less powerful discourses. That which takes on the guise of truth does so because it fits with previously received knowledge established by the intellectual or political authorities of the day. What others would posit as 'truth', Foucalt refers to as the nexus: power/knowledge. The impulse to deconstruct the discourse, determine the constraints and trace the operations of power/knowledge have been evident in recent Australian studies. Richard White's *Inventing Australia*, Graeme Turner's *National Fictions* and Sylvia Lawson's *The Archibald Paradox* are divergent studies of culture which take new points of departure. They participate in the contemporary impulse to reach beyond the assumed unity of man and nation as framed through liberal humanism and affirm the endless play of difference within Australian culture. They now mark the margins of the tradition.

In the case of Lawson, 'he' was discovered and established at the centre of a tradition by writers in and after the decade of the 1920s. It was then that he became the 'voice of the Bush' for generations of commentators up to the present day. The quotation on the dust jacket of the 1978 book on Lawson which touched off this unravelling of phallocentrism, logocentrism and phonocentrism embedded in the discourse on Australian tradition was a text on Lawson titled *In Search of Henry Lawson*. The title is the text's 'proper name'. It is what the whole work is known by. In this case the title allows for a decentring of the subject known as 'Henry Lawson' by calling into play a series of linguistic possibilities. Are readers to focus on the 'search' or its object? Does the title suggest that despite years of critical acclaim and cultural adulation, we still do not know who Henry Lawson is? Or that we do know and are to be engaged in a quest of rediscovery? Will Manning Clark's text recreate for the reader the quest or its grail? Can the two be separated? And if readers 'find' Henry Lawson, will they find themselves—'Honest Australians . . . real Australians'? These questions are made possible because the discourse has placed Lawson at the centre of the tradition which is based on a series of dichotomies or polarizations. The oppositions are themselves the product of the discourse.

The face of Lawson, which stares out from the book's dust jacket beside the enigmatic title, arrests the reader in its gaze. It 'presents' Lawson to the viewer as the man behind the text. It holds out a promise to the reader that 'he' will be found. The cover illustration reproduces the 'official' Longstaff portrait of Lawson, painted in 1900 when the writer had reached the peak of his powers, which now hangs in the Art Gallery of New South Wales: rugged face, bushy eyebrows, familiar handlebar moustache, curiously dark and deep-set eyes. To a large and often unremarked degree one's visual sense of Australian identity revolves around the selectively reproduced images of this man. Yet, even in the repeated visual assertions, the face becomes so familiar, the image so constantly reproduced, that in the end it becomes a form, a mask, a mould for national identity which commentators, advertisers, and the media strive to fill, to imbue with meaning—significant meaning, but their meaning. This is the way the game is played. The search for origins results in a dispersion of 'Lawson', dissension among critics and a playful sense of disparity within the culture.

THE CALL FOR AN INDIGENOUS CULTURE
BEFORE LAWSON

Every nation has its story of unique beginnings. Foucault reminds us that the will to know, to establish a reality and a truth for the already there, signals a primal desire to find an original identity. He writes: 'What is found at the historical beginning of things is not the inviolable identity of their origin, it is the dissension of other things. It is disparity.'[17] We registered this disparity with regard to Henry Lawson. It can be found as well with reference to the literary and cultural histories which reach back beyond Lawson in their search for an indigenous, white cultural heritage.

We can illustrate the elusive character of origins by examining the call for an indigenous literature, heard in both Australia and England throughout the nineteenth century. Elizabeth Webby remarks in her analysis of early reviews of Australian literature that the reviewers looked upon the new colony's cultural productions as a parent to child, commenting, in moralistic and paternalistic tones, upon the efforts rather than the achievements of the writers.[18] Reviewers gently suggested that the young colonial poets look to the Australian landscape for their 'similes and metaphors' to discover a 'fresh-ness of originality'. 'Let him select from the treasures by which he is surrounded—let nature be his exclusive study—and Australia will have it in her power to boast of the productions of her bard.'[19] This Wordsworthian call to nature hardly suited the bush poet in a land of gumnuts and mallee scrub. He would find not verdant, nurturing pastures but a harsh, alien plain of exile in the new (step) motherland. Nonetheless, the narrative structures its meaning by constructing a family romance between parent and child, which becomes parent and son. It suggests that that he will find his identity through his relation to nature which boasts of his originality through his appropriation of her treasures. These elements structure the discourse circulating between old and new worlds.

Brian Kiernan details another element in the search for origins. His studies indicate that from the 1830s, as Australian writers and critics awaited the birth of an indigenous literature, they frequently looked to America rather than England for models.[20] They noted with interest America's 'coming of age' through its literature of the 1850s. William Walker, an Australian critic and reviewer, lectured to the Windsor School of Arts in New South Wales in 1864, making possibly the first of many extant references to the model which American literature might provide. The years leading up to the Centenary celebrations in 1888 provided an additional context for identifying the unique cultural features of the colony. The debate on what constitutes 'Australianness' emerged gradually through the late nineteenth century. But for critics of the twentieth century, the decade of the 1890s is distinguished as the time when Australia produced a body of literature which could be identified as indigenous rather than derivative, with the bushman as the central presence who viewed his country from the inside. His creator was most often compared, however, with Mark Twain or Bret Harte. To be named, he had to be compared with spokesmen for other colonial cultures and placed within the broader discourses on national identity arising out of (in these instances) a romantic conception of art. Australian commentators on national identity consistently borrow their idioms from an American (British, German . . .) romanticism, validated in the new land. To call him 'original' (based on the English or American model) is at once to assert and deny the concept of originality. As de Man reminds us, 'origin always depends on prior existence of an entity that lies beyond the reach of the self, though not beyond the reach of language that destroys the possibility of origin'.[21]

However, by the 1930s Henry Lawson had the undisputed pride of place as the author of a tradition. Empirical studies of the period suggest that this was not Lawson's reputation in his own time. The poems of Banjo Paterson were far more popular than those of Lawson. *The Man from Snowy River* sold more copies than any other volume of poetry before or since. Miles Franklin's novel *My Brilliant Career* was said by A. G. Stephens, literary editor for the *Bulletin*, to be the first truly Australian novel. But Lawson's centrality has been legitimated in the annals of Australian literary history, beginning with Nettie Palmer's *Modern Australian Literature* (1924). There is more to tell, however, than this identification of Lawson as founding father which Palmer's text announces. It is interesting to note the way in which Palmer's text asserts that Lawson is central to the code of Australian nationalism. The writer places herself behind the authority of a British critic to make her assessment. She

39

writes, 'In an appreciation of Lawson's stories, the English critic, Edward Garnett, said that they expressed a continent. That phrase may suggest what we have to demand from our literature, that it shall to some extent express our virgin and inarticulate continent.'[22] We note some interesting components in Palmer's discourse—a deference to English authority, even in an assertion of a native voice; a reference to the land as female, virgin and silent; and an indirect assertion that Lawson's stories express the voice of the silent land. Ironically, the discourse, like that registered earlier from the David McKee Wright emblem on the Manning Clark dust jacket, asserts that the 'voice' gives the continent (and its people) a presence even though the word 'voice' is used to refer to the literature as interpreted by foreign experts. David McKee Wright was an Irish poet, Edward Garnett an English scholar and reviewer.

After reviewing the scope of Australian literature, however, Palmer places Lawson more confidently in the study. She writes in the conclusion, 'there has been no one to follow Henry Lawson. His work remains the most intimate revelation of our life in prose'.[23] Nettie Palmer's text, its evocation of Lawson's voice and his intimate revelations, the authority of its articulation through Garnett and the reiteration by later writers and critics of these views, including H. M. Green in *A Literary History of Australia* (1961) and the writers featured in the *Oxford History of Australia* (1981) establish his undisputed place and presence at the origin of the Democratic Nationalist tradition.

VALIDATIONS

Lawson's importance is validated historically in W. K. Hancock's *Australia* (1930). It is a seminal history of the nation. Although Lawson's vision which became identified with the myth of the bush emerged in a gradual evolutionary process, Hancock is the historian of repute whose history authorizes the paternal authority of native sons. Hancock's study is divided into four parts: 'Foundations', 'Political Economy', 'Politics', and 'Civilization'. The text provides an interpretative framework for understanding Australian nationalism which historians, politicians and social commentators have expanded upon for generations. Hancock discusses Lawson in the final chapter, 'Art and Literature', where he parallels the historical growth of nationalism with the psychological growth of consciousness. 'Lawson's stories brought self-recognition',[24] he writes, meaning in the context of the argument, historical accuracy and psychological awareness, which Lawson's stories are seen to portray to bushmen, Australians and 'civilised persons in Europe'.[25] He concludes that through the writers of the *Bulletin* school, and essentially through Lawson, 'Australian nationalism expressed itself as a repudiation of

English conventions and standards, as a vindication of equality and democracy and an assertion of the supreme worth of the average man'.[26] Hancock's history did at least three important things: it validated the code of Australian nationalism as anti-English, democratic, and egalitarian; located it primarily in the 'authentic' works of Henry Lawson; and cited the dominant themes in his work as the dominant themes in Australian society.

Brian Kiernan draws a parallel between Hancock's *Australia* and de Tocqueville's *Democracy in America*, a central text which had explained another colonial nation to Europe a century before. He maintains that the links Hancock established between nationalism and egalitarian democracy as hallmarks of the literature and the national character became stabilised and accepted formations from the 1930s in the discourse on national identity. But even as they became orthodoxy, they began to come under attack.[27]

LAWSON AND DIVERGENT APPROACHES TO THE CODE OF NATIONALISM

The texts of Palmer and Hancock introduce a structure for the debate about the Australian tradition which survives today. The discourse suggests that the origins of an indigenous culture and the presumed ability to trace these origins in literary fictions and historical events are vitally important. But although Henry Lawson has become a touchstone by which to judge Australian culture, appraisal of his significance is by no means uniform. For the Democratic Nationalists, his name conjures up a myth of origin for Australian nationalism. His is the voice which enunciates the cultural code upon which Australian nationalism is built. The code has a history of social formation worthy of note. At its best, this code embodies a vision 'of social harmony, of confidence and optimism and resistance to any sense of defeat by the harsh Australian environment'.[28] This comment comes from an article by John Docker, in his attempt to delineate the dominant characteristics of 'the literature of the 1890s' from the perspective of the Democratic Nationalists. The interpretive code has been applied to the 'classic' Australian short stories which have come to represent the tradition through Lawson. Within the nationalist tradition 'Lawson' stands for a utopian social vision, a positive personal attitude and a character who embodies this vision and this attitude in his struggle against a hostile landscape. Literary and social critics refer to this optimistic national perspective as the 'Whig faith in progress', linking it to a British political philosophy of the eighteenth century. It is a perspective shared by many but claimed as essential to writers of the school of Democratic Nationalism.

The detractors from the code of Democratic Nationalism are designated accordingly as 'Anti-Whig' writers. They include modernist and New Left critics who challenge the liberal optimism of the Democratic Nationalists. They see in the code, and specifically in Lawson's work, evidence of 'racism, an anti-intellectualism, militarism, and anti-semitism',[29] among other faults. This litany of sins, which enraged critics sympathetic to the positive mask of nationalism, comes from Humphry McQueen's attempt to document what he called the fascistic elements present in Australian literature and culture, and most centrally in the works of Henry Lawson. McQueen calls attention to the hegemonic character of the code, those ideological components which tie it to ruling-class values of the English parent culture. Both views can be culled from the literature. Which one is chosen depends on the ideological frame of reference of the writer. They exist simultaneously in the discourse on national identity, which is grounded in Australian history but tied to the social, political and economic institutions of Western capitalism. The point to be made here is that when critics describe Lawson as a socialist or a fascist, they engage in the construction of either/or categories and they reduce the complexity of his writings to a single mould which fits their chosen image of the national character.

The contrasting positions outlined above share the assumption that the Australian character, whether praised or condemned, is a masculine subject. The bush against which he forms a sense of identity is represented metaphorically as a feminine other. In Lawson's fiction the bush is an evocative presence. It can be awesome, endless and enduring. Yet it is also harsh, parched and unforgiving. It forms a constant, silent and ultimately unconquerable backdrop for the bushman. 'A blasted, barren wilderness that doesn't even howl', Lawson relates in 'Hungerford'.[30] 'The grand Australian bush—the nurse and tutor of eccentric minds, the home of the weird', he comments in 'The Bush Undertaker'.[31] The 'resistance to any sense of defeat', posited as a tenet of the Whig faith in progress, is always a tenuous one. The bushman resolves neither his struggle for survival against the landscape nor his battle for authority against the British civilisation. Like his digger counterpart, he often ends his days in bitter resignation—dazed by the bush, crazed by the drink or dead in the struggle. The struggle with the land-as-other determines the nature of this character, the Australian character. Meanings which can be attached to the land are potentially without limit. These meanings become fixed and regulated, however, by the structure of social relations existing within the culture at the time. In broad terms, the code of nationalism structures the native son's battle with the land in relation to the parent culture, England, and his identity won through his battle with the land is also a replacement for his colonial status within British culture.

In a significant sense, 'Henry Lawson' has become a metaphor for Australia—not the man himself, not the stories he wrote, but the story of the man and his work. Vance Palmer in *Legend of the Nineties* remarks that 'Lawson *himself* was a portent' (emphasis mine).[32] The ongoing strength and vitality of the Lawson mystique can be registered through the response to two recent publications concerning Henry Lawson: Colin Roderick's *The Real Henry Lawson* and Brian Kiernan's *The Essential Henry Lawson*, both published in 1982.[33] As the titles suggest, critics continue their search for the real, the essential, the true Henry Lawson. The new texts emerge in response to the contentious claims made about Lawson in the 1970s by such writers as Humphrey McQueen and Manning Clark. The dust cover of the Roderick study states: 'So much has been published about Lawson recently that the author felt it necessary to tell the story of the real Henry Lawson in straightforward style and with strict regard to accuracy.' Such an assertion is a very curious introduction to a text which has no preface, no footnotes, no acknowledgements of source material and no bibliography. Even the pretences of academic legitimation are absent here. The air of familiarity of the critic with the writer replaces the usual paraphernalia of scholarship. But the assertion that there is a real Lawson behind the facade of rhetoric motivates the text. Roderick's view of Lawson, as a writer of genius marred by a manic-depressive personality inherited from his maternal ancestors, is not a 'new' nor particularly 'true' depiction, but one the critic has adhered to for at least ten years. His study does not do much more than settle the score on a scholarly debate between Roderick and Manning Clark, brewing since the publication of Clark's text, *In Search of Henry Lawson* in 1978.

Brian Kiernan's study, *The Essential Henry Lawson*, appeared amidst much trumpeting by the popular press concerning the dramatic discovery of lost and previously unpublished manuscripts of Lawson's works, which Kiernan includes in his text as being among 'the best works of Australia's greatest writer'. The fact that the manuscripts had been found, catalogued and partially published by the staff of the LaTrobe Library in 1981 was conveniently muted by the press in its sensational coverage of this publishing event. The *Advertiser*, Saturday Review section, included a full front-page article about the Kiernan study, followed by the publication of three Lawson prose pieces over three successive days.[34] The photo which announces the event pictures Kiernan in the foreground, holding up for inspection the discovered texts, framed by the massive stone quadrangle of Sydney University. Thus the university, the scholar and the press are represented together to establish the event within a legitimating field of scholarship tied to the academy. No other writer in Australia could command the excessive attention and extensive coverage granted to Lawson. The notice given to two scholarly studies, the contentious critical reviews, the press commentaries, and the letters to the editor which flowed in as a response to the press coverage, may not have settled questions as to the real or essential Henry Lawson, but they attest to the vitality of 'Henry Lawson' as a cultural object.

In 1986 Oxford University Press published an anthology edited by Cecil Hadgraft entitled *The Australian Short Story before Lawson*. It contains a 56-page introduction which attempts to establish, evaluate and describe a canon, 'even a tradition', for the Australian short story prior to Lawson. Hadgraft reports that at least forty anthologies of short stories were published by Australian writers between 1887 and 1894. He attests to the fact that the short story was a popular form of Australian writing prior to Lawson—a fact which has been neglected by scholars of the Australian literary heritage. But the introduction upholds the centrality of the Lawson canon. Hadgraft writes, 'even the best are not the equal of many to come'.[35] Mary Lord reviewed the new publication for the *Australian Book Review* in an article titled 'Retrieving the Baby'.[36] She reports that the history of the short-story writers prior to Lawson is virtually unknown. She refers the reader to Harry Heseltine's preface to the 1976 *Penguin Book of Australian Short Stories* in which Heseltine writes that Henry Lawson was 'the chronological founder of the Australian short story . . . and the source of most that is imaginatively important in it'. She reiterates that Nettie Palmer's *Modern Australian Literature* (1924) was the text which first credited Lawson for leading the way.

The publication of Hadgraft's edited anthology and its critical appraisal by Mary Lord contain many of the familiar narratological features of the Australian tradition. The publication introduces new data about writers before Lawson including Edward Dyson, 'Price Warung', 'Steele Rudd', John Lang, Marcus Clarke, Rosa Praed, Barbara Baynton, Frances Adams and Ernest Favenc. But both the introduction and subsequent review place the new data within the previously established tradition. They call for a re-evaluation of the tradition, while at the same time they uphold the position of Lawson as founding father. The event continues the circulation of the discourse within the rules of limitation delimited by Foucault as: author function, commentary and discipline.

This exemplar demonstrates the ways in which the critical texts make history. They place newly found and previously established objects within a field. The objects of history acquire an objective validity after the fact. It would be a mistake to assume that texts on Lawson and the Australian tradition hold the key to a true Australian identity, or that they uphold the values thus assigned, or that those values are 'honestly Australian'. But there exists no Australian identity outside the literature. Language is not a substitution for the real. Writing, itself, creates the reality it attempts to describe. As expertise accrues, the texts create a knowledge and a reality for the facts they appear to describe. A tradition takes hold. The ideas concerning national identity are given structure, form and existence in the discourse. And the discourse has modes of operations whereby subjects are produced and a cultural order is maintained. It limits and regulates what is known, even as that diffuse knowledge comes into being. It reduces a complicated series of facts to a unitary field of history. It assigns authority to certain speakers (professors and scholars in this case) who legitimate and carry on the tradition. Lawson's life and his stories are given status as truth by both his defenders and his detractors. The interpretations, taken as truth, come to form a framework for literary critics, social historians, political commentators, popular novelists, advertisers, cartoonists and film-makers. Operating across class divisions and social institutions, they continue to exclude race and gender as considerations as they continue to expand the received knowledge on 'Lawson', 'Mateship', and 'The Bush' as touchstones for enunciations about the character of Australian culture.

We can return to David McKee Wright's statement which introduces Manning Clark's text, *In Search of Henry Lawson*, with a renewed sense of insight and amusement. 'There is not one word in all his work which is not recognised . . . as honest Australian.' The double negative confounds one's sense of grammatical honesty even as it makes resonant the sense in which Lawson has come to be 'the articulate voice of the real Australian'. He fathers the tradition. The authority of his writings lends it a presence and a voice. In so far as we all are the effects of language, we in Australia are most certainly, but in diverse and contradictory ways, the effects of the discourse on Lawson and the national identity.

RETHINKING THE QUESTION OF ORIGINS

As the previous analysis indicates, Henry Lawson has been the focus of a search for identity by writers of the Democratic Nationalist, modernist and New Left perspectives. Recently a new generation of texts within Australian cultural studies have begun to appear which challenge the tradition. Some adopt the approach of a history of ideas. They attempt to locate origins differently within the articulation of a history of knowledge about Australia. Until recently, the academic institutions which provide legitimation for the cultural production of knowledge paid scant attention to Australia as an entity worthy of study. One of the bicentenary projects has been to support the growth of Australian studies within tertiary education. Books like John Docker's *Australian Cultural Elites* (1974) and *In a Critical Condition* (1984), Tim Rowse's *Australian Liberalism and National Character* (1978), G. A. Wilkes' *The Stockyard and the Croquet Lawn* (1981) and Robert Dixon's *The Course of Empire* (1986) announce this transformation of ideas about Australian culture within academic institutions. The texts investigate social, economic, political and cultural conditions both within and outside Australia which have fostered the growth of Australian nationalism. The studies delineate such features as patterns of national growth, historical divisions and periods, political and ideological investments in the growth of nationalism, as well as relations between economic, political and cultural events within the country.

These new texts contribute to the discourse in significant ways. They place 'Australia' firmly within a field of institutional and scholarly activities. They witness a desire to define Australian culture through critical practices which, like all critical practices, have intellectual and political implications. The discourse is not stable. There are moments of transformation where dominant ideas and interests shift, causing rifts. But the recent activities begin to make possible studies of Australia from Foucaultian understanding of culture as 'a body of disciplines having an effective force of knowledge linked systematically, but by no means immediately, to power'.[37] Even as political ideologies and institutional practices come under scrutiny, they continue to frame the conditions for the emergence of new ideologies, new knowledges.

Sylvia Lawson's text, *The Archibald Paradox*, provides another mode of analysis. Her object is the immensely popular newspaper the *Bulletin* which in the decade of the 1890s supported a literature of, for, and by the people and came to be called the 'nurse and guardian' of Australia's fledgeling prose.[38] She treats the paper as a set of habits, an institution, a repetition of a set of writing styles, in short, a discourse which works across time and between the various sections of the paper. She cautions that political historians have used selected themes and influences of the *Bulletin* to stand in for the whole. Further, those selected themes have evolved into a myth of Australia. Lawson concludes that:

There was, after all, no simple representation of a rugged bush or frontier ethic; nor were there single, stereotypical and uncontested notions of man and woman, bush and city ... The inhuman, reactionary and repressive voices were at times as loud as those calling for democracy, and there was indeed a great fear of gender difference, and of woman as that nineteenth-century world had constructed her. But all the voices existed together, with inconsistency, clash and discord as well as consonance and integration. In the play of tensions and contradictions, there was room for readers to move, a relative freedom to grasp usable alternatives.[39]

Nonetheless, Sylvia Lawson does give credence to the special place of Henry Lawson. 'He became the folk-hero, the familiar figure on the stage, taller than his characters, always there, shambling and innocent-wise', she writes. She concurs that Lawson created the myth of the bushman who becomes 'the white man or—in Joe Wilson's wife, the drover's wife and Mrs Spicer—the white woman. They are identified in their plights within the hard landscape, the alien continent over which the governors have so casually assumed dominance'.[40]

Sylvia Lawson's analysis increases awareness of the textual discontinuities and plurality of voices which are both incomptable with, and coexistent within the discourse on nationalism. The discourse is so fraught with contradictions that, if recognized, belief in the tradition could not be sustained because of the incompatibilities, and yet all these voices do coexist. The text takes us further toward a realization of the possibilities for discursive transformation, even if literary history tends to reduce the differences which exist in the primary texts to repetitions of the same.

Richard White's study, *Inventing Australia: Images and Identity, 1688–1980*, like Sylvia Lawson's text, participates in the post-modernist impulse to affirm difference. Following Foucault, White traces the diverse images of Australia as they have been constructed over time to reflect 'the national interest' as defined by competing power groups within the dominant society. In the introduction he explains:

> A national identity is an invention. There is no point asking whether one version of this essential Australia is truer than another because they are all intellectual constructs, neat, tidy, comprehensible—and necessarily false. They have all been artificially imposed upon a diverse landscape and population, and a variety of untidy social relationships, attitudes and emotions. When we look at ideas about national identity, we need to ask, not whether they are true or false, but what their function is, whose creation they are, and whose interests they serve.[41]

The *Bulletin* features in White's analysis. He demonstrates how the paper codified the image of 'The Coming Man' to the nation. Extracts from Henry Lawson's writing are sprinkled liberally through White's text, although Lawson (atypically) does not have pride of place. The Lawson extracts give evidence for White of the culture's shifting attitudes. He contends that the 'real' Australia, symbolized in the *Bulletin* by the bush, mateship, freedom and egalitarian principles, grew out of attitudes of a new generation of

Australians who used the symbols in their own self-interest as a reference point for their revolt. The reputed irreverence of Lawson and his crowd of Bohemians of the Bush, he maintains, though French in impulse, can be traced to a British radical tradition and to Irish nationalism.[42] The characteristics were not endemic to the new image of Australians. The text places origins in doubt.

White's treatment of the changing constructions of the national image and this examination share a common point of departure. But White's text does not examine the construction of sexual difference which gives rise to notions concerning identity. He explains that 'national identities are invented within a framework of modern Western ideas about science, nature; race, society, nationality'.[43] But not gender. Woman is absent (again) from his list. Nonetheless, the text does refer to the absence of women from the tradition, and it notes the masculine bias inherent in the nationalist code, the exclusion of women from artist communities of the 1890s and the difficulties faced by women writers who had to compete with men for attention and recognition on male grounds. White's analysis, like that of *The Archibald Paradox*, provides a radical departure from Australian cultural studies of the past.

Graeme Turner studies the dominant patterns in Australian literature and film which give the culture a specificity of meaning in *National Fictions*. He discusses Lawson in a central chapter entitled 'Characterisation and Individualism'. Turner suggests that despite the democratic theme in literary nationalism, individualism in Australian literature is not a central concern. Rather, it is modified by the convention of mateship. Through an analysis of Lawson's short stories, 'Telling Mrs Baker', 'The Union Buries its Dead', and the character of Steelman, Turner concludes that

> the Australian commitment to certain kinds of independence masks a basic suspicion of difference and of individuality. This manifests itself in a particular mode of characterisation which sees character as overwhelmingly the product of social and ethical determinants, of interest primarily for the purpose of moving the plot, providing a setting, or creating a world.[44]

In this section, Turner retreats from his structuralist analysis to rely on a more modernist conception of character. He searches for examples of individualism, of the kind familiar to readers of American literature, and finds, instead, in Australian texts and films, unindividuated characters, locked into the bonds of mateship and subsumed by their environment.

If one poses the question of identity differently, by seeing the concept itself as one of the effects of discourse and surveying the relationship of man to the land, a different perspective comes into view. Within Australian literature it is not the lone individual submerged in his setting but the relationship between them (man and the bush) which defines each. It is not that man is always a victim within an Australian context. Rather, the discourse doubly inscribes the Australian character into a dual relationship—to the parent culture on the one hand and to the land on the other. The discourse maintains the authoritarian influence of the British parent culture through a particular form of neo-colonialism. It constructs the land as a particularly raw, harsh and unforgiving other which cannot be mastered. The 'real' Australian is caught within this system of representations. A post-modern analysis would begin with the knowledge that the 'individual' is not a separate entity. He exists in and through a system of meanings and ideological practices. Individualism and national identity themselves are disputed concepts which discourse seeks to settle and unify. Man's mastery over the land which in a nationalist tradition attempts to secure the illusion of coherent identity is known to be impossible now in a post-modern world. Only a nostalgia for the lost individual remains, with America as a dubious model.

Questions of how the discourse on national identity constitutes the categories of the masculine and the feminine have been posed here: how the discourse defines the nature of what is spoken and what is repressed; who speaks, for whom, and by what authority. This chapter has traced the various elements which constitute as well as challenge a national tradition. Lawson as founding father and the commentaries on Lawson have been analysed with reference to Derrida's concerns with the phallocentric, logocentric and phonocentric impulses within Western philosophy. The evolving tradition has spawned a diversity of interpretations, schools of thought and ideological positions. This chapter has examined this tradition with reference to Foucault's work on discursive formations and, in particular, with regard to the limitations and controls which the principles of author, commentary and discipline impose on the open possibilities of discourse. More recent post-structuralist approaches have been cited which interrupt the uniformity of the tradition and introduce ways of analysing national identity as a construction.

In terms of methodology these approaches call into doubt the status of the text, the land and woman. The texts which form the dominant discourse on Australia operate to establish a unified entity called Australia; the right of white Western possession over the land; and a rational critical mastery over the meanings of nationalism. They control the diffuse nature of the data and experience. For example, the texts are silent about the dispossession of Aboriginal inhabitants. They fail to recognize the Chinese presence in a colonial history. And they mute the significance of white women and non-Western European migrants. The dominant discourses mask these elements of the culture which escape or overflow or are elided by the controls and limitations of the discourse.

WOMEN AND QUESTIONS OF NATIONAL IDENTITY

Recently feminist theorists have begun to register the ways in which discursive operations which establish meaning for a culture are also at work to reduce feminine differences to the order of masculine sameness. They attend to the evidence of diversity, plurality and diffusion which is reduced to singular meanings through the operations of discourse. Feminist historiography challenges the dominant discourses and opens up the possibilities for transformation. A central issue, as I have attempted to show in relation to the commentary on the Australian tradition, is the question of mastery. That is, when one reads a text or interprets the meaning of landscape or woman as object/other, one takes up the position that it is possible to know it, to master it—the text, the land, the woman, the unknown. This knowledge of the other must be read into the object, then taken away from it and appropriated by the speaker. In a critical gesture, its difference is denied. The otherness of the land/woman or of a text, the multiplicity of meanings, the infinite referentiality of signs are reduced, censored and suppressed in the act of interpretation. Thus, the act of interpretation establishes a relation not only to knowledge but to power. To know the other is to control it by purging its plurality of meanings into a singular representation of 'truth'.

Mastery over the other both imposes authority over it and represses its difference at the same time. Mastery over the texts, like mastery over the land and women, is an operation which denies difference, radical difference, in Kristeva's sense of the term. Feminist readings, like those of Anne Summers and Miriam Dixson, have called attention to the myriad of ways in which traditional interpretations of Australian culture avoid or exclude 'the woman question'. These feminist readings—although they break the male monopoly on speech, politicize the discourse and move women from passive receptors to active producers of meaning—can still require a (false) position of mastery. But what is the alternative? From what positions can a woman speak?

There is more at issue here than the sex of the author or critic. The critic, whether feminist or not, in the very articulation of the problems of meaning, produces meaning. Interpretation, when it reduces a text to a determinate meaning, becomes yet another instance of the law. The issues are strategic and political and relate to critical practice. There are several alternatives. One is to read for process, rather than for meaning, as does Sylvia Lawson in her study of the *Bulletin* as discourse; another is to interrogate the changing ideological assumptions underlying assertions of truth, as does Richard White in *Inventing Australia*; another is to search for the repressions of race, class and gender within patriarchy and signify the differences muted by a universalist history, as do Henry Reynolds in *The Other Side of the Frontier* and Jill Matthews in *Good and Mad Women*. The strategy adopted in this study attends to the linguistic processes of signification which attempt to establish meaning for Australia and Australian men and women. The new texts interrupt the discourse and make possible a new space of articulation.

I want to turn attention now to another level of that articulation, one which attends more specifically to questions of feminine representation. As I do I hear the words of Miriam Dixson echoing in my ears. 'Australia,' she writes, 'is like the body of an unloved woman'.[45] The simile brings together two dominant signs of otherness in a specifically Australian context. The comment reminds me that speakers stand within a field of meaning specific to a particular culture. Women position themselves in relation to that field. Australian women writers speak from within metaphors of landscape in which they are named as other. Male critics of women writers imagine women to be in the same space of signification as the feminine landscape. We will take up these ideas and extend the ways in which woman is implicated in the discourse even as she exceeds it, in the next few chapters.

CHAPTER 3

THE BUSH AND WOMEN

The bush is the heart of the country, the real Australian Australia.

Francis Adams, *The Australian*

The central image against which the Australian character measures himself is the bush. 'The Bush is the heart of the country, the real Australian Australia', wrote Francis Adams, a journalist who migrated to Australia from England in the 1880s. In his travel guide published in London in 1893 he lauded the 'true Bushman' as 'the man of the nation'.[1] But he also tempered his praise with a recognition of the dangers which attend bush life, dangers which later writers would concur made the bush 'no place for a woman'.[2] Adams remarked that 'The Anglo-Australian has perished or is absorbed in the Interior much more rapidly than on the sea-slope or in the towns.'[3] Adams' descriptions reveal several attributes familiar to the discourse on the Australian tradition: the male-as-norm and land-as-other; the bush as central and city as peripheral to self-definition; and the personification of the bush as the heart, the Interior—a mysterious presence which calls to men for the purposes of exploration and discovery but is also a monstrous place in which men may either perish or be absorbed.

When Adams wrote of death in the bush he may have been thinking of the fate of Burke and Wills, Australia's most celebrated explorers, who perished in July 1861 during their attempt to traverse the continent from south to north. His use of the term 'absorption' suggests the power of the bush, like the fantasy of the primal mother, to suck up its inhabitants, assimilating them into its contours and robbing them of a separate identity. This is a powerful fantasy in Australia. It is one of the ways in which the feminine is present in the bush tradition—not necessarily in actual figures of women inhabiting the bush, but in responses to the bush itself. The landscape provides a feminine other against which the bushman-as-hero is constructed. Further, these narratives engage the reader in a process through which his or her own subjectivity is constructed. The fantasy of the bush as an absorbing landscape, capable of sucking up its inhabitants, circulates through the narratives of history, fiction and film. It structures meaning for human events as well.

That this particular fantasy continues to circulate in contemporary culture can be shown from its recent evocation in the popular film *Picnic at Hanging Rock*. The film was directed by Peter Weir and derived from a 1967 novel of the same name by Joan Lindsay, allegedly based on a real occurrence. Only with the publicity surrounding the film did publishers reveal that the book's claims to truth were a hoax. The film premiered in 1975 and received wide acclaim at the 1976 Cannes film festival. Critics praised the film for its depiction of 'the awe-inspiring power of the Australian bush, which alienates some and hypnotically absorbs others,' into the enigma and mystery of its animistic force.[4] The film, through commentary, takes its place within the associated meanings, figures and tropes of the Australian tradition.

Film operates differently from literary narratives. In film, the film-maker and the audience actively participate in the production and construction of meaning. Although the film text appears to present the viewer with a reflection of the real world, it conveys this effect through technical features (music, sound, visuals, dialogue, lighting, editing, camera angle, focus, etc.) as well as through its modes of representation which naturalize the play of codes and discourses (codes of ideology and representation; discourses of politics, aesthetics, philosophy, and the like) within it. In addition, as Laura Mulvey explains, 'cinema poses questions of the ways the unconscious (formed by the dominant order) structures ways of seeing and pleasure in looking.'[5] Film provides erotic pleasure for the viewer through the image of the woman. It positions the audience in the role of a masculine spectator. He is the bearer of the gaze, whereas woman is the object of the look. The bearer of the gaze has power and control over its object. Woman as object is coded for visual and erotic impact. She connotes 'to-be-looked-at-ness'.[6]

In *Picnic at Hanging Rock*, the gaze of the spectator is directed towards both a mysterious Australian landscape and the innocent schoolgirls who inhabit and ultimately succumb to it. The opening sequence establishes these relationships between audience and spectacle. The camera focuses on a primal landscape over which hangs a dense fog at what could be the dawn of time. Only chirping birds break the eerie silence. The morning fog descends to ground level providing viewers with a glimpse of the Rock in the distance against a backdrop of rolling thunder. As the thick fog lifts viewers are allowed full visual access to the dual aspects of the scene: a harsh, barren plain of dry grass and stunted trees and the distant rise of majestic, imposing volcanic rock. The film's title is superimposed upon this scene accompanied by a voice-over, later identified as the voice of Miranda, cautioning 'What we see and what we seem is but a dream'. From the outset the film as narrative opens up the possibilities for mediation between real and imagined worlds. It provides us with an instance of the formation of an Australian Imaginary, according to Lacan's use of the concept. The camera then pans the parched bush to include a view of the Ladies' College accompanied by the gentle sound of flutes. Inside a bedroom, viewers watch the sleeping Miranda wake to look out towards them. She is alone, erotic, on display, and 'ours'. As the scene shifts from nature to culture, the bush to the school, the wilderness to civilization, the sounds of Nature, both gentle and ominous, are replaced by the cultured but exotic strains of the pipes of Pan.

The audience participates actively in the film fantasy, in which three young women and one of their teachers will be absorbed into the bush, from a doubly inscribed position. That is, there is a separation of the erotic identity of the viewer from the girls and the landscape, represented as objects of desire on the screen. At the same time the spectators identify with the schoolgirls, and especially Miranda, as mirror images of themselves. This allows two things to happen at once within the viewers' subjectivity: it sets up an identification with the girls as subjects like themselves and a separation from the girls who also become fetish objects for the viewer. The audience gazes upon the innocent, pubescent Victorian maidens with fascination and desire, while it views the landscape of the Rock as a mystery which will pose the ultimate threat of loss of identity. A question is set up: who will possess Miranda—Michael ('us'), the besotted youth through whose eyes the spectator engages with her image as an object of desire, or the dominating, enigmatic forces of Nature? The natural world threatens at every turn. Cicadas land on shirtsleeves; ants infect the picnic cake; even greenhouse plants grasp at human hands. 'Civilization' battles with the forces of nature while at the same time the delicate, wind-blown, idealized images of the innocent young girls fuse with those of the majestic bush. Both are erotic objects to be looked at and displayed.

Mulvey explains that the pleasure of the gaze in film is derived from three looks: that of the camera which can gaze on the scene where there is no spectator; the audience whose gaze corresponds with the male gaze of the film's protagonist; and the characters within the film to each other. In terms of both the story and the spectacle, an identification is set up between the audience and the main male protagonist in the film. In *Picnic* his place is occupied by Michael, a British son of the gentry visiting his relatives in the colonies. Michael and then Albert, the Australian 'common man'and servant to the gentry, who becomes Michael's 'mate', voyeuristically spy on the girls. Spectators follow their gaze as the camera offers a closeup of Miranda's knee as her hand peels back black stockings to reveal bare legs, and, later, her delicate face frozen in slow motion as she waves to the French teacher before ascending the Rock, as well as the flesh of hands, arms and feet exhibited by the girls for our pleasure as they languish at the base of the Rock prior to their disappearance. Through the active look of the camera, the audience unites its gaze with that of the voyeuristic young men, to enjoy the passive images of the girls on the screen.

After the girls' disappearance, Michael, as the representative of the Father's Law, emerges as the character who must solve the mystery. He mounts a one-man search party and, Oedipus-like, sets out on a quest of discovery. As he approaches the Rock he is viewed from above, from the imagined position of an all powerful mother, in full control of 'her' family, watching her son 'swimming' helplessly on the rising ground, unable to mount the crevice and penetrate the womb-like cave where one of the girls will be found. Exhausted and overcome by the bush, Michael passes the 'key' to the journey (also presented as a fetish in the form of a close up-shot of a scrap of torn white lace) onto Albert, the Australian native son, who masters the precipice to find a lone survivor. Throughout the film the look of the camera constantly shifts between the three kinds of look identified by Mulvey: from a dominating perspective within the Rock—the enigma of nature, the impossible place where there can be no spectator; to the look of the audience which corresponds centrally with the gaze of the two youths, Michael and Albert; and to characters with each other. The young girls and their teachers view each other erotically—they glance lovingly, stroke sensuously, reflecting each other in photos and mirrors in an intensely engaging and pleasurable exhibition for the viewer, beyond the deteriorating ritual constraints of the school and its God's police headmistress, Mrs Appleyard. For Michael, and through him the audience, the desire for woman merges with a desire for meaning which in turn merges with the desire for a fixed self.

In terms of an imaginary fantasy for Australian viewers, *Picnic* imagines the bush as the most powerful and mysterious object in the film. The bush obstructs man's possession and mastery of the girls, of logical narrative meaning and a coherent self-identity. In psychoanalytic terms, the film evokes a spectator's fantasy of the bush as both a pre-Oedipal mother and an Oedipal, phallic mother. The bush as pre-Oedipal mother draws one towards total fusion with itself and recreates a desire for the lost unity between the child and the world before the imposition of the Father's Law and the child's entrance into language and culture. The Oedipal mother signifies separation, loss and repression of this fantasy. She controls the family in the child's imaginary and organizes the pleasures of fusion and rejection. Ego identity is constituted in relation to the maternal image, with the Oedipal mother coming to represent castration.

The film engages the viewer in a primal scene of seduction between mother and child, outside the constraints of the Father's Law. As the school girls become one with the bush without distinction they signify an attachment between mother and child beyond the cultural order of rules and restraints and reasonable controls. This is an intolerable threat to the ego within patriarchy. The paternal position is empty. The children are absorbed. In the film the sense of threat for the audience is enhanced by the shifting angles of the camera's gaze as well a sounds of wind, thunder, growling animals and dark, ominous music presented as emanations of an animistic landscape.

As the girls and later Michael, Albert, and the search party approach the place of disappearance the camera closes in on monstrous primeval faces staring out from the Rock on to the girls (the audience), its victims, and then shifts its gaze to an elevated position within the Rock, allowing Nature and the audience to perceive the insignificant people far below, from a position of maternal omnipotence. (In the imaginary the maternal threatens to absorb the infant, whereas the paternal guarantees him or her a place in culture as a whole person, separated from the mother and her imagined power.) Always, as the scene is presented and represented through the haunting memories of several characters, we are saved from the primal scene of seduction by the piercing scream of Edith, the schoolgirl left behind. The primal mother, as a 'fantastic land of monstrosities' (recalling Marcus Clarke's signification), exhibits an omnivorous appetite of insatiable need, outside of articulation.[7]

The film *Picnic at Hanging Rock* illustrates the paradox that the bush is both 'no place for a woman' and, at the same time, the place of Woman with reference to a Western symbolic order as it locates the feminine. The young women in the bush become the bush, without distinction. They are absorbed into its contours. Through them, viewers play out a fearful fantasy which circulates within the Australian imaginary. In terms of Australian identity, this film depicts the ultimate threat, that the land might actually absorb its inhabitants. Mastery over the land (and thus the self) would be denied. It is a powerful male fantasy, but one in which women participate as both subjects and objects of the gaze. In *Picnic*, on a narrative level, the mystery is never solved; identity is not secured. In terms of the film as spectacle, however, the category of femininity is preserved; the erotic identity of the viewer and the desire of the ego for autonomy are fulfilled through the pleasure of the gaze.

Christian Metz has said that

> the power of unreality in film derives from the fact that the unreal seems to have been realized. Unfolding before our eyes as if it were the flow of common occurrence, not the plausible illustration of some extraordinary process conceived only in the mind . . . Film is like a vacuum which our dreams readily fill.[8]

There is evidence that *Picnic* has had this powerful effect on the subjectivity of Australian viewers. Our dreams of both women and the bush become nightmares as we negotiate the terrain of identity, but female spectators, as both subjects and objects of the gaze, are positioned differently. To view the film in an unproblematic way, female spectators must participate in the (masculine) fantasy. But women are identified as *both* self and other, subject and object of the gaze, man and the object of men's desire. Female subjectivity is constructed through the filmic codes. Nonetheless, it is also possible to recognize the images as representation and to adopt an oppositional stance. From this dissident perspective, it is possible to understand that 'woman' resides in a void of meaning, a place not represented or symbolized.[9]

The power of the fantasy of an absorbing primeval mother nature, evoked in the nineteenth century by Marcus Clarke, Francis Adams and others, and re-enacted in *Picnic at Hanging Rock*, continues to motivate personal, social and cultural responses to the bush. This can be seen with reference to a series of recent tragic events. The first surfaced in a small news item in Adelaide's *Sunday Mail*, in December 1986. It reported the disappearance of two teenage boys from their separate caretaker positions in remote areas of a cattle station in Western Australia. The article carried the headline: 'Missing Boys: Mystery Deepens', with a central column sub-heading 'Phone call a hoax'.[10] Images of two adolescent boys, one a photo of a fair-haired youth dressed in a school uniform, the other of a darker youth, smiling and in casual dress, formed border columns for the article. The visual and linguistic cues (photos, mystery, hoax) signalled a repetition of the Hanging Rock fantasy for readers. The text describes how the boys 'vanished without a trace', a phenomenon said to 'rival the fictional mystery of Hanging Rock for intrigue'.[11]

Four months later the mystery would be solved with the discovery of the skeletal remains of the two boys in a remote desert region 400 kilometres south-east of Halls Creek. Even at the time of their disappearance, speculation as to its cause might have surmised that the boys could have been anywhere—together or apart; on a holiday or on the run from a difficult situation; safely camping outback or in danger through lack of supplies. They could have been abducted or the victims of foul play. As it turns out they were allegedly attempting to escape from inhumane conditions imposed upon them by the property manager of a remote outback station. They perished when their car broke down, they ran out of water and were unable to summon help. Human error and inexperience were responsible for the mystery, not the inanimate forces of nature. The boys were not absorbed into the bush—

although that fantasy was re-created by the news item and, later, reactivated for its readers by the tasteless photo of one of the boys' parched bones, scattered amidst desert scrub, which announced the tragic discovery on the front page of the press.

A month later a nine-year-old mentally retarded boy would disappear in rugged bushland in Wilson's Promontory National Park in Victoria. At the time of this writing his disappearance has not been explained. But the last press report quoted the grieving mother of the boy as saying 'I believe my son was probably consumed by the forces of nature'.[12]

Tragedies like these sparked a front-page editorial under the headline: 'Realities of a harsh land no joke'. The editorial was prompted by the death of an American tourist, taken by a crocodile in the far north of the country. But the event was used to further encode the meaning of the land in the Australian tradition. The editorial, which opened with reference to the harsh land, ended with the following warning: 'We are Australians. And we must learn to beware of Australia's capricious wonders as much as we love them.'[13] In this instance, the death occurred on water not on land; the woman was American, not Australian; and her death was the result of an ill-considered decision to swim where crocodiles were known to breed. The editorial, which is ostensibly about her death, is actually about 'Australianness', which arises out of man's relation to what is imagined as a harsh landscape, the bush, represented as a capricious wonder. Imagined in this way, nature becomes an indomitable feminine force and man its passive victim.

People do die in the bush. And those deaths are tragic. But they could have been prevented. The victims died through misadventure, inexperience, loss of direction, misjudgement, exposure, lack of supplies, foolhardiness, and the like. The bush, itself, was not absorbing, consuming or capricious. These are imaginary constructions for the landscape which attend a long history of white settlement. The white Australian bush, for example, is not the bush of the Aboriginal dreamtime which has sustained tribal life in the outback for over 40 000 years, nor the mythic 'land of milk and honey' as represented in the American colonial tradition which later became signified as the 'whore with the heart of gold' when she yielded her riches in the 1850s. This chapter will argue that the relationship of white Australians to the bush produces very different bush from that of Aboriginal Australia. It also produces a very different 'woman' from her construction in other lands. The discourse on the Australian tradition is a crucial site of narrative construction for 'femininity'. That meaning which this culture pours into the category of the feminine also engages its readers in cultural and social formations of the feminine which inscribe female subjectivity. The process of signifying landscape through a variety of metaphoric expressions deserves further scrutiny.

THE COLONIAL CONTEXT

Within the Australian tradition the nature of man's relationship to the land is a central concern. The land as an imaginative construction, a fantasy, has taken many forms. Representations are not stable but heterogeneous. In the early days of exploration the land was imagined as a playground for man's rational-cum-scientific interests. Wild, untamed Nature, through Romantic constructions, came to be a source of man's knowledge and pleasure. Men of science discovered, through Captain Cook's voyages, a wealth of Australian flora and fauna previously unknown and unclassified. The zoological oddities contributed to the idea of Australia as a land of oddities. 'Nature . . . seems determined to have a bit of play, and to amuse herself as she pleases,' wrote the Reverend Sidney Smith from London in 1817.[14] When Nature yielded scientific riches she was described as playful, capricious. She was not amusing herself, of course, but the new colonial inhabitants. Her riches, the plant and animal life which defied classification into the linear order of the Great Chain of Being, would eventually provide scientists with data to support a new theory of organic evolution.

At the same time, scientists, philosophers and moral reformers began to take an interest in the native population. The Aboriginal people were variously described for popular readership. Some writers hailed them as noble savages, others dismissed them as wanton barbarians, still others studied them as the possible connecting link between man and the monkeys in the Great Chain. All natives were named as objects for white man's scrutiny and placed on the lowest order of human life. But the Aboriginal women, who 'only seem to require a tail to complete the identity' were especially damned.[15] During convict days the antipodean land of oddities came to be seen as a suitable dumping ground for criminals: 'the dwelling place of devils in human shape, the refuse of Botany Bay'.[16]

During the time of transportation, Australia became a 'howling hell' on earth, a hostile wilderness. The women unlucky enough to be sentenced to the penal colony were invariably described as unregenerate reprobates, much worse a class of criminals that the men, women being 'generally the refuse of London'.[17] During this time the image of Australia in England was one of exaggerated horror. As Coral Lansbury suggests, the representations may have served as an ideological device to control working-class crime in Britain. The moral reformers in England created an image of moral depravity for the colony in Australia in order to mask and control the threat of civil disruption from within their own society. The signifying force of the feminine as evil, the she-devil, operates to name both the land and its inhabitants. But convict women, all damned whores, were especially damned.

The imaginative construction of the land as an alien wilderness is familiar to contemporary readers of Australian literature. Marcus Clarke's novel of the convict system, *His Natural Life*, represents Australia in similar terms as a land of exile and terror from which there is no escape. In Clarke's text Australia is represented as 'a fantastic land of monstrosities' which tells its 'story of sullen despair' in 'the language of the barren and the uncouth'.[18] In his preface to the poems of Adam Lindsay Gordon, Clarke extends the metaphor of a monstrous, alien landscape, describing the spirit of the bush as one of 'weird melancholy'.[19] We recall Lawson's use of similar descriptions of the bush—'a blasted, barren wilderness that doesn't even howl'.[20]

EXPLORING THE LANDSCAPE

To the early explorers, however, the land was imagined as an Arcadian paradise. Thomas Mitchell wrote evocatively of the allure of the luxuriant, verdant landscape of Victoria. 'Of this Eden it seemed that I was the only Adam', he reported, 'and it was indeed a sort of paradise to me'.[21] He coined the phrase 'Australia Felix', a phrase which later writers used to express the possibilities for the whole continent. John Lort Stokes, Captain of the *Beagle* during the exploratory voyages of 1837–43, referred to the pliant, virgin land which met his gaze as 'the Plains of Promise'. As the explorers penetrated the bush, often without success, they began to recognize its dangers and its mysteries. Charles Sturt, unable to reach his goal during the 1849 expedition into Central Australia, wrote:

A veil hung over Central Australia that could neither be pierced or raised. Girt around by deserts, it almost appeared as if Nature had intentionally closed itself upon civilized man, that she might have one domain on earth's wide field over which the savage might roam in freedom.[22]

Charles Eyre wrote in a similarly imaginative vein as he headed west from Adelaide towards Western Australia. He detailed his self-confessed obsession with this landscape/this woman in the following way. He penned his desire to penetrate 'the vast recesses of the interior of Australia, to try to lift up the veil which has hitherto shrouded its mysteries from the researches of the traveller'.[23] For both Eyre and Sturt the land takes on the features of a veiled, seductive, exotic, unknown, but desired maiden. This same fantasy is evoked for viewers in the opening scenes of the film *Picnic at Hanging Rock*.

3 THE BUSH AND WOMEN

As land exploration and settlement progressed through the nineteenth century, the land came to be seen as harsh, raw, obdurate, cruel, barren and fickle.[24] The bush of Lawson's stories, 'that everlasting maddening sameness of stunted trees [which] makes a man want to break away',[25] becomes more familiar to Australians, replacing the earlier Arcadian fantasies. In the twentieth century the metaphor for the landscape as a body of lack is encoded in Hancock's pastoral history, *Australia*. In this text the land is represented as a wilderness, a void, a threat to be mastered. Hancock details this mastery in a central chapter entitled 'Filling in the Vast Open Spaces'.[26] In *The Legend of the Nineties* Vance Palmer remarks of the pioneers' vision, 'Even the most patriotic spirits thought of Australia as a lean, unlovely mother . . . an enemy to be fought.'[27] It is not surprising, then, to find Miriam Dixson commenting that 'Australia is like the body of an unloved woman'.[28]

What is articulated in these constructions about the bush comes not from the bush itself but from the fantasies of those who view it. The bush functions as a locus of desire. Animated by man's desire, it takes on the seeming attributes of woman, whether described as a passive landscape or an alien force; a place of exile or belonging; a landscape of promise or of threat. This myth of the bush precedes actual seeing. And it is one constantly reproduced in the twentieth century through postcards, television, films, newspaper articles, picture books and ecological campaigns. Meaghan Morris, in a different context, has written of how this construction structures and motivates the visitors' vision. She describes the bush of the Australian imaginary as both void and plenum—'a reservoir of places where nothing might be, or anything might happen'.[29] She writes that the myth of the bush is both powerful and seductive *because* its meanings are reversible. The outback both seduces and repulses. It presents the fantastic possibilities of a spiritual quest and vision and also the nightmare fears of madness and death. These images of the bush come to us through our heritage of texts through which outback Australia is understood in all the force of its mystery, power and threat as 'our' possession. Texts 'make sense' of the world. Narrative is the place where our material history, our social relations and our subjectivity as Australians are produced.

On the function of narrative to construct identity, Teresa deLauretis suggests that:

> In its 'making sense' of the world, narrative endlessly reconstructs it as a two-character drama in which the human person creates and recreates *himself* out of an abstract or purely symbolic other — the womb, the earth, the grave, the woman; all of which . . . can be interpreted as mere spaces and thought of as 'mutually identical.' The drama has the movement of a passage, a crossing,

61

an actively experienced transformation of the human being into—man (emphasis in original).[30]

In this passage deLauretis calls attention to the fact that the subject who reads and writes and speaks is a masculine subject—man, constituted in relation to the feminine as a category of discourse, a symbolic other. Our symbolic other, in Australia, is the land in her many disguises.

Nineteenth-century colonial outcasts from Britain identified the land as a place of exile. To them it was alien, foreign, strange. Speakers who identified with the land, either on behalf of British imperialism or Australian nationhood, imagined it as a threat to be mastered, an object to be possessed, an other to be incorporated into or appropriated by the self. When the early explorers successfully penetrated Australia's inland barriers they evoked the land through Romantic metaphors—a bountiful gift, an exotic paradise, a pre-lapsarian Eden. When wealthy pastoralists established outback stations, they imagined it as a passive, pliant virgin awaiting marriage and consummation. But an ambivalence remained. The bush took on the characteristics of danger, particularly for the bushman of the nationalist tradition. It threatened him with assimilation, isolation and death. It represented a force which might reduce him to madness, melancholia or despair. Man's identity, which might be secured heroically by his possession and control of the land as a primary object of desire, was called into doubt by the threat of the bush as a form of the monstrous feminine.[31] The native son is rendered powerless in the face of this force. He becomes its victim.

NO PLACE FOR A WOMAN

All Western discourse positions woman as both subject and object. Discourse establishes a surfeit of representations for feminine otherness. Is there an Australian specificity which mediates this process in ways that implicate actual women who live in Australia? In other words, how is life in Australia similar to and how is it different from that in other Western phallocentric cultures? What is the relationship between the various representations of the feminine and the construction of subjectivities within actual women in Australia? We all are the effects of discourse. Meaning does not exist anywhere except where it is lived and made. The pre-eminent meaning encoded in the nationalist myth of the land-as-woman is that of a harsh, cruel, threatening, fickle, castrating mother. She is dangerous, non-nurturing and not to be trusted. This is 'no place for a woman'! But it is also a familiar place of Woman within the Australian tradition.

What can this tell us about women as actual subjects in discourse? When women inhabit the bush in the histories and fictional accounts, it is seldom in their own right. They appear as daughters, lovers, wives and mothers in relationships to men. That is, they are (always) already spoken for. How are they represented? Daisy Bates and Caroline Chisholm would appear to be early models who break away from a dependent role in relation to men. Both were public figures of renown, who worked independently, both in and out of the bush, in isolation and in the public eye. They were in fact married, a detail I had to check. Daisy Bates was bigamously married, first to Breaker Morant, a union which was never dissolved. The marital status of these two pioneering women (regardless of its legality) did not alter their effectiveness in the public sphere. But they have been inscribed in the culture, however ironically, as God's police—women who looked after the moral interests of the nation under the paternal metaphor. The articulation of the stereotype of God's police is attributed to Caroline Chisholm, a moral reformer who in the 1840s called for the emigration from England of 'God's police—wives and little children—good and virtuous women',[32] to provide the material for the reconstruction of an unregenerate culture of ex-convicts to a 'respectable society' based on the English model. The Father's Law, as represented by Church and State institutions, would be materially embodied in the nation's women. Daisy Bates, the 'protector of the Aborigines', fits the type. Both women have been located historically within the stereotype of God's police.

When women attempt to intervene in the public and political arenas of culture they assume the symbolic space of difference in a relation of similarity to men. As Luce Irigaray writes, 'Woman? "Doesn't exist." She borrows the disguise which she is required to assume. She mimes the role imposed upon her.'[33] Women are excluded as subjects of representation. Identity, autonomy and authority are denied them in their own right. Further, within the Australian tradition, women actors are represented as having a variety of characteristics similar to those ascribed to the harsh 'natural' environment. Their subjectivities and our own consciousness of them as historical agents are constituted by and through the discourse. As subject and object, 'woman' becomes a site of shifting signification with reference to dominant codes of meaning. The Australian myth of woman as God's police coalesces with attitudes towards living women as subjects within Australian culture.

Anne Summers suggests that the two predominant, enduring stereotypes for women in Australia are those of the 'damned whore' and the 'God's police'. Despite this formulation and the historical remnants of convictism which support it, it would appear that the 'damned whore' is not the predominant underside of the code for Australian femininity. Rather, it is the bad mother. In a society which still can refer to a legitimate sex act between married partners as 'having a naughty' and can call to a new bride as she departs for her honeymoon 'Don't forget to pack the Disprin', sex is not an important cultural category of transgression. But motherhood is. The problem is that, until recently, the mode of existence for the bad mother—the one who is harsh, obdurate, fickle, threatening; the one who fails to nurture her children; the one who cannot be trusted; in other words, the construction of the cruel mother which has served as a metaphor for the bush, was largely a fantasy.[34] This was the case until the fatal evening in August 1980 when Lindy Chamberlain stepped into her shoes and inadvertently into the Australian tradition.

The Chamberlain case is interesting for the purposes of this study not in terms of Lindy Chamberlain's innocence or guilt but for the ways in which the media portrayed the event and the attitudes and opinions which coalesced around her. Within two days of the disappearance of the nine-week-old infant Azaria Chamberlain at Ayers Rock, police were convinced that they had a murder case. They surmised that Lindy was lying in her assertion that a dingo took the baby from the tent in the public campground at the base of the Rock. Although they could detect no motive, no evidence, no murder weapon, no body and no witnesses, they concurred that the mother had murdered the baby. A trail of suspicion dragged at Lindy's heels, aided no doubt by the media accounts of rumors of bizarre and unusual behaviour which led to her personification as an evil, demonic monster, in league with the devil. In pubs across Australia the patrons stood up and cheered months later when she was convicted for the murder of her child and sentenced to life imprisonment in Darwin's Berrimah goal, far from her family and new-born child, born while she waited in prison for the outcome of her second inquest and trial. She has since been pardoned for the crime and exonerated by the courts, but not forgiven by a large percentage of the Australian population. It took seven years to sort through the paranoia, lies, rumours, evidence, forensic tests and conflicting accounts between the police and Aboriginal trackers, the scientists and eye witnesses, lawyers and expert witnesses, which led to her pardon. Still many Australians are prepared to debate the issue. They have not forgiven Lindy.

Critics and cultural commentators remain baffled as to how this event could have captured the imagination of the nation and inflamed such harsh and irrational judgements for seven years. How could it be that the police, the press, trial witnesses, the jury which convicted Lindy of the death of the child, the inquiry which finally pardoned Lindy but failed to restore her innocence, and the hostile public which continues to denounce the mother in the most vitriolic rhetoric were all convinced without sound evidence of a mother's guilt? A recent *Time (Australia)* cover story suggests that 'the question must ripen for a few years yet'. The writer comments that 'it is too early to expect everyone to dispassionately reassess their weird jumble of Azaria mythology, so deeply held and so passionately defended for so long.'[35] A few critics have attempted to analyse the cultural phenomenon. They resort to a context of witchcraft, demonology, scapegoating and the like to make sense of it. They 'know' that it was a uniquely Australian phenomenon, this 'sacrifice in the desert', but no one can pinpoint exactly why .

My investigation of cultural representations resonates with reasons as to why and how the bizarre event could have occurred. The media positions viewers and readers to receive meaning in certain ways. The codes of meaning through which the population interpreted the death of Azaria Chamberlain and the character of her mother must have existed in the culture long before the event took place. Reports of the death of the baby gave shape to 200 years of historical constructions about the land waiting to solidify around a woman and an event. The disappearance of the child at Ayers Rock allowed Australians to pour a century of fear and frustration, evidenced by representations of the bush as cruel mother, on to a woman who became the archetypally evil mother. The event was placed in a field of meaning and then explained in relation to that field. The meaning did not emanate from Lindy Chamberlain herself nor from events which actually occurred at Ayers Rock in August 1980. The 'meaning' which materialized around the infant's death already had been constructed within an Australian imaginary. The infant victim stood in the place of all the repressed and irrational fears about national identity—that the native son might succumb to the cruel mother; that the mother might ruthlessly harm her innocent children; that mother nature can victimize her sons; that identity, potency, authority of the self over the other is never secure. These powerful imaginative associations are embedded in a consciousness of what it means to be an Australian. It is likely that they were activated by the press in its construction of the Chamberlain case. It is not the 'reality' or the 'facts' of the case which deserve closer scrutiny but the modes of representation which enabled the population to read the events according to pre-existing systems of meaning.

FEMINIST PERSPECTIVES ON WOMEN IN AUSTRALIA

Given the fact that women as actors are curiously absent from much of the discourse, the signification of the feminine becomes all the more pertinent to a study of the place of women in the Australian tradition. But it is also necessary to acknowledge what it has been possible to say by women as subjects contributing to the discourse on Australia from evolving feminist perspectives. Within six months of each other, in late 1975 and early 1976, two texts appeared which interrupted the male monopoly on historical interpretation. They were Anne Summers' *Damned Whores and God's Police* and Miriam Dixson's study *The Real Matilda*. These two inaugural studies attempted to rewrite the history of women in Australian society and to analyse underlying structures which contributed to women's inordinately low status when compared to the position of women in other Western capitalist cultures. The timing of their appearance was important.

The year 1975, International Women's Year, was a watershed for women in Australian political life. The Whitlam Labor government had previously appointed a Women's Advisor and established an I.W.Y. Secretariat and a Women's Advisory Committee within the Prime Minister's Department. The government had set aside two million dollars in an International Women's Year fund to support projects to enhance the position of women in society. A national Women and Politics Conference in Canberra drew many of the nation's feminists together to focus on the status of women. Funds were granted for a project whose major aim was to locate and document sources relating to the study of women in Australia. For that year, at least, the concerns of women were to receive high political profile.

Summers' and Dixson's historical studies appeared at the end of 1975 and the beginning of 1976 respectively. They were followed by the publication of bibliographic materials which annotated primary and secondary source materials relating to women in Australian society. Documentary texts, like Ruth Teale's *Colonial Eve: Sources on Women in Australia* (1978) and Kay Daniel's and Mary Murnane's *Uphill all the Way: A Documentary History of Women in Australia* (1980) followed.[36] They have provided researchers and historians with valuable documentary evidence concerning the history of women in Australia. Recently feminist histories, like Jill Matthews' *Good and Mad Women* and Kereen Reiger's *The Disenchantment of the Home*, have appeared. More are promised. The new texts adopt diverse approaches which attend to the problems of gender construction, challenge the dichotomous categories which divide the public world of men from the private world of women, and attempt methods which interrogate the interaction of political and personal worlds.[37] The early texts by Summers and Dixson, however, continue to exert an influence as major interpretative studies. Their authority has not yet been eclipsed.

Each study has both advanced and retarded what it is possible to know and articulate about women's place in the Australian tradition. The texts are progressive in several ways. They play a role in the development of Australian feminism in their complex treatment of political, social and personal issues as they had been formulated in theory. They revise the traditional paradigms of history and restore feminist perspectives to the field. In their appropriation of theoretical concepts, especially from Marxism and psychoanalysis, they have broadened the scope, methods and directions of mainstream and feminist history.

The texts have also had a retarding influence. They fill in some of the gaps in Australia's historical past. But they reproduce the tradition of a separate sphere for women which the studies set out to challenge. They present a separate case, largely to a separate audience of readers. They document women's position of inferiority within the culture. The texts now appear on reading lists for studies of Australian history, literature and culture, usually in an appended category—that is the real, Australian History (male), then come: Women, Aborigines, Chinese, that is, the others. This situation is, however, a decided improvement over their former standing, noted by Humphrey McQueen in his index to *A New Britannia?*, as: 'Women, ignored, page 13'.

Although Summers and Dixson do not share the same ideological assumptions concerning the nature of women's oppression, both rely on liberal social theories as the basis of their studies. Dixson uses a humanist psychological model, Erikson's identity theory, to explain women's low self-esteem within Australian culture. Summers uses a more activist, interventionist model of socialist-feminist analysis to detect systems of oppression within the capitalist and patriarchal order. But both approaches rely on phallocentric and logocentric assumptions which do not account for the construction of the concept 'woman', defined in relation to man, within language and representation. Both texts, but in different ways, assume that women are autonomous subjects in culture with equal access to language. Both posit a faith in the 'real' woman, who might attain her own autonomous and independent identity, if only the social, political, economic and psychological systems of oppression could be abolished. In Dixson's text the central problem is men—the settlers who came to Australia as convicts, outcasts, Irish peasants, or diffident administrators, all lacking in self-esteem. Their own psychological needs caused them to demean women, as a psychic defence against their own inadequacy. In Summers' study the problem is male power and female colonization. Her analysis is social and systemic. But both writers conclude that woman's dilemma, at a fundamental level of consciousness, lies in the internalization of social, political and cultural structures which determine and maintain her inferior status. Thus, in the final analysis, the unconscious, and specifically the female unconscious, becomes the repository for patriarchy. This would seem to establish an impasse.

Miriam Dixson analyses woman's inferior status in Australian culture with reference to humanist perspectives in social psychology, specifically the theories on ego identity developed by Erik Erikson. The study applies identity theory to the formation of Australian national identity. Like Summers, Dixson affirms that women are either left out of the debates on nationalism or are characterized as 'cast outs' or moral guardians. These anti-woman attitudes evolved because the men who came to Australia, either as convicts or as colonial authorities, brought with them feelings of low self-worth. They depicted women in a negative light to keep them a step below the men on the social ladder. She explains, 'the women of the males on the lowest rungs of the ladder internalized the proferred definition of female worth and they became what "their" males needed them to become.'[38] Dixson also cites the 'imprinting' of nineteenth-century British upper-class values onto the Australian personality and sexual mores. Thus, Victorian prudery, 'a sense of awkwardness or fear about the flesh of woman,'[39] came to pervade Australian history, literature and social life. The study examines how sexual opresion and psychic repression constrain women, but it could not register how the interrelated systems of psychic, political and institutional constraints act on the very production of the concept of the self. The categories of masculinity and femininity which underlie and structure her argument are not questioned.

Anne Summers uses a socialist-feminist model to analyse the position of women. The constructions of damned whore and God's police which divide women into evil, tainted, sexual creatures or good, pure, sexless wives and mothers serve in her terms as examples of the ideology of sexism through which the ruling class validates its political, economic and cultural practices. She calls it an 'external' system, 'imposed' upon women, which 'strips' women of their own culture by the imposition of an alien one, 'an artificial contrivance', which prevents them from 'being able to construct their own identities'.[40]

Summers recognizes the difficulty of her argument in which the 'artificial contrivance' of sexist ideology becomes the 'reality' of female economic, social and political dependence on men. She resorts to the psychological concept of 'internalization' as an underlying source of women's 'cultural impotence'. She writes, 'they acquire a conception of "self" which is based on a contradiction which they resolve by submitting to male dominance.'[41] There are several problems. She speaks on behalf of women she cannot know, women whose lives have been represented by and through the master texts. In addition, she analyses their oppression with the assistance of a contemporary psychological concept of the divided self. Summers represents the 'real' woman as caught within a culturally colonized 'false self'. She reiterates in another place that the only territory women possess is that of the body: 'their bodies are all that women indisputably possess'.[42] As we have noted before there is no real or essential self. Even the body is given meaning through its historical and ideological constructions.

There are certain dichotomies which frame and structure the arguments of both Dixson and Summers: true and false self, natural and cultural roles, external impositions and internal constraints, social and psychological realities. Because both writers hold to a liberal humanist concept of an authentic self, they pose the problem of woman's inferior position in culture in terms of the imposition on women of stereotypes of female sexuality, which women (voluntarily?) 'become'.

If one dismantles the idea of the autonomous subject and locates the construction of both subjectivity and the unconscious in discourse then it becomes possible to say more about the problem of patriarchy and to analyse woman's position differently. 'Woman' is the effect of the binary oppositions male/female, external/internal, social/psychological, and the like which define actual women and the category of femininity as the mirror opposite of man/masculinity. All the oppositions have a privileged term which contains its opposite. Questions about the authority of the 'self' are resolved by the dispersion of women/the feminine into the signifying place of the other. Language establishes the illusion of a unitary subject (the 'self') by laws, rules, procedures which harness the fragmenting force of the feminine other—the dark core, the chaotic body processes which threaten to overflow the boundaries of unity.

The dichotomy between 'damned whore' and 'God's police' is not about women at all but two sides to a masculine projection of female sexuality as it mirrors the dilemma of self-definition. The damned whore can function as a scapegoat for man in convict society; God's police serves as the redemptive counterpart historically brought into play to master the threat of the damned whore (that is, lawlessness, madness, sexuality) all of which threaten the authority of masculine sameness. It is not only women who are thus defined, but also men. The process of naming, however, not only places readers in masculine positions of representation, it also subjects women to the operations of discourse which sustain the concepts.

The Big Dichotomies in language precede and make possible the social, political, economic and psychic positions examined in Summers' text. This is not to say that women are not oppressed. They are both socially oppressed and discursively repressed within a phallocentric culture. Historical interpretation represents women within the master discourse. Deconstructing the discourse can give evidence of a plurality of meanings and shifting subjectivities through time and circumstance.

DECONSTRUCTING THE WOMAN IN AUSTRALIAN CULTURAL STUDIES

The 'Bush Mum' Revisited

Dixson and Summers attempted to analyse the biological, social, political and cultural position of women from liberal humanist and socialist-feminist frameworks. Their texts took the arguments as far as possible with the tools of analysis available at the time. Utilizing their insights it is now possible to approach the subject from another perspective—to interrogate the linguistic signification of women/the feminine in the organization of knowledge as power. Knowledge about woman involves the power to name, to master, to control the undecidable through the complex processes of signification. I will illustrate the difference in approach, which requires a difference in critical textual strategy, with reference to the idea of the bush woman.

In *Damned Whores and God's Police* Summers relates that although women are seldom presented in a positive light (when they appear at all) in the histories of Australia, one of the few depictions of women which might be seen as positive is Manning Clark's description of the bush woman. In Henry Lawson's stories she takes the form of the drover's wife. Here is how she is represented in Clark's history and recalled in Summers' text: 'out of such squalor and hardship, which drove the menfolk into erratic, unsteady ways in the primitive huts of the gentry, a matriarch quietly took over the central position in the family, and in the huts of the servants a "Mum" came into her own'.[43] Summers challenges this view as an example of Clark's idealization of women in the bush as 'copers'. She claims that in both the literature and the history of Australia this depiction is unrealistic because it fails to recognize the real hardships which women faced in the bush, including the physical threats of rapacious men. The latent suggestion of rape as the most violent and repressed form of women's oppression, absent from any consideration in the country's 'objective' histories, re-emerges, if indirectly, in Summers' description of women as a colonized sex in her text's central chapter.[44] Clearly, a number of underlying ideas which from the framework of the study come together in Summers' remarks on Clark's depiction of the bush woman.

Summers calls Clark's commentary on the bush Mum an idealization which disguises male power and the rapacious instincts of men in the bush. Clark's history mutes evidence of physical violence against women. This is a fair critique of masculine violence to women within an empiricist or a Marxist historical framework. But there is more to say. If we re-read the text as discourse in order to interrogate the linguistic organization of knowledge as power, Clark's history reveals the power of patriarchal ideology as well. It partakes of the operations of language which give men the power to name, to represent and to speak for women. The bush Mum as a signifier in both Clark's and Summers' texts is an effect of knowledge/power. The context of Clark's description deserves more careful consideration. He writes:

> contemporaries coined the phrase that the bush was 'no place for a woman.' Yet, paradoxically, those who possessed the pluck and the will to endure acquired a prestige and a power in a society whose composition seemed designed to confer a power on the man even in excess of that on which Moses and the apostle Paul had conferred a divine sanction. Out of such squalor and hardship, which drove the menfolk into erratic, unsteady ways in the primitive huts of the gentry, a matriarch quietly took over the central position in the family, and in the huts of the servants a 'Mum' came into her own.[45]

Read semiotically this passage illustrates how men and women are constituted through phallocentric systems of reference. It reaffirms the earlier discussion in which we saw how the bush has been constructed as both 'no place for woman' and the place of women. The text reproduces that meaning. In addition, it makes meaning with reference to already established dichotomies of class and gender within a nationalist discourse. Within this passage woman acquires a prestige and power which is not her own but is designated to her through the authority of God, Moses, St Paul, and finally men (especially Australian men). The men belong to two distinct social classes—the gentry and their servants. Yet their class difference is elided. The passage acknowledges that 'men' in Australia have inordinate prestige and power because of the specific 'composition' of the society. This 'composition', however, is discursive before it enters the realms of fiction and history. The women in Clark's description are not presented as autonomous individuals. Their status is that of wife and mother. For both women 'her own' is her place in the network of family relationships. She usurps the 'natural' place of her bushman husband. In reference to the 'matriarch' the text reads, she 'took over the central position' not actually in the bush but in the family. This 'unnatural' event can occur because the bushman (whether he be from the gentry or the servant class) has become 'erratic, unsteady'. Only in such a 'primitive' place could such a role reversal take place. His wife preserves his position for him. The position is one of authority and of central importance to the maintenance of the social order, the family and the state. It stands for 'civilization' in the primitive bush. The position (not the woman) saves the populace from being driven astray, that is, dazed by the bush as alien Other, a form of the feminine. The status she acquires is a masculine status. The mother has become the phallic mother who possesses power. But the matriarch 'took over' this power whereas the Mum 'comes into' it; this represents two different modes of acquiring power and aligning the reader with the position of the bush Mum rather than the matriarch.

Clark is right to call the situation a paradox. It is a paradox not because of what the women become, but in terms of how the text represents them as both self and other, masculine subject and feminine object, within signification. Both positions are made possible within a gender order where female difference is defined in relation to men within a symbolic order of sameness. At the same time, the male/female dichotomy which is upheld, despite the role reversal, subsumes class considerations. The gentry woman becomes a 'matriarch', while the servant woman retains the title 'mum'. But she is given extraordinary status through the rhetorical device of capitalization of her title, 'Mum'. Nevertheless, all the engendered ideological connotations of sex and class attached to the terms 'matriarch' and 'mum', even if capitalized, continue to co-exist textually. Although they seem to uphold her autonomous status, they actually deny it.

If we continue to unravel the web of meanings, the titles matriarch and 'Mum' have further significance. Historically, men escaped the servant class to become pioneer bushmen—selectors and drovers within a nationalist history. The gentry, although no doubt more successful in their attempts to tame the bush due to larger property holdings, became aligned with old-world values against which the nationalist tradition has been formed. The bush Mum, as drover's wife, took on exalted ideological status as the feminine equivalent to the drover. In Clark's study of Lawson he refers to 'The Drover's Wife' from within the same discursive frameworks which operate in the above passage. He writes, 'Lawson knew that her heroism, the halo of glory with which he endowed this bush Mum, was of a high order.'[46] Clark's discourse reveals an ideological commitment to working-class rather than ruling-class culture, to pioneers rather than gentry, to competent women rather than unsteady men. But the categories which structure the argument also reinforce class and sex divisions. The master discourse which regulates social composition produces the representation of the bush Mum. Clark's passage maintains characteristics of a specifically Australian code of national-ism through the discourses on Christianity, capitalism and patriarchy all of which fuse, reinforce and naturalize each other. Men and women, 'bush Mums' and 'matriarchs', are signified by the network of related meanings. And the text engages the reader as a subject in its processes.

The discourses on the Australian tradition, of which the feminist reinterpretations form a part, create what they repress as well as what they assert. They define sexual identity through the exclusion of 'woman' (what she might be outside of the symbolic representations) and the substitution of culturally specific concepts of masculinity and femininity. What woman might be in her absolute difference from man is not a revision of the second term: male/female (rediscovered), but an impossible subject within patriarchy.

CURRENT FEMINIST APPROACHES TO QUESTIONS OF NATIONAL IDENTITY

Although no monographs have appeared to date which move beyond liberal humanist assumptions to question women's difference within the Australian tradition from post-structuralist perspectives, a growing number of journal articles have begun to suggest a variety of new approaches to women, the feminine and Australian nationalism. Among feminist critics pursuing new approaches within literary studies are Susan Sheridan, Sneja Gunew and Bronwen Levy. Sheridan introduces the shift in the terms of debate in her review of the anthology *Who is She: Images of Women in Australian Fiction*.[47] The review calls attention to the assumptions which underlie many contributions to the anthology that women have an essential female nature or share a common set of experiences which mark them as different from men or that women have a distinct voice which can be traced through the annals of literary history to reveal a separate female tradition. Instead, Sheridan suggests that the 'female voice' is actually a position of the woman writer in relation to representations of femininity in language. She suggests new modes of reading which would register woman's relation to language and socio-cultural production—new modes made possible by semiotics, psychoanalysis and French feminist theory.

In her article ' "Temper Romantic; Bias, Offensively Feminine": Australian Women Writers and Literary Nationalism' Sheridan challenges the democratic spirit of literary nationalism, put forward most recently by John Docker and others, by analysing the absence of women from the literary canon of the 1890s.[48] She demonstrates how the nationalist tradition establishes literary value in terms of the masculine norms of realist and vernacular writing. 'Popular' 1890s writers like Ada Cambridge, Roas Praed and 'Tasma' were excluded from consideration within the canon because their writing deviated from the norm. In addition, critics have discounted these women because they wrote for what were deemed English ruling-class papers rather than the *Bulletin*, 'the Bushman's Bible', even though it is now realized that this view of the *Bulletin* is an urban myth.[49] Sheridan focuses on the way the *Bulletin* handled 'the Woman Question' to reveal the depth of its offensiveness to women, whom it denigrated as innately conservative, class-bound and irrational. In a variety of ways, she studies the processes of literary production whereby masculine values were elevated to national traits. Her study of women like Barbara Baynton, who did write for the *Bulletin*, reveals how they had to work both within and against the narrative conventions of the popular romance. Nonetheless, although from limited positions of authority, these writers mounted a considerable challenge the masculine definitions of Australian culture.

Sheridan extends the argument concerning the masculine construction of national identity and women's position of marginalization in her chapter 'Women Writers' prepared for the bicentenary publication of *The Penguin New Literary History of Australia*. The article considers women writers and a nationalist literary tradition as it evolved in the 1930s and 1940s.[50] In a similar vein, Bronwen Levy has examined the construction of the contemporary woman writer in Australian literary criticism.[51] Her article reminds us that language is a crucial site of political struggle for marginalized groups. Through an examination of the critical reception of Shirley Hazzard's novel, *Transit of Venus*, Levy, like Sheridan, politicizes the received modes of understanding women, art, culture and the connections between them.

In an incisive series of articles on migrant women writers, Sneja Gunew calls into question the whole categories 'Australian Literature' and 'Australian identity' as linguistic constructions formed with reference to a dominant cultural order. Her article 'Migrant Women Writers: Who's on Whose Margins?'[52] analyses the oppressed and marginalized position of both Australian women writers and migrant writers in terms of how each group is situated in relation to the literary norms of the dominant culture. Both women writers and migrant writers adopt similar techniques— first-person narration and the confessional mode, for example—through which to voice their otherness. With reference to Lacanian psychoanalysis and Derridian deconstruction, Gunew articulates the position of the migrant writer as a construct of Australian culture (the child under the guardianship of paternalistic parents) and also Australian culture as an object of the migrant's gaze (the place in writing from which migrants can interrogate social and cultural conventions, notions of linguistic competence and gender certainties). In her article 'Framing Marginality'[53] Gunew extends the argument to consider the negotiation of differences constructed *within* the margins by writers and readers of texts by women, migrant and Aboriginal writers. The article interrogates the idea of Australia as a multicultural society and the ways in which the 'migrant condition' undermines national and personal assumptions of a unified entity, be it the nation, the ego or the self.

In historical studies, as well, feminist writers have begun to challenge the received tradition from new critical perspectives. Patricia Grimshaw reviews the nationalist history, identifies it as a masculine myth and details the feminist historigraphic responses to it in her article 'Women in History: Reconstructing the Past'.[54] Marilyn Lake contextualizes the male myth embodied in the bush legend by considering two conflicting ideologies of the 1890s and the ways in which each promoted a different style of masculinity. She argues that the *Bulletin's* bushman as Lone Hand, separated from the demands of family, was elevated to heroic status while his domestic urban counterpart, promoted by the moral reformers, church groups, the women's temperance movement, the parliamentarian William Lane and others, lost status within cultural practice.[55] Lake suggests that the dominance of the *Bulletin* style of masculinity endorsed men's rejection of domestic responsi-bilities and had 'profound implications for women and children . . . [for whom] there were particularly injurious consequences of the style of mascu-linity propagated by the champions of the Bushman'.[56] By making gender a category of historical analysis, she challenges the masculine assumptions within the nationalist tradition and calls attention to its selective represen-tation of both men and women.

Judith Allen delivers a broadside to the whole discipline of history in her article 'Evidence and Silence: Feminism and the Limits of History'.[57] She begins by detailing feminist approaches to history in the 1970s. Feminist researchers have criticized the patriarchal bias of the discipline. They searched for and found women pioneers to be added to history in order to make it more accurate and comprehensive. Some have written women-centred histories in an attempt to remove feminist questions from the mainstream and take 'women' as a group seriously. Other approaches have shifted the focus of history to study the effects of power relations in social and domestic life and to question the divisions between them.

Similar approaches and techniques have marked the endeavours of feminist researchers who have challenged the pervasive masculine bias across a range of disciplines. Women writers, artists, historians, geographers, educators and pioneers have been discovered, researched and added to the margins of the discourse within specific domains of knowledge. The research contributes to our store of knowledge about women. But it also co-opts women within the phallocentric foundations of Western thought and extends its domain of influence over women's lives. Allen concludes with what might be a summary position for feminists working from post-structuralist positions across the fields of literature, history, philosophy, art history and the like. She writes:

Phallocentric disciplines like history are constituted on the exclusion of women—literally, professionally, conceptually, methodologically and epistemologically. Concern about women's marginalisation through institutional, disciplinary or interdisciplinary separation are located firmly within this illusion, the fear of incoherence and loss. It is only when we realise that we lose nothing in recognising and acknowledging our position outside traditional academic disciplines, that we find where our strength lies. The source of this strength is, paradoxically, that we have no choices. For feminists there is no choice but to start and continue on from this position, most of the time separate and external to traditional knowledges. Our historical silence is then merely an effect. It is the beginning, not the end of our history.[58]

Recent critiques of phallocentrism, whether forwarded by feminists, deconstructive critics or semioticians, work in ways that are separate from and external to traditional knowledges. They attempt not to say something new about women, but to interrogate the textual and discursive formations of women and the feminine within and across the boundaries of scholarly disciplines. They include the work of film makers, as well. Feminist film maker, Helen Grace, whose film *Serious Undertakings* subverts dominant modes of production and reception in cinema, calls attention to filmic codes, gender politics and the fictions of national identity. The film by Ross Gibson and Susan Dermody, *Camera Natura*, traces masculine desire in the representation of Australian landscape and the construction of the national character. Feminists examining philosophic and psychoanalytic traditions, like Genevieve Lloyd, Moira Gatens, Elizabeth Grosz, challenge the liberal humanist and orthodox Freudian assumptions underlying the disciplines and the absence of women from these discourses.[59] These approaches mark a new beginning, both within and beyond feminism—a new place from which to interrogate the construction of women, men and the national culture.

To illustrate further how the Australian tradition is an effect not of history nor of discipline-based frameworks but of phallocentric logic controlled and regulated through discourse, it is necessary to return once again to the dominant texts about Australian nationalism. The texts are not about women, indeed, they hardly mention women as historical subjects. They employ constructions of masculinity and femininity, however, which function to reproduce gender divisions in the various articulations on the nature of the Australian character, especially in relation to man's imperialistic battle with the land. These issues are the focus of the next chapter.

CHAPTER 4

LANDSCAPE REPRESENTATION AND
NATIONAL IDENTITY

Many nations have adventured for the discovery of Australia, but the British
peoples alone have possessed her.

Sir Keith Hancock, *Australia*

Woman is never anything more than the scene of more or less rival exchange
between two men, even when they are competing for the possession of
mother-earth.

Luce Irigaray, 'This Sex Which is not One'

This chapter brings together and expands some of the concerns traced in
Chapter Two: In Search of a National Identity and Chapter Three: The Bush
and Women. It is primarily about landscape representation. But the territory
it explores is at once physical and linguistic, sexual and social, literal and
figurative. A historical question I want to address is: how is it that the land
known as *Terra Australis Incognita* came to be named, tamed and, in
Hancock's words, possessed by British interests—initially on behalf of
Empire and eventually on behalf of Australian native sons?[1] On another level
the question becomes one about identity. How has man as subject confronted
this land as alien other and attempted to define himself through his attempts
to understand his origins in the land; to come to terms with his experience of
its space and boundaries; to assimilate its strangeness into himself and his
symbolic order? These are the processes through which people who came to
live on the land and fill in what Hancock called its 'vast, open spaces' have
constructed their images of identity as Australians.

The question when approached through semiotics, or the study of the
social production of meaning through sign systems, becomes: How is it that
processes of self-representation and identification with the land came to be
registered in discourse with reference to a speaking self who is masculine,
and an object of discourse, an other (in this case the land) which is feminine?
In Hancock's nationalistic history as in other texts referred to earlier,
Australia is imagined, through metaphor, as the body of a woman. It is this

77

'woman', that is woman-as-sign within Western political discourse, to whom Luce Irigaray refers when she comments that woman is never anything more than the scene of a rival exchange between men.[2]

I chose to introduce this chapter with the opening lines of Keith Hancock's 1930 history. Social and political commentators cite this text as seminal in the construction of an Australian national identity. Tim Rowse in his study *Australian Liberalism and National Character* cites Hancock's work as representative of one of three dominant approaches to nationalism.[3] Hancock's book provides the outlines for understanding Australia as an egalitarian democracy within an imperialistic framework. The other two approaches taken up by Rowse are those of the modernist New Critics who re-evaluated the Australian tradition in the 1950s and 1960s, leading up to and including Manning Clark's progressive historical revision, and the New Left critics, represented by Humphrey McQueen's critical history *A New Britannia?*. I will examine constructions of the national character with reference to Rowse's categories before turning to questions of women writers and their relationship to the land.

Until the 1930s the concept of a national character, marked by its distinct difference from England, had little currency in the texts which took Australia as their theme. But with the publication of Hancock's *Australia* the idea took shape and gained academic authority, traces of which survive to this day. The text encodes a nationalist history. But its primarily a history of land settlement. Hancock calls it a 'history of progressive mastery'. The idea of the land, signified as woman, as a body to be shaped, conquered and civilized by man, is a central preoccupation of the text. The Australian identity which emerges is the matey, egalitarian native son of the Democratic Nationalist tradition.

As R. W. Connell pointed out in 1968, 'the themes developed or crystallized by Hancock have been taken over by his successors with only minor modifications . . . The result has been a homogeneous tradition of social comment and criticism.'[4] That homogeneous tradition is coming to an end. It is no longer possible to read history simply in terms of colonial conquest and Western appropriation of a foreign land and its indigenous people. Yet the structuring ideas embedded in Hancock's nationalist history and the narratives on Australia which preceded it have not been fully explored. There is more to be said; in particular, there is more to be said, on both literal and figurative levels, about women.

When Anne Summers, in *Damned Whores and God's Police*, challenged the absence of women from the definitive texts which constitute an Australian tradition, she specifically cited Hancock's *Australia* and Connell's critique. She wrote, 'A . . . flaw of Hancock's work, one which eluded Connell and the

Hancockians he selects, was that Hancock used the terms 'Australian' and 'men' synonymously: the Australian he described was a wholly male universe depicted from a man's point of view.'⁵ Summers took up a position of a socialist-feminist writer. She engaged in a social, political and systemic analysis of male power and female colonization. She took the argument as far as she could with the tools of analysis available to her at the time. As we saw in Chapter Three, however, her critique remained encapsulated within a humanistic philosophic tradition which upholds the autonomous identity of the male or female historical subject. There is a meaning which she could not register then, but we can now. 'Manzone Country' is the name Summers givers to one of her chapters and the name she gives to Australia as the object of analysis. And what her text and that of Hancock signify, through language, is that 'Manzone Country' is woman. The land signified as woman is the site of origin for national identity.

It is rare for commentators on the Australian tradition to register or analyse the significance of the enunciation of the land-as-woman. ⁶ Yet if one re-reads the texts on Australia which constitute a historical tradition, from Dampier's *A New Voyage Around the World* (1697) to Manning Clark's recent five-volume history, what becomes apparent is that although references to actual women as historical agents seldom appear, references to the idea of woman, embedded in linguistic constructions of landscape, proliferate. They are so familiar that they have become commonplace; so disguised by other elements of the narratives that they have escaped notice. Perhaps it is time to register the metaphor of Woman in the landscape and to rethink the authorial Man who comes to represent the national character.

THE PRE-TEXTS OF A COLONIAL CULTURE

For centuries Australia existed as an empty space on the map of the world, as body of desire. Man, as the agent of history, confronted raw nature, as a vast and empty Other, and named it his Australia Felix. The land has taken on the attributes of masculine desire. This desire acts as a generative force in the narratives of exploration and settlement. We can register the force of desire operating through the discourses on Australia by attending to the naming of the land and man's attempts to claim it for the self. This dimension of the present study is not unlike that adopted recently by Tzvetan Todorov in *The Conquest of America: The Question of the Other.* In that text Todorov explains:

> Language exists only by means of the other, not only because one always addresses someone but also insofar as it permits evoking the absent third person. But the very existence of this other is measured by the space the

symbolic system reserves for him . . . [A]ny investigation of alterity is necessarily semiotic, and reciprocally, semiotics cannot be conceived outside the relation to the other.[7]

Within the Australian tradition, the land is the not-me, that which is opposite. As other, it can be imagined as either similar to the writer and function as an object to be assimilated into the symbolic order so that it becomes identified with the self; or different from the writer, but not beyond the realm of understanding. In either case the land is named through linguistic processes of inclusion and exclusion. That is, it exists either within the writer's/speaker's frame of reference and is linked to him or her on a historical, cultural or moral plane; or it is outside the subject's imagined frame of reference and is represented as alien, foreign or strange. If it is imagined within the subject's frame of reference it is imagined as a locus of desire within the Father's Law. If it is imagined to exist outside the subject's frame of reference it can take on the characteristics of alterity, of otherness beyond the symbolic order, for example, as a howling wilderness or gaping abyss. The categories are fluid. Within any one text contradictory or shifting significations for the land are likely to occur. But the naming is not arbitrary. It takes place within a symbolic order of masculine sameness with reference to masculine and feminine categories.

A dominant impulse in the narratives of exploration and discovery is one towards ownership, mastery or possession of the land, which might consolidate and guarantee identity to the subject. At least mastery over a threatening landscape allows the illusion of a unified identity to be countenanced. To challenge the illusion of unity of the subject, we can interrogate the processes of naming to ask not what identity is but how it has been constructed as masculine identity with reference to the otherness of the land. In so doing it is possible to trace a rich and diverse network of contradictory significations for woman, man and the land which the illusion of unity disguises.

A writer, says Roland Barthes, 'is one who plays with his mother's body . . . in order to glorify it, to embellish it, or in order to dismember it to take it to the limit of what can be known about the body'.[8] These 'playful' processes have been at work in the naming of Australia as a feminine (if not always specifically maternal) body. These imaginative constructions are also determined by ideological constraints informing the subject's relation to power/knowledge. As Michel Foucault reminds us, a central question to be asked when analysing discursive formation is: who speaks, for whom and by what authority? He writes:

> discourses are not once and for all subservient to power or raised up against it, any more than silences are. We must make allowances for the complex and

unstable process whereby discourse can be both an instrument and an effect of power . . . Discourse transmits and produces power; it reinforces it, but also undermines and exposes it, renders it fragile and makes it possible to thwart it'.[9]

By re-reading the discourse we can register both the psycho-social and political disparities embedded within it.

The discourse on the Australian tradition not only attempts to establish a national identity through the relationship of man to the land but also to foreclose and maintain the interests of dominant social, religious and political institutions. The land, then, is not only a metaphor for feminine otherness through which man attains a (precarious) identity but also a shifting site of battles—moral, political, religious, economic—invested and traversed by the relations of power/knowledge. Writers of authoritative texts, in their attempts to master knowledge, construct the land as an object and instrument of power.

There are several processes which attend the writing of history, according to Foucault. One common preoccupation, which we detailed in Chapter Two, is the pursuit of origins. This process attempts to capture the essence of things, to find pure truth and to posit identity behind the masks of origin— which is a place of loss. Another process involves a tracing of descent, or genealogies, through the discourses of history which deal with differences and disunities. According to Foucault history itself produces unities. It has no origins, no ultimate meaning, no continuity except that which emerges through the operations of power/knowledge. The discourses construct the meanings which appear to supply coherence to human endeavour.[10] We will use these insights as tools with which to examine the dominant historical discourses, reveal discursive practices and analyse how constructions of femininity function textually in the production of concepts of Australian identity. The Australian tradition, constructed with reference to Lawson as founding father, registers the bush as the landscape on which Australian identity is constituted. We can register the linguistic signification of the bush within a nationalistic tradition by recalling its evocation in the texts of the nineteenth century as they are said to lead up to Lawson. In so doing we register the second of the two impulses of historical construction about which Foucault writes, the tracing of descent.

THE DISPERSEMENT OF 'WOMAN' AND THE IDEA OF AUSTRALIA

The first British explorer credited with visiting the land known as *Terra Australis Incognita* was William Dampier. In 1697, ten years after the publication of Locke's *Second Treatise on Government*, Dampier provided the British peoples with the first detailed descriptions of the land and its inhabitants. The land of his experience was described negatively, in terms of lack. He related that it held no gold or spices, houses, water or crops, only pestering flies and miserable savages. But he imagines for the reader a land of more promising aspect:

> I could not but hope to meet with some fruitful lands, Continents or Islands, or both, productive of any of the rich Fruits, Drugs, or Spices . . . that are in other parts of the Torrid Zone, under equal Parallels of Latitude; at least a Soil and Air capable of such, upon transplanting them hither, and Cultivation.[11]

This conception of the use-value of the land is derived from Locke's theory of private property, which assumes the right of ownership to land, based on human enterprise. In his *Second Treatise on Government* Locke wrote:

> And hence subduing or cultivating the Earth, and having Dominion, we see are joined together. The one gave Title to the other. So that God, by commanding to subdue, gave Authority so far to *appropriate*. And the Condition of Humane Life, which requires Labour and materials to work on, necessarily introduces *private possessions* (emphasis in original).[12]

The assumption that the masculine (man, Empire, Civilization) has an unquestioned God-given right to subdue or cultivate the feminine (woman, Earth, Nature) and appropriate the feminine to masculine domination is a constant structuring principle of Western discourse. As an ideological construct, it underlies British imperialist interests and shapes the Australian tradition. As a psychoanalytic construct, it makes possible the inscription of the subject into culture.

The land evokes man's pleasure when seen as a resource for exploitation and appropriation; otherwise, it remains a 'waste' land. As Lenore Coltheart demonstrates in her thesis on the settlement of the Northern Territory, 'the "consummation" of "waste" lands was the mission of the Victorian age in Australia, a duty recognized as divinely ordained.'[13] This can be illustrated in the words of John Lort Stokes, Commander of the *Beagle* during its 1837–43 voyage of exploration. He wrote, echoing Locke's sentiments, of: ' . . . the feeling of pride engendered by the thought that we are in any way instrumental to the extension of man's influence over the world which has been given him to subdue.'[14] Stokes looked to the northern coast of Australia and imagined:

> a noble city . . . sprung as though by magic from the ground, which will serve both as a monument of English enterprise, and as a beacon from whence the light of Christian civilization shall spread through the dark and gloomy recesses

of ignorance and guilt . . . Providence has entrusted to England a new Empire in the Southern seas.[15]

There are several impulses at work in this discursive moment. In the semiotic play of sameness and difference detailed here, there is a double movement—a movement between the signifiers of Empire and Christianity. The noble city imagined as a 'monument of British enterprise' marks Australia as a place co-existent with the self and the demands of Empire. The noble city imagined as a 'beacon from whence the light of Christian civilization shall spread through the dark and gloomy recesses of ignorance and guilt' registers the uncivilized land as an alien body of barbaric difference to be rescued from an unregenerate state of Nature. The sacred trust of Providence (the Law of the Father) is the 'magic' which might transform a threatening landscape into land of social cohesion.

Stokes called the continent the 'Plains of Promise'. But the notion of threat, sounded with reference to the 'dark and gloomy recesses', represents an unsettling element in the text. The fear that the land might come to absorb its inhabitants is a common feature within the discourse on the Australian tradition, as we recalled earlier with reference to the film *Picnic at Hanging Rock*. In the literature of exploration the threat of absorption can be registered as operating on a sub-textual level in the discourse concerning the expedition and disappearance of Charles Leichhardt. Leichhardt began his journey north to the Gulf of Carpenteria in October 1844. When he did not return for fourteen months, he was presumed dead, absorbed by the alien bush. His reappearance evoked the mythic motif of Jonah and the whale: a man swallowed by the vast interior and then miraculously rescued. The newspapers reported his return as a 'return from the dead'. Further the *Sydney Morning Herald* described the interior landscape which Leichhardt had traversed in excessive terms which subdued any suggestion that the land might have the power to absorb its inhabitants. The paper reported that his journey had:

> established the broad fact that our continent possesses an Australia Felix to the north as well as to the south . . . a land of mingled sublimity and beauty; a land of majestic rivers and graceful streams . . . a land . . . of wheat and barley, and vines and fig trees, and pomegranates; a land of oil-olive, and honey; a land wherein thou shall eat bread without scarceness; a land where stones are iron, and out of whose hills thou mayest dig brass.[16]

It would not be the last time the newspaper resorted to journalistic excess. But it is excess to a purpose. In this description we note several semiotic impulses. The references to wheat and barley, and later to brass and iron, suggest that

83

the Plains of Promise can be put specifically to agricultural and industrial uses. But the excessiveness which swells at the centre of this description: 'a land of wheat and barley, and vines and fig-trees, and pomegranates; a land of olive-oil, and honey . . .' evokes the image of both a biblical promised land and a nurturing maternal body—a pliant, waiting, passive Mother Earth, needing only an eager European presence for consummation. The threat that the dark continent might absorb its pioneers into its vast, open and empty centre has been quelled. Jonah has escaped the whale. Leichhardt's return was acclaimed in public speeches, in prose and poetry and song. The sombre reports of Leichhardt's contemporary, Augustus Gregory—an explorer who neither harboured Arcadian visions nor found them—sank into obscurity, while the imagined vistas of Stokes and those evoked by the *Sydney Morning Herald* were widely quoted and credited with the status of truth.

The early aspirations of Empire would be sorely tested in the light of the actual experience of settlement. Increasingly, through the decades of land exploration and settlement, the imagery of the magical body gave way to the language of threat. When it defied the settlers' attempts at mastery it was described as 'hostile,' 'harsh,' 'obstructive,' 'deceitful,' 'cruel,' 'impoverished' and 'raw'. Still, as long as imperialistic assumptions concerning the land predominated over the discourse, the land was imagined as a desired (rather than feared) feminine other, capable of being mastered and subdued. The colonists were aided in their assumptions of mastery by the four-stage theory of social evolution propounded by Locke and later in economic terms by Adam Smith. It held that human societies naturally progressed through four developmental stages: hunting and gathering, pastoral, agricultural and commercial. The white man aided the delivery of Australia into and beyond stage two. Thus, a pastoral historian in 1911 would report that 'the soil was, as it were, electrified by the touch of colonization.'[17]

We can register the signification of the land as a terrain on which the white man battles for his rightful possession in William Harcus' 1876 emigration guide. Harcus wrote:

> To successfully plant a young Colony . . . seems to require special qualities, physical, moral, and intellectual, which are possessed in their highest form by the Anglo-Saxon people. It is a small matter to supplant the Aboriginal inhabitants of a barbarous country and to secure possession of their land . . . .
> It is battling with Nature, conquering the soil, holding on against capricious seasons, fighting with the elements and compelling the earth to yield what it never yielded before . . . a reward for man's toil . . . that the real triumphs of an old people in a new land are seen. [18]

Harcus speaks for Empire. In this discourse the whole of Australia, land

and people, are imaginatively assimilated into the self. His assertions uphold the authority of white, male, Western civilization as a presence which must be established and maintained in the advancing cause of progress and civilization. Imperialistic assumptions of mastery over the barbaric natives and capricious Nature take the forms of moral, economic, physical, rational and sexual possession. The terms of possession are military—battling, conquering, holding on, fighting and, finally, finding triumph. Victory is assured. Nature will 'yield what it never yielded before', if not crops in abundance, then enhanced power to a flagging British Crown. Nature here is imagined as a phallic Mother Nature, who is desired not for herself but for the power she symbolizes.

AN AUSTRALIAN NATIONALIST TRADITION

In the colonial period of Australia's history, the dominant groups whose interests would shape the image of Australia resided in Britain. In the late nineteenth century, however, the colony took on a cultural and political identity as a new society. The discourses which speak from a nationalist Australian tradition obscure Australia's ties with an imperialistic past. Hancock's historical study, Australia, encodes these new nationalistic attitudes in the literature which identifies with the land on behalf of Australian nationalism and not British Empire. The nationalist texts contain ambivalences: between the speaker's identification with either Britain or Australia, and towards the land itself as an object either loved or loathed.

The Theme of Two Mistresses
These differences can be registered with reference to a theme which recurs in the literature—the theme of the two mistresses. In 1880 a popular emigration guide sounded the now familiar call of Empire to master and subdue the land. 'As the soil of old countries become impoverished and needs rest and recuperation, it becomes imperative that fresh virgin ground must be found to meet the ever increasing wants of the stockholder and husbandman.'[19] In this description, England is named as the old and impoverished motherland which will be replaced by the pliant young virgin. The master, stockholder or husbandman, is guaranteed rights of ownership and possession through land use on behalf of Britain. By the 1930s the terms of reference have changed. Hancock, reflecting on the ambivalence inherent in the theme of two mistresses, writes: 'A country is a jealous mistress and patriotism is commonly an exclusive passion; but it is not impossible for Australians, nourished by a glorious literature and haunted by old memories, to be in love with two soils.'[20]

The historian of Democratic Nationalism admits to a dissonance between the desire for Australian nationalism, imagined as a jealous mistress, and a residue of imperialist loyalties to the motherland, located in its literature and old memories. His political loyalties are with Australia, but he reserves a space for British cultural traditions—'Culture' being a desirable attribute of the parental heritage which did not necessarily follow in the wake of progressive mastery of the land.

What occurred, historically, between the writing of these two texts was Australian Federation. Politically, the old British authority was supplanted by a new order. But the idea of the land as a desired (even if illicit) object, answerable to male needs, remained constant. The difference is that the master was no longer British, but Australian. Hancock represents the interests of the new native sons vying with the old imperial father for authority over the land.

The nature of both the subject (man) and object (the land) is radically different depending on whether one speaks for Empire or for Australian nationalism. In the texts quoted above the literature of Empire assumes man's victory over the land as the logical consequence of white man's burden. But the native son, who would conquer the land on behalf of more limited national needs, has diminished status. And the land, in the light of actual experience, defies his attempts at mastery. It offers a variety of unexpected responses to male demands and desires, including drought and bushfires and floods and poisonous snakes. Victory is never assured; his status remains in question. His desire for the land is represented as an ambivalent loyalty to two soils—old mother and new mistress. The Australian tradition, in Hancock's text, represents a coming to terms with man's limited potential on the land. But the limitations will be blamed on the 'fickle' land-as-woman, the land which denies man's desire for full possession and, thus, challenges his identity on the Australian soil.

Hancock's 'Australia'

Hancock's *Australia* begins with the sentence which opened this chapter: 'Many nations adventured for the discovery of Australia, but the British peoples have alone possessed her.'[21] Possession, unchallenged, remains the basic prerogative of imperial power. Having established the singular British claim to ownership based on the male/female coupling, he continues by describing the physical and economic assaults on the land by pastoralists who 'raided the desert'. Personification of the land as woman continues. She comes to life, responding to the assault as a cruel, avenging mother. 'The very soil has suffered from the ruthlessness of the invaders . . . To punish their folly the land brought forth for them bracken and poor scrub and other rubbish.'[22] But Hancock's history is one of forward-looking optimism. So, despite huge, threatening distances, he confides, 'The Australians are not depressed by the contemplation of their vast, open spaces.'[23] The land would povide the frontier for their 'coming of age'. Like the explorers of Empire before him, he uses the same belief in the progressive history of land-use, derived from Locke and Adam Smith, to justify the white presence on the landscape. Out of 'bracken and poor scrub and other rubbish' (could this include the Aborigines?) the pastoral industry is established: 'the trampling of hundred of sharp little hoofs has consolidated illimitable grasslands for the use and comfort of man . . . From the flame and burn of dreary scrub arise corn lands and a rich permanence.'[24]

As Hirst points out, Hancock imagines the pastoral pioneers of the 1830s as forebears of Australian nationalism to the businessmen of the 1930s.[25] His assumption is that the early explorers were working on behalf of the later Australian capitalists. The assumption is that men of Hancock's generation had a legacy from the past and an obligation to the future. Within the Australian tradition, the bushman as a national type does battle on behalf of his successors. Within Hancock's text he is called the 'native son' whose story will be told by Henry Lawson, but Hancock's allegiance is with the pastoralists who built an industry, and not the legendary bushman. Despite this conflation of identities, Hancock's 'native son' is seen, however, to be battling the forces of nature, rather than the more amorphous and uncontrollable human forces of world trade, low prices, depression and other pioneers.

Heseltine and Modern New Critical Approaches

Not all commentators on the Australian tradition agreed that physical mastery of the bush alone would guarantee success. Harry Heseltine, who featured in the modernist New Critical re-appraisal of a national democratic literary heritage, alters the earlier perceptions of the bush as a physical fact to be conquered. What for Hancock was a landscape which tested the manly strength of character, for Heseltine becomes a psychic plain 'of horror, of panic and emptiness'[26] which threatened to drive its inhabitants insane. He writes: 'the bush becomes a metaphor for the self. Just as the heart of the continent is a burning, insane emptiness, so too at the heart of man is the horror of his prehistory.'[27] This sounds a new and ominous note in the discourse; it marks the departure from an initial naive realism to a modern existential metaphysics of the bush. In terms of imaginary and symbolic constructions, Heseltine's 'horror of prehistory' parallels the horror of seduction and absorption of a pre-Oedipal mother, imagined in the writings of

Francis Adams, Marcus Clarke and others and dramatized in the film *Picnic at Hanging Rock*. Only now the horror of the other is an internalized other; the other as the beast in man.

Heseltine claims that attempts to 'physically subdue the bush and so control its power to subvert the mind',[28] whether in life or in literary imaginings, are doomed to failure. The bush is *more* than a physical force. It confronts man with 'the primal energies at the centre of his being'. The only solution is to 'acknowledge the terror at the basis of being, to explore its uses, and to build defences against its dangers.'[29] This is the response of Oedipal man, within the Father's Law, vitally aware of the threat to self-unity posed by maternal otherness—that is, a state of non-being outside the law. Its threat is that of insanity, madness or death.

What has changed in these readings is not the concept of the feminine, but of human nature, defined with reference to the masculine norm. Heseltine's existential humanism projects on to the bush the unconscious, irrational fears of the inner man as opposed to the older, rational, pragmatic, empirical view of man which saw the bush as a testing ground for political mastery and rational self-control. But whether perceived as a physical or an existential landscape, the bush retains its imaginative construction as both (and at the same time) a passive and an alien force which we witnessed in the early writings of Francis Adams and Marcus Clarke. The land is an unarticulated landscape until imagined as a void, a wasteland, a pliant virgin, a plain of promise. In the Australian imaginary it takes on the contours of an unknown feminine Other which is both desired and feared. It must be seen, named and conquered (e.g. in Heseltine's words, acknowledged, explored and defended against) if a national identity (which is also a masculine identity) is to be assured.

Although the external adherence to masculine/feminine dichotomies, determined not by the writer but by the inscription of the self within the symbolic order, has not changed, the *significance* of the bush, as a powerful feminine force, has shifted for the writers. Francis Adams registered the fear of physical and cultural absorption by the bush. He becomes a literary successor to the geographic explorers of its contours. Marcus Clarke had registered its alien, sinister qualities. In his novel, *His Natural Life*, he transforms the bush into an autobiographical projection of a son's exile from a lost motherland. By the time of Hancock's writing, physical invasion and political conquest of the land by 'Independent Australian Britons' had been assured. He can write, as a democratic historian, from a position of (equivocal) mastery. Heseltine, a literary critic, registers man's sense of metaphysical horror in his psychic confrontation with the bush. In all these descriptions, it is not actually the bush, but the self, whose identity is in question. The landscape is a neutral surface inscribed by a network of meanings; these provide a framework to allow a series of identifications between men. Through the discourse, men can acquire a proper name as Australian. The articulation of the landscape brings into play this masculine regime of desire.

McQueen and New Left Approaches

Humphrey McQueen belongs to a band of New Left intellectuals whose radical revisions challenged the frameworks of both the Democratic Nationalists and the modernist New Critics. His Marxist approach analyses the ways by which the interests of Australia's labouring classes were integrated into the capitalist system. He writes, 'My purpose is to reveal the components of this radicalism and nationalism and, in penetrating beneath the surface of words, confront the attitudes and attributes which were their substance and dynamic.'[30] But one does not have to penetrate beneath the surface of words to reveal the operations of power. And power is not confined to the ruling class. Although McQueen and others who share his approach engage in a localized struggle against power, it cannot be totalized nor explained adequately by reference to a hierarchical organization of ruling-class versus working-class interests. As Foucault demonstrates, power is serial, as well as hierarchical, and exists in a multiplicity of relationships, revealed in and through the linguistic operations of discourse. McQueen's location of 'the feminine' within the text, though muted, reveals another site of power/knowledge. He begins his treatise by presenting in a kind of dialectical opposition stanzas from two poems about Australia. The first, by William Charles Wentworth, is said to represent a Whig tradition within Australian culture. It reads:

> And, oh, Britannia! shouldst thou cease to ride
> Despotic Empress of old Ocean's tide—
> Should thy tame lion—spent his former might—
> No longer roar, the terror of the fight
> Should e'er arrive that dark, disastrous hour,
> When, bowed by luxury, thou yield'st to power;
> When thou, no longer freest of the free
> To some proud victor bend'st the vanquished knee;
> May all thy glories in another sphere
> Relume, and shine more brightly still than here;
> May this, thy last-born infant then arise,
> To glad thy heart, and greet thy parent eyes;
> And Australasia float, with flag unfurled,
> A NEW BRITANNIA IN ANOTHER WORLD! [31]

Written in 1823, by a prominent colonial administrator, the poem personified Australia in glowing terms as the last-born infant son (born of the loins of the despotic English Empress) who will replace the flagging strength of the British lion, with a proud new social order in the antipodes.

The second poem which McQueen used to introduce his study is a derivative of and dialectically opposed to the first. It was written by Charles Harpur in 1853.

> And, O Britannia, shouldst thou cease to have
> One born obstructionist, one titled Knave;
> Shouldst e'er thy Treasury only Truth employ,
> Nor longer hire brute Hessians to destroy;
> Shouldst e'er arrive that bright auspicious hour
> When thou shalt abdicate all wrongful power,
> And not in seeming, but in substance free,
> To God, as monarch, only bend the knee;
> May this, thy last born daughter then arise
> A barbarous Britain under other skies,
> And Australasia spread, with flag unfurled,
> All thy worst features through a wider world. [32]

Harpur, son of convict parents who resisted the barbarous features of native culture, presents an image of Australia as a flawed and weakened last daughter of a failing British power. The two poems, depicting masculine imperialistic strength and feminine deceitful weakness, preface McQueen's study. Is it this flawed feminine weakness which McQueen fears has overtaken a self-satisfied neo-colonial culture? His iconclastic critique of Australia's bourgeois values—within the radical national mystique—will not challenge masculine/feminine dichotomies. In fact, McQueen is not only masculine in approach, but militantly so, despite his sympathy with feminist historians and acknowledgement of the neglect of women by nationalist historians in his index. In the Introduction, he quotes with approval the advice of another socialist historian who warns that 'only vigorous intellectual imperialism and collective assault will make the mark'. Otherwise, the limp ghosts of long-departed liberal mandarins will forever 'weigh like a nightmare on the brain of the living'.[33] Thus, McQueen sets himself up as a beseiged battler combating wave after wave of received cultural history. He sets up an us-against-them dialectic in which he will attempt to replace one set of truths with another. But the result will be masculine, ethnocentric and hierarchical. His critique becomes yet another attempt to form the basis for yet another Australian identity as opposed to that of Britain, a battle between father and son fought on the political terrain of the feminine against the flawed daughter and the weak liberal mandarins. By the completion of his study, McQueen recognizes his own entrapment. He writes, in the second commentary of the introduction, written after the text had been completed, 'at every point [the text] remains encapsulated within the tradition it so violently denounces'.[34]

Common Assumptions

Each of these texts by Hancock, Heseltine and McQueen adds substance and weight to an understanding of the Australian tradition. The texts themselves create and accrue a knowledge and reality which they appear to describe. They attempt to define a 'natural' entity, the self imagined in the Australian character, but the processes of naming relate to symbolic representations which extend beyond the self. The changing historical representations about Australian identity challenge received ideas concerning the construction of the individual, but they are all informed by abiding latent presuppositions of the dominant culture, despite their manifest differences in approach. They do not challenge the notions of racial and sexual superiority of the white, male, neo-colonial tradition. They take for granted the concept of the self as a whole unity of self-presence. The texts presuppose this concept of the unified self. The concept operates to quell the threat of fragmentation which class relations and the idea of the feminine pose to the body, the mind, the psyche and the social order.

Within the discourse, the place of woman-as-sign retains a certain internal consistency in relation to the dominant order of knowledge. The representations of the bush as woman name the bush as a hostile threat, a barrier to be overcome. But this barrier also presents a rite of passage for the bushman— whether the landscape and its test is imagined as a physical, psychic or moral force. The bush in the male imaginary exists as loved and feared object of desire. But within the Australian tradition an inordinate and unresolved fear of the object dominates the discourse. Yet there have been times in the nation's history when the land and its precious treasures were passionately desired. Did the signification of the land as a harsh, cruel and alien threat take on new meanings when it brought forth gold and the dream of a utopian social order based not on the 'quality' of the man, but on his access to wealth?

DISPERSEMENT OF 'WOMAN': THE GOLD RUSH

The gold rush of the 1850s marks a new departure in Australia's history. Until that time the new white settlers who occupied Britain's last colonial outpost had come either unwillingly as transported convicts or reluctantly as their colonial masters who owed primary allegiance to and derived their identity from the mother country. South Australia, the first territory to be opened to free settlers in 1836, had thus far attracted few settlers in search of pastoral lands. The force behind the representation of the land as a terrain of exile and alienation which threatened to absorb or defeat its inhabitants owes a great deal to the historical facts of colonization. But, suddenly, with the discovery of gold in Guyong, beyond the Blue Mountains of New South Wales, in 1850, the land beckoned to new settlers, inviting men in to explore its treasure and its promise.

Between 1851 and 1853 the population of New South Wales grew from 77 000 to 200 000 with 80 000 men on the goldfields. In the decade of the 1850s the population of Victoria increased six times. The diggers fantasized that the gold discoveries would usher in a golden age and make real the dream of a classless, egalitarian society. By 1852 the Governor of New South Wales feared that the chaos and confusion, represented by the phrase 'Jack is as good as his master', would bring about the 'subversion of the social order'.[35] If ever there was a time in Australian history when it seemed possible to invert the social order and subvert the control of the ruling class, this was the time. In terms of discursive formations, the gold rush, as represented in the definitive texts on Australian nationalism, presents an interesting case. How does it contribute to the formation of the concept of identity and what role does 'the feminine' play in the representations of this period?

A distinction must be made between the imaginative Arcadian constructions of Australia as a home for the landless poor of Britain, which appeared in the guidebooks for emigration in Britain, and the historical reconstruction of the period, which began in Australia with Hancock's history. The interests of Empire demanded that emigrants be persuaded to take up lands in Australia to rescue the 'vast, empty spaces' and consummate the European presence in the antipodes. The gold rush provided added impetus within Britain to market the idea of Australia. In 1852, Samuel Sidney, an English aristocrat who extolled the Arcadian virtues of Australia for the abused British workers, published his major work, *The Three Colonies of Australia: New South Wales, Victoria and South Australia*. It sold 5000 copies in its first year of publication and helped to convince countless numbers of men to migrate to the promised land. He wrote that Australia had progressed: 'to be the wealthiest offset of the British crown—a land of promise for the adventurous—a home of peace and independence for the industrious—an El Dorado and an Arcadia combined, where the hardest and easiest, best paid employments are to be found.'[36]

In terms of the history of Empire, Australia offered hope to the Chartist aspirations of worker ownership of land, provided Britain with a new source of agricultural production at a time of industrialization and could be mythologized to mask the self-interest of the rising commercial sector of Britain. But in terms of a modern Democratic Nationalist tradition, the gold rush attracted settlers whose descendants would become Australia's native sons.

Hancock's Australia provides an interpretative framework for succeeding generations. But the text reveals a deep ambivalence. The ambivalence finds expression within the schema of a family romance, a battle between the fathers and sons. The gold rush provides time of consolidation of Australian nationalism in the form of egalitarian democracy represented by the digger. Hancock writes, 'the "digger" spirit is perhaps the typical Australian spirit.' The text depicts the ideal digger as 'the independent fellow seeking his own fortune and paying his own fare'; one who 'laid stress upon the difference, the uniqueness of Australia; and [his] own difference, [his] own uniqueness, as Australian'.[37] Hancock represents the period in terms which evoke a sense of Lacan's description of the mirror phase when the child as a fragmented subject recognizes its image in the mirror and identifies with the image of a unified ego. This corresponds with the child's entrance into language and the symbolic order as an 'I'. For Hancock the gold rush represented to Australians 'the one epoch in their past in which History has fashioned for them a mirror, so that they might behold themselves reflected as they would be, as they surely are . . . the first authentic Australians, the founders of their self-respecting, independent, strenuous national life, the fathers of their soldiers'.[38] And how do these independent Australians forge their newly-won sense of a distinct identity? By conquering the land, imagined as the abused body of a woman.

> As they threw themselves upon the land, scouring the river flats, scarring the sides of rugged mountains, forcing their way to the heads of tortuous gullies, so they imposed themselves upon colonial society, casting down its barriers, fighting for a foothold in its multitudinous crannies, pushing their way towards its summits where a noisy crowd of the new-rich flaunted its good fortune.[39]

Although less noble a description of conquest, Hancock's military imagery of the assault on the land on behalf of the new settlers mirrors that of Harcus of conquest on behalf of Empire. And yet there remains a dissonance of attitudes. Hancock imagines the digger as adolescent, Harcus's man of Empire was mature. Hancock's own subjectivity—as an historian torn between two soils, two mistresses—leads him, once again, to identify with British moral values which coexist with his national political loyalties. He reports that the diggers who came in search of gold and remained to settle the new land were 'predominantly vigorous, independent, law-abiding Britishers who . . . struggled for decent comfort when they were disappointed of riches, derided the colonial gentry, demanded democracy and observed the Sabbath "with order and decorum" '.[40]

Throughout the volume Hancock imagines the evolving national character in terms of individual maturity. The country had grown from an 'untidy, vociferous urchin' towards 'strenuous, independent' manhood. Within this schema the gold rush is a period of adolescence. Thus, the diggers inaugurate their 'love' for the soil, the new mistress, through a brutal collective assault— scouring its flats, scarring its sides, forcing their way into its gullies, overcoming barriers, fighting and pushing for a desired pride of place—through possession and mastery.

What is signified when Hancock writes that the diggers cast down the barriers of the colonial society in their quest for gold? There appear to be at least three imperatives of domination at work in the rhetoric—imperatives of sexual, economic and political mastery. In sexual terms, the land is raped for its riches. Economically, the acquisition of wealth allows for the erosion of class barriers inherited by the colonial culture to be overturned. Politically, the redistribution of wealth shifts the power balance away from the ruling class and towards the common man—the carrier of Australia's egalitarian democracy. The land becomes the scene of a rival exchange of power between the colonial father and the egalitarian digger. The battle is said to have become historical fact at Eureka, when diggers rioted against the unjust and intrusive policies of police inspectors concerning licensing fees. At the same time, however, the competition between the men for land, gold and fortune erodes the collective values of mateship and ensures a repetition of a social order inherited from the father. Still, the sense of battle between father and son is based upon a competition over the land as female body.

Once again landscape functions as the nexus of a network of meanings which allow a series of identifications between men. The imagined competition between fathers and sons, and the lesson of the gold rush and Eureka—that one must win by mastery—becomes a dominant motif in the text. The imperatives of mastery form a framework through which the events of a nationalistic history can be represented. The motif is reiterated throughout the text to give meaning, coherence and continuity to the processes of historical construction. It will be repeated after the gold rush, in the years of early land settlement beyond the boundaries of the cities. Hancock writes, 'to the early settlers, the Bush was an unfriendly wilderness. It would not accept them as it had accepted the Aborigine; they must master it, and mastery . . .

came so painfully and so slow.'[41] He describes that slow process in a later chapter called 'Filling the Vast Open Spaces.'

That Australia was a land of vast open spaces was a concept that both the imperial father and the egalitarian son could agree upon. Neither saw nor acknowledged the presence of over 250 000 Aborigines on the colonial landscape. The Aborigine was not perceived as having rights of ownership in terms of the Lockean appropriation of the land. In 1911 James Collier had written:

> [The Aborigine's] inability to till the ground or even make use of its natural pasture . . . was the capital offence, and it was irredeemable. . . .Their disappearance was a natural necessity. It came about in obedience to a natural law. It was effected by natural processes, and followed the lines of the substitution of vegetal and animal species all over the world. [42]

In this passage the concept of nature is employed in the cause of colonial conquest. The Aboriginal peoples are objects represented within the hierarchical schema of vegetable, animal, Aborigine, Man. The Aborigine is wholly excluded from representation; the Aborigine becomes an inferior species, a lower order, the not-human, because of the inability to conform to the doctrine of progress through which the white race laid claim to and held suzerainty over the continent. The passage utilizes the framework of social Darwinism to serve the interests of imperialism. To the colonial administrators in the 1850s, to Collier in 1911, and to Hancock in 1930, Australia was a 'waste' land, whose soil 'was electrified by the touch of colonization'. [43] It was a body open to mastery for the purposes of European civilization. What is herein represented is the conquest of civilization over barbarism; activity over passivity; history over nature. History comes to be seen as the valorized achievement of man over Nature. Nature is the raw material providing a passive context for (white) man's activities. The Aboriginal peoples become absorbed into the concept of Nature. Their presence is repressed.

Palmer and Ward on the Gold Rush

Although less explicitly sexual in their descriptions of national identity, Vance Palmer, in *The Legend of the Nineties* and Russel Ward, in *The Australian Legend*, reinforce the notion that the gold rush represented Australia's adolescence, rather than full maturity. The texts also continue to assert the political and economic dominance of the common man who comes to represent the Australian character. The gold rush advanced the common man's political consciousness through a greater possession of the land, claims Palmer. It extended the principles of egalitarian democracy, born out of the bush ethos, by access to and possession of wealth, claims Ward. Like

Hancock, Palmer and Ward share a sympathy with the 'natural vigour' of the diggers, yet their praise is checked by the suggestion of immaturity of the men and of the national spirit. How does this relate to a construction of the feminine, as the 'not-me' of masculine identity?

Palmer adopts an intimate tone to confide that 'it must be admitted that there was a good deal of grossness in the social life created by this new distribution of wealth. [The digger] was a rowdy, uncompromising fellow, with the restless energy of an upstart and an impulse, when he had made money, to assert himself emphatically.'[44] A dominant form of this assertion was for the digger to dress his 'ladies' in extravagant costumes which gave objective expression to his new-found wealth. The women in Palmer's text are represented as objects through which the digger measured his success and a means by which he could flout the conventions of old-world respectability. The women have a function as the 'not-me' which mirrors and establishes male identity on the goldfields and demonstrates differences between men marked by wealth. The 'ladies' become markers of exchange between men. Although Palmer's sympathies do not lie with the gross displays of wealth and temperament, he judges the nature of the Australian character solely by the activities and attitudes of the men. In relation to the gold-rush era, he confesses that the 'natural vigour' of the digger would 'enlarge the freedom of his adopted country, changing its social and political structure'.[45]

Russel Ward describes the immaturity of the men on the goldfields in different terms. He praises the men for their ordered lives and 'rude notions of honour', which future historians would question. But Ward chastizes the digger for his racism. He confesses that the gold-rush era tainted Australia's national life with a new element of virulent racism against the Chinese. The Chinese, 40 000 of whom worked on the diggings in Victoria alone, were charged with bringing leprosy and smallpox to the country, fouling the water, jumping the white man's claims and generally displaying 'monstrous and unnatural vices'.[46] The Chinese community by other accounts is known in Australian migrant history as being one of the most unassuming, law-abiding, abstemious and self-contained groups to enter the country. The charges levelled by the diggers against the Chinese are imagined attributes which serve to exclude the Chinese from white Australian gold-rush society. And they are similar to claims which had been and would be levelled against the Aboriginals, particularly the women, when they were seen to stand in the way of land settlement.

Within these narratives by Hancock, Palmer and Ward, Australian identity is a masculine identity. Further, native Aborigines, white women and the immigrant Chinese are all textually reduced to categories of otherness. The tactics of discursive reduction in relation to the Chinese immigrants and Aboriginal natives have several effects. In terms of naming, their radical difference as a diverse cultural group is reduced to a sameness marked as different from the dominant white cultural norm. This reduction establishes, upholds and extends racial, sexual and class divisions. It maintains the right of the white man to decide who speaks and on behalf of whom. It allows the native white speaker to control the threat of sexual, moral and physical corruption which he fears in himself by locating its cause in the other. Further, it narrows the possibilities for speakers who attempt to represent excluded peoples in a different way. Their argument against bias can only be expressed in pre-existent terms of a discourse of mastery and subjection. These processes of discursive mastery operate to mark the Aboriginal inhabitants and Chinese immigrants as other, and at the same time reduce their radical difference to the order of the same.

The gold rush becomes regulated through the discourse and reduced to a moment in the growth towards nationalism. It is represented as one of a continuous series of events through which the Australian native son grows from infancy through adolescence to maturity. The gold rush is a time when 'the urchin' reverses the colonial power structure, inverts the old order and lays claim to the land and its riches. In this sense the gold rush belongs to the story of the rise of egalitarian democracy. But the egalitarian character of the myth only applies to the inverted relationship between father and son. And even here, the differences between pastoralists, bushmen and gold-rush diggers coalesce into a common type. Further, it is through repression of Aborigines, Chinese and women in general, the native son establishes his place as he is inserted by the discourse within a hierarchical system of power relations and sex, race and class divisions inherited from the old order.

A common element in the texts of Hancock, Palmer and Ward, all of which make reference to the gold rush as an adolescent phase in the nation's history, is a moral judgement that the digger failed to control his passions. The lust for the land (Hancock), gross displays of wealth (Palmer) and racism (Ward) deny what has been implicit in the concept of national character, that is, rational control and moral responsibility within a Christian tradition. In the end, Hancock, from his 1930 vantage point, concludes that the Australian people have not yet come of age because they have failed the test of 'spiritual achievement',[47] although we recall that he did note that the digger observed the Sabbath 'with order and decorum'.

What emerges in the argument is a construction of 'human nature' derived from nineteenth-century liberal philosophy and rational theology.[48] The underlying assumptions are that the state is a collection of (white male) individuals. Its faults are the faults of the people. National character is reducible to personal attributes. The ideal of egalitarian democracy demands that certain standards of conduct be achieved. Rapacious lust, personal licence, material acquisitiveness and racial prejudice (except when tied to the imperialistic interests of the Commonwealth) must be controlled. Underlying all these texts is the challenge to the common man, the Australian character, to act responsibly and uphold the prevailing social order. With their assertion of anti-British and anti-privilege sympathies they fall within what has been called a radical democratic tradition; but their assumptions concerning human nature, the State and its progress to maturity tie them to conservative, colonial and imperialistic frames of reference. Further, the otherness to be mastered within the self, in both old-world and new-world conceptualizations, is that of the passions which must be controlled by reason; the body which must be ruled by the spirit. These dichotomies of reason versus passion, the spirit versus the flesh, underline sexual divisions within the symbolic order. They came to affect actual women who were cast into the patriarchal roles of damned whores and God's police in cultural practice.

Modernists and Manning Clark

In the decades which succeeded World War II, the consensus among academics as to the constitution of 'human nature' shifted away from a rational-spiritual framework to one which stressed the non-rational social and psychological attributes of man. The bush, 'gashed, devastated, scorched by its own patriots', came to be viewed as a place of cultural emptiness.[49] Social critics re-evaluated the democratic tradition and found in the national character evidence of human frailty and perversity which crossed over boundaries of class. Within the dominant discourses on nationalism a bourgeois humanism challenged the proletarian version of the national character. No longer did the convict-digger-unionist-soldier represent a march of progress towards the ideal of egalitarian democracy. The claims of universal humanity overtook the discourse. Socialist historian Ian Turner lamented that it was an 'elitist assault on the levelling tendencies of egalitarian democracy'.[50] The historical revision of Manning Clark bears witness to this shift in approach, which represents an ideological shift, a rupture within the dominant ideology. His analysis of the gold rush depicts a 'sorry history of dark deeds'.[51] The chaos and confusion which threatened the stability of the social order, according to Clark, actually stabilized the evolution of a middle-class, racist and imperialistic urban culture. From the outset his interpretation defies the proletarian approach. Clark maintains that the mad dream of wealth established in full glory 'Carlyle's aristocracy of rogues', it allowed the digger to lynch the swells.[52] The men on the goldfields suc-cumbed to cupidity, licence and all the 'wilder passions' that assail the human heart. Clark reads the historical records and concludes that the hapless digger responded to his new-found wealth with attempts at suicide, long bouts of drinking, despondency and despair.

Mateship gave way to lynching, plundering and abuse. 'The violators and robbers of the soil', he writes, 'slid naturally into violating and robbing each other.'[53] And although Clark suggests that the 'ladies' presented a moderating influence on the goldfields, the diggers could not always be trusted to treat them with respect. Clark tells a story of two German girls who attended a dance. 'The diggers competed for the honour of a dance with one of them with that same glint in the eye with which they searched for gold dust.'[54] He represents the desire for gold as an 'unholy hunger' which transformed men into demonic, rapacious creatures of greed, and left them spent with feelings of overwhelming defeat and despair.

What the Democratic Nationalists had presented as a period of ado-lescence leading to the 'coming of age' of an authentic Australian identity, Clark depicts as the coming of European civilization which robbed the continent of its authentic Aboriginal past. The description of the gold rush introduces Volume Four of his five-volume history of Australia. It covers the period from 1851 to 1888. The final chapter, which carries the same title as that of the whole volume, 'The earth abideth forever', treats the centenary celebrations for the anniversary of the founding of New South Wales, in terms of human defeat.

One of the structuring elements within the text is the reiteration of the theme of two mistresses which we referred to earlier, in relation to both the emigration guide and Hancock's history. We can focus on that motif to explore a semiotic shift which is also an ideological transformation. Clark asks 'What did the centenary celebrate?' He relates that British civilization, which promised the 'pursuit of material well-being and the freedom of the individ-ual' enslaved the Australian colony to 'the bitch goddess of success and the goddess of respectability'.[55] But the eternal mother earth, lying in wait beneath a Western culture's materialistic desire, prepared its revenge. The year 1888 was one of severe drought. The drought, says Clark, was 'the revenge of an ancient, barbaric continent' upon the men who 'wantonly robbed it of its wealth'.[56] Clark's history is a challenge to liberal social theory and its attendant faith in progress. Clark defies the liberal consensus of the white man's march to progress over the Western and non-Western world. He pushes against the boundaries of Western consciousness with an evocation of the 'ancient, barbaric' land. In Clark's history the white man is the intruder upon the natural environment, which he depicts as an enduring maternal presence. But he builds his argument on past Western, humanistic traditions. His commentary establishes a different political perspective. But it exists within the order of sameness which produced the earlier histories. The 'ancient, barbaric' land which avenges its despoilers was present in Hancock's history and in Eyre's journals. It gains complex expression in Henry Handel (Ethel Florence) Richardson's novel, *The Fortunes of Richard Mahony*. In fact, much of Clark's commentary on the gold rush reiterates elements of Richardson's fiction, redressed in the guise of historical truth. [57]

Clark leaves the white man with his two mistresses: the bitch goddess of success and the goddess of respectability. The bitch goddess of success was brought to life a century earlier by William James as a detested symbol of American materialism; the goddess of respectability retains the British mantle of Christian morality and mark of Western culture. Although given bulk and form over three generations of historical speculation, they are not unrelated to Hancock's mistresses, the British past and Australian present, imagined as divided loyalty between the two soils. Clark brings the mistresses to life in the dress of Western capitalism where they mirror man's diminished status. He reverences the ancient soil as an emblem of the enduring 'natural' world. But there is no 'natural' world. He returns to a Romantic evocation of the Eternal Feminine, employed in this instance as an instrument of moral power in the patriarchal universe of the sinned against and sinning. Man abandons his mistresses when they appear to have failed him, and longs to return to the imagined security of the pre-Oedipal womb in retreat from an unresolved battle with the father. The loss of a vision of potency for Western man accompanies a longing for the archaic Earth Mother, not in conquest but submission. This is not a different version of history but the other side of the history of progressive mastery.

The Oedipal complex structures this battle within the discourse on Australian tradition. What is repressed is the relation to the maternal body, imagined as an abyss. She has been replaced in an imperial framework by the pliant virgin and in a colonial and nationalistic context by the castrating mother. The fantasies of control, of mastery, of possession of the land and the fears of denial, threats of madness or death—these regulate man's relation to the land. The fantasies set up a homoerotic economy of desire established among men. The imagined relation to the mother/land is, paradoxically, the condition of men's failure *and* their salvation. We are reminded, once again, of Luce Irigaray's remark: 'woman' remains 'the scene of a more or less rival exchange between men, even when they are competing for the possession of mother-earth'.

How does mateship figure in the battle between sons for possession of the land? Mateship is a defining characteristic of the Australian character, the pioneering bushman. It stands for manly independence, an assertion of equality and a loyalty between men. It is an ethos associated with the little Aussie battler and not the squatter, pastoralist or capitalist investor. The signification of the land figures in the construction of mateship in a somewhat paradoxical way. The bushman imagines the land as harsh, raw, harsh, obdurate, fickle—in Lawson's terms, that maddening everlasting sameness that makes man want to break away. Mateship is his refuge. The colonial explorers and pastoralists, however, imagined the land either as a pliant virgin or as a wasteland awaiting consummation. The bush was a barrier which they successfully mastered. They are represented as the detested squatters within the bush tradition.

How is the difference in ideological perspective registered in the connection with the land? For the woman/the earth to be the site of a rival exchange between men, she must be desired. Desire for possession sets up a competition among men. But if the land is loathed or feared, as it is in Lawson's stories, then it offers no prize. Men retreat into mateship; but mateship on these terms is a community of defeat. Further, mateship is a male community. It excludes women (except as honorary members in circumscribed contexts, within a union or the Communist Party, for example. The exclusion of women, which parallels the loathing and fear of the feminized landscape, creates the condition and possibility for mateship. For the bushman, the land continues to be the enemy when, in fact, economic and political forces are more strongly at work. In the end, the nationalist myth perpetuates a ruling-class ideology. The bushman is defeated; but the capitalists (although excluded from the tradition) have won. The harsh attributes of the landscape justify man's defeat and make it appear natural. 'Man', however, has not been defeated, especially not the 'man' of the ruling class or gentry, leaseholder or stock company. When the digger/bushman is represented as a national type and the type is then invested with the attributes of Australian nationalism, these class contradictions can escape notice.[58] The discourse appears to subvert the ruling-class ideology, but in fact it operates to tie the tradition to that ideology.

The naming of colonial Australia and definitions of national identity detailed here, from texts of early exploration, nineteenth-century settlement experience and twentieth-century historical formulations, offer a variety of ideological perspectives and attitudes towards Australian nationalism. Cultural production is susceptible to ideological transformation. Yet, despite differences among speakers, there are common linguistic elements in these discourses on Australia which mark them as belonging to a common genealogy, a common line of descent. All of them attempt to establish a space for the subject as a stable masculine subject through the linguistic representation of dichotomies between self and other. The discursive representation of the land as the feminine other against which man measures his identity, the muting of differences betwen men, the repression of Aborigines, Chinese and women—analysis of these features demonstrates some of the ways in which the idea of otherness functions to reserve the space of the stable subject, the homologous male speaking voice which comes to represent Australian culture, within a dominant discursive tradition.

As we have noted, questions concerning the authority of the self are resolved through the dispersion of women, the landscape, Aborigines and Chinese migrants into the signifying place of the other. The other takes on many imagined attributes and forms. The attributes include: passivity, compliance, allure, vengeance, barbarism, terror, ignorance and guilt. The forms include: chaos, the void, a wasteland, the body of the mother/mistress, a barrier and a passage. Since the speaking subject is posited as a male speaking subject—one who has power, authority, status—the category of otherness, although fluid, is one through which the feminine is signified. According to Teresa deLauretis 'Woman' as an idea embedded in the textuality of Western discourse is posited as 'the object and foundation of representation, at once telos and origin of man's desire and of his drive to represent it, at once object and sign of [his] culture and creativity'.[59]

An examination of the linguistic signification of woman in the metaphors of landscape and the metonymic placement of man in the bush as the site of national identity provides some clues as to how 'woman' is posited within an Australian specificity, a masculine symbolic order. Within the Australian imaginary the bush is the site of otherness through which a precarious masculine identity is established and maintained. The bush is signified as both 'no place for a woman' and the place of Woman. As we register the contradictions, the crises in meaning, we begin to deconstruct assumptions concerning the self as a stable subject and, at the same time, register a new, yet to be explored space for women and men beyond the boundaries of the Australian tradition.

WOMEN WRITERS AND THE BATTLE WITH THE LAND

What happens when women writers enter the discourse on the Australian tradition? The whole concept 'woman writer' is one of an uneasy coexistence. As a writer she assumes a position of authority over the text and the tradition she addresses. As a woman she is marginalized within the tradition and also retains the place of other within the symbolic order. To speak with authority she must wear a male disguise. Women as well as men attain identity as writers by subjecting themselves to the laws of language, that is, the Law of the Father. In so doing women attain status and authority which is derived from a masculine system of representation. Women exist within the same norms of sexuality, the same discourse and the same phallic economy as men.

But women writers have had a different relation to power, to knowledge, and to the representation of Western colonization of the land, even as speakers within a Western culture and consciousness inscribed within the symbolic order. The imperatives of masculine sexual, political and economic domination of the land have not been those of women. The perspectives of women writers, who occupy positions as subjects as well as objects in the history of representation, have defied and resisted the male norm. Man in Australia inherited a land he could not and did not conquer. Perhaps for this reason his love affair with the land is represented within the tradition as ambivalent and ongoing. He continues to approach with fear and respect, loathing and desire. His relationship to the land and to his own identity as Australian remains open to question. But it revolves around the question of mastery.

Women writers, who have seldom spoken from positions of political authority, and whose 'public' voice has most often been the 'private' voice of literature, have registered conquest of the land as an alien concept. A resistance of the dominant masculine desire for mastery over the land marks their writings. Another mode of enunciation pervades their texts and signals a difference in approach to the themes of the sexual, political and economic dominance of the white man over the land as feminine other. There are several issues which need to be addressed concerning woman-as-other who is also a writing subject. One is the matter of the grounds on which women's writings are produced and received; another is the critical judgements made about the writings of women; another is the question of similarity and difference of ideological perspectives among women and between women and men.

Henry Handel Richardson and the Critics

Manning Clark's late bourgeois challenge to the white man's right to mastery had been expressed before. But the earlier radical departure from accepted imperialistic norms of the culture failed to find as receptive an audience. Henry Handel (Ethel Florence) Richardson wrote her goldfields trilogy, *The Fortunes of Richard Mahony*, between 1917 and 1929, after completing nine years of historical research on the gold rush and her father's involvement in that event. The trilogy provides a complex and compelling interpretation of the gold-rush epoch which announces in fiction a number of themes seized upon as fact by later historians. But until Manning Clark revitalized its radical ideological perspective, the trilogy had been categorized as a work of imaginative fiction and had been excluded from the so-called Democratic Nationalist canon of the Australian tradition because of its complex psychological and metaphysical themes. Volume One of the trilogy, *Australia Felix*, published in 1917, opens with a 'Proem' which introduces the dilemma of male identity in relation to the land. It depicts the scene on the diggings in the following way: 'The whole scene had that strange, repellent ugliness that goes with breaking up and throwing into disorder what has been sanctified as final and belongs, in particular, to the wanton disturbing of earth's gracious, green-spread crust.'[60] The text describes the gold-rush diggers as 'prisoners to the soil'.

> A passion for the gold itself awoke in them, an almost sensual craving to touch and possess; and the glitter of a few specks at the bottom of pan or cradle came, in time to mean much more to them than 'home', or wife, or child.
>
> Such were the fates of those who succumbed to the 'unholy hunger'. It was like a form of revenge taken on them, for their loveless schemes of robbing and fleeing; a revenge contrived by the ancient, barbaric country they had so lightly invaded. Now, she held them captive—without chains; ensorcelled —without witchcraft; and, lying stretched like some primeval monster in the sun, her breasts freely bared, she watched, with a malignant eye, the efforts made by these puny mortals to tear their lips away.[61]

What the discourse on the tradition has represented as mastery of the self by defeating the land, Richardson names as mastery of the land through defeat of the self. The text reiterates the self–other dichotomy, however. It pits nature against culture, woman against man. In this sense Richardson confirms the perspectives of a masculine history and reinforces the terms of woman's repression from culture. The Australian landscape is imagined as a revengeful mother, denying man his goal. It is an image similar to those conjured up by the explorers Sturt and Eyre when they could no longer advance their expeditions. The difference is that Richardson's narrator identifies with the land against its would-be masters. Her subjectivity has been captured by the processes of representation. She, too, is an effect of the discourse. In the end, the poor, forlorn and divided spirit of Richard Mahony is absorbed back into the earth: 'The rich and kindly earth of his adopted country absorbed his perishable body, as the country itself had never contrived to make its own, his wayward, vagrant spirit.'[62]

Richardson's three-volume trilogy surveys the scene on the goldfields with a subversive detachment. The novel has not been accepted as part of the literary canon of the Democratic Nationalists. This is not surprising. The text denounces and names as sham the pretences of masculine identity which the tradition struggles to uphold. H. M. Green attacks just this quality in the trilogy. 'Not only', he writes, 'is there . . . no trace of sentimentality, but there is no idealization', either.[63] In terms of critical appraisal the novel has been placed within the received male-defined categories which structure the tradition and judged in relation to those norms.

In addition, the novel as fiction has been separated from historical interpretations of the gold rush. Academic disciplines are structured hierarchically with reference to their ability to produce 'truth'. History is judged to be more true, less subjective, more informational, less experiential, more trustworthy in its adherence to empirical methods than is imaginative fiction. Manning Clark's history marks a radical departure from historical representations of the past. The text does not assume Western control of the land as a fact of nature, nor white male mastery as a sign of human progress. It appeared in the 1970s, at a time of world-wide challenge to Western suzerainty, when Clark himself was active in the anti-war movement. And yet Clark's depiction of the white-man-as-outsider on the Australian landscape bears a close affinity to Richardson's 1917 treatment. Although his text bears the marks of a Christian moral pessimism absent from Richardson's trilogy, both depict the land as an awesome, enduring, powerful and positive force against the white man as alien intruder. Both invert the relationship of man to the land. Clark's history lays the groundwork, in a way her fiction could not, for re-evaluating the ideological components of Australian nationalism.

Richardson's text is radically sceptical concerning the processes of formation of a colonial identity. It has been treated as an anomaly—not history, not realistic enough to be tied to the *Bulletin* school, too Australian for the New Critical demands of universalism. The text stands in an uneasy relationship to the canon of writers identified with the school of Democratic Nationalism. In the 1960s and 1970s, when modernist critics re-evaluated the tradition, they included her work in their 'revised' canon of Australian writers who explore the more complex metaphysical and psychological dimensions of the human soul (along with the poetry of Christopher Brennan and the novels of Patrick White, Martin Boyd and Christina Stead). But the New Critical treatment of Richardson's trilogy establishes a commentary on her work which maintains the power of the interest group. They place her text within a tradition they espouse, thus creating a truth they appear to describe. Clark's history repeats the process.

Heseltine suggests that the Australian tradition is broader than that represented by the social and political realism of the 1890s school. He discovers an underground tradition in the 'dreams and myths' of the people. The dream organized around a hope of unearned, suddenly acquired wealth which ends in defeat may be a unique Australian formulation, he surmises. In this, *Australia Felix* provides an exemplary pattern to be found in a variety of nineteenth- and twentieth-century fiction. Rape of the land, revenge by the earth mother, absorption back into the land is the pattern he identifies. He concludes that the 'passage through the trials and disturbances of a competitive male world towards final acceptance by a dominant maternal spirit, it may be, is a uniquely Australian response to the human condition.'[64] This is the male myth. To what degree can it be said to be shared equally by Heseltine, Richardson and the fictional character of Richard Mahony?

The questions of who speaks, to whom, and by what authority are pertinent here. Heseltine speaks as a modernist literary critic, to a bourgeois audience, from a masculine, metaphysical perspective. The fantasy of acquired wealth which he identifies with the Australian character and also attributes to the 'poet'/writer is not Richardson's fantasy, but that given to a character in her fiction. The male rite of passage which Heseltine describes relates to his formulations of an Australian identity which Richardson's novel challenges. His treatment masters the scepticism of her text. Richardson's depiction of the earth as a devilish witch who deflates masculine, acquisitive, possessive values and denies mastery can also be read, as it is in Clark's history, as a radical resistance to the bourgeois ideology Heseltine espouses.

Although there have been changes in the discursive formation of an Australian tradition, those changes have not been accidental, nor neutrally additive, but selective, in the accumulation of knowledge as power. And although Clark and Heseltine use Richardson's text in differing ways, and according to opposing ideological perspectives in relation to the white man's will to power, neither acknowledges her. Her position is muted. Clark appropriates her fictional constructions to his historical account; Heseltine elides the ironic distance in her work between the writer and the text. Both enlist the novel to serve their cause.

MALE STANDARDS AND FEMALE DISSIDENCE

Aside from, or in addition to, these questions of critical reception, interpretation and appropriation of the woman writer's views, Australian women have written about the land in fiction in ways which offer a variety of perspectives which challenge man's assumption of mastery over the land. Novels like Katharine Susannah Prichard's *Coonardoo* (1929), Eleanor Dark's *The Timeless Land* (1941), and Mary Durack's *Keep Him My Country* (1955), for example, despite differences in ideological perspectives, all depict the land as an enduring, maternal presence destroyed through the white man's attempts at conquest.[65] The women writers perceive a different relationship of the male to the earth as opposed to the female to the earth. That relationship, however, remains encased within a masculine order of sameness. The narratives of exploration and settlement and subsequent nationalistic histories fantasise a desire for possession of the earth as a mother or lover, a desired or despised, loved or loathed object. In the novels of these women writers, the feminine landscape frustrates masculine desire. The fiction written by these female novelists reconstructs the battle in terms of a tragedy rather than the victory of white presence. But the texts do not attempt to rewrite masculine/feminine positions within the symbolic order. They depict the land in ways that are equally problematic. The women writers reiterate masculine constructions in their representation of the feminine. One might say that the fiction by women writers supports, even as it seems to challenge, the codes of national identity.

Representation attempts to fix a constructed meaning on historical events. But the social formation of meaning depends on the individual's relation to what is represented. The woman writer cannot escape the relations which structure her difference and desire within the phallogocentric norms of culture. She can challenge and question her heritage. But if she speaks on behalf of the land as it has always already been conceived in the discourse, the woman writer takes up a position within the male imaginary. She mimes the role she is required to assume. Her ideological perspective may become a site of resistance to dominant modes of representation of knowledge as truth. But at the same time her assumption of the role and voice of an imagined femininity more fully inscribes women within the dominant phallic economy. This dilemma can be illustrated with reference to the texts of Henry Handel Richardson, Katharine Susannah Prichard, Eleanor Dark and Mary Durack.

In Richardson's *The Fortunes of Richard Mahony*, the hapless Richard is absorbed back into the 'rich and kindly earth'. The depiction of the land as a kindly mother is repeated in Eleanor Dark's *The Timeless Land*. The images invert rather than transform those embedded in the texts of the acknowledged historical formulators of the Australian tradition. Concerning attempts at male dominance over the land, Dark's text reads: 'Nature, undisturbed and unchallenged for countless centuries, has reached a might and stature which made Man feel less than pigmy-size . . . the land was determined, it appeared, to make [the pomp and circumstances of Empire] look rather silly.'[66] When Governor Phillip, the first Governor of New South Wales, thinks of acquisition of the land on behalf of Britain, we are told:

he felt a power which was even stronger than the power of his race, an influence from the land itself . . . which human folly and human brutality could not harm, could not even touch. He saw now that they had delivered themselves up to it, that no word or deed or authority of his could stay its quiet, unhurried processes of envelopment and absorption. 'Acquisition!' The ageless silence swallowed the presumptuous word. What had been thrust upon it as shame and degradation and hypocrisy became merely human life, the overlaying man-made creeds and customs and conceptions fell from it, leaving it nakedly re-born.[67]

The same themes of imperialistic ownership, desire for mastery and presumptions of authority which have been the mark of Whig faith in progress are here reduced to human folly. The final insight of the fictional Phillip, shortly before his death, recalls the language of Hancock in his description of the gold rush. The difference is that whereas Hancock asserted that a ruthless possession of the land would guarantee political and economic dominance for the Australian native son, Dark's text throws these assertions into doubt. The land:

> would accept them only when, with difficulty and humility, they had learned that she was not theirs, but they were hers. He saw [the white colonists] driven by their reckless greed, and by an obscure urge for conquest of so aloof and invulnerable a foe, exhausting her earth, fouling her rivers, despoiling her trees, savagely imposing upon the pattern of her native loveliness traditional forms which meant beauty in other lands. He heard them crying out to her insatiably: 'Give! give!' and was aware of her silent inviolability which would never give until they had ceased to rob. [68]

The land will not give. It defies attempts at mastery. It endures as a silent maternal body. But it is the same land as imagined by its male subjects. The descriptions are those also found in the historical texts of Hancock, Clark and McQueen. The difference is that the political, social and moral order which man is said to have created by reference to the land as other, is now reinforced textually by a narrative voice which represents the land to that same order. In the first instance, cited above, the land threatens absorption, that is, it occupies a position homologous to the imaginary space of the pre-Oedipal mother imagined and repressed within the symbolic order. In the second instance, the personified landscape takes on the attributes of vengeance—a God's police, the moral, Christian, ethical mother who will subdue the sinful character of the new colonists. Many of the imaginative constructions of the land which we registered earlier in the narratives of exploration and settlement are invoked in Dark's text. The writer as subject upholds the authority of the masculine speaking voice. The place of the feminine remains a place of otherness. The landscape as represented here reinforces, even as it challenges, the economies of masculine desire.

In Katharine Susannah Prichard's *Coonardoo*, the land is identified with the Aboriginal woman, Coonardoo, who loves, nurtures and protects Hughie, the white station owner's son. She is the 'well in the shadows', the spirit of the earth, who by 'mysterious affinity with that ancestral spirit . . . was responsible for fertility, generation, the growth of everything.'[69] The Aboriginal presence in the land, their spiritual identification with nature, forms the backdrop for the novel. But white possession of the land, disruption to tribal life, and imposition of white moral values on the Aboriginal people gradually erode Aboriginal existence and taint the native population. Hughie brutalizes Coonardoo as a result of guilt over his sexual possession of her. Coonardoo and her culture are destroyed at the end, due to the sexual and economic exploitation by the white man. Coonardoo is Hughie's other, constructed with reference to the Jungian categories of masculine and feminine. The politics of the novel defy and at the same time reinforce white colonial authority through the maintenance of the Big Dichotomies: masculine/feminine, white/black, culture/nature, which, as Susan Sheridan observes, 'obscures the crucial historical relationship of colonial exploitation and violence.'[70]

In Mary Durack's *Keep Him My Country*, the white man is ultimately successful in his pioneering efforts in the new land. Her novel exhibits a post-war optimism and faith in progress which marked the texts of Whig historians. Her depiction of the land, however, defies the masculine dictate: 'to master and subdue'. Durack prefaces the novel with two verses from an Aboriginal love song.

I talk to my country in the night,
I talk of my love . . .
I talk to my country for she is woman
The water and the soil of life,
That the smoke of her fires encircle him in the night
And her strong loins hold him . . .
I cry to my country that her voice shall sing in his blood
And her hot suns fire him.
I cry to my country—

'Keep him that he may come to my side
'For I wait through the burning heat of the day
'And the long quiet cold of the night.
'I wake when the whirlwind scatters my fire to the dry bush
'And its embers die under the falling rain,
I wait for my lover.'

(Aboriginal love song extract) [71]

This love poem, appropriated from Aboriginal culture to serve the ideological needs of white Australian nationalism, certainly binds women to the demands of male desire in its depiction of the woman/land as objects of both desire and possession. In the novel, the white hero, who stubbornly resists the land as a harsh and cruel landscape to be feared and fought, is gradually won over by the love of an Aboriginal woman who gives herself and her country over to the hands of the white man. The ideological perspective is that of the white conquering hero. But even here, we note that the depiction of the land is unusual within the tradition. It is loved (and conquered) rather than feared and despised.

It remains true that the feminine is a sliding site of signification constructed with reference to the masculine as norm. It is also true that the feminine is strategically defined with reference to who speaks, for whom and by what authority. Women as well as men can speak for conservative, white imperialistic interests. What is interesting is that these four women writers, who do not share similar ideological perspectives, all depict the land, in defiance of the tradition, as a loving, mysterious, powerful and positive force. Nowhere in these writings is the land/woman vilified and named a scapegoat for man's defeat. For Richardson, from a metaphysical perspective, and Dark and Prichard from socialist perspectives, conquest of the land is an alien concept. Male sexual, economic and political dominance is not the imperative of these writers. Within historical and fictional representations of the land as other, patriarchal, imperial, colonial, bourgeois and national ideologies intersect and support each other. In the fiction by these women writers, patriarchal ideology is inverted to invest 'the feminine' with a power over man which is absent from the accounts of male writers. But other ideological perspectives, shared by both male and female writers, remain intact and, thus, reinforce the dominant modes of representing national identity.

The difference between male and female writers relates both to their positions in relation to power and to their perspective as marked by gender. Although they attempt to say something different about power relationships between man and the land, they are contained by the same systems of representation which constrain them. The representations of the feminine landscape are no more true in the accounts of female novelists than they were in the narratives of the male writers. Women are not the land. The land is not a mother—either barbaric or nurturing. These texts demonstrate how the land continues to be a shifting site of signification for the feminine, whether evoked by male or female writers. The women writers complete the masculine representations by filling in the missing content—the other side. Both men and women write within the dichotomies discussed earlier; they all are contributors to the power/knowledge nexus which sustains the Australian tradition. Both men and women as subjects within a masculine culture are implicated in the naming of the land as a feminine other. That otherness as constructed in texts of both male and female authors also upholds race, class and gender divisions within capitalism and patriarchy. The demands for order, civilized congress, 'a proper name' for Australia and 'her' people, proper meanings within a Christian moral context and concepts of property ownership and appropriation pervade the texts by both male and female writers. Women can create a space for a dissident perspective by denying the pretences of male identity, mastery and authority. But as long as they continue to represent identity in terms of dichotomies between self and other, where the self is a masculine subject and the other is a feminine object, they do little to challenge the masculinity of the cultural order. Further, the degree to which the women writers identify with and take on for themselves the constructions of feminine otherness demonstrates how actual women become inscribed within the masculine economy.

How is it possible to go beyond the dichotomies, to represent the two sexes differently? A feminist project within a post-structural perspective has been to attempt to dismantle the structures which support the present phallocentric system. As Cixous reminds us, 'Phallocentrism IS. History has never pro-duced or recorded anything but that. Which does not mean that this form is inevitable or natural.'[72] By dismantling the logic of phallocentrism it may be possible to begin to displace women's place within the discourse and allow for difference, to reinscribe meaning differently. The feminist critics described at the end of Chapter Three are involved in this project. I will attempt this approach in Chapter Six through a textual deconstruction of the idea of woman embedded in the short stories of Barbara Baynton. But before turning to Baynton we need to look at the phenomenon of Henry Lawson—'the first articulate voice of the real Australian.'[73] In the annals of Australian life and literature Henry Lawson is seen as the founding subject for the 'true' Australian character. Women writers, including Baynton, when they write into the tradition, accept Lawson as the founding father. We will turn now to the constructions of 'Henry Lawson' as cultural object and the effect on the Australian tradition of Lawson as fictional father.

CHAPTER 5

HENRY LAWSON: THE PEOPLE'S POET

Australia is Lawson writ large.

Manning Clark, *In Search of Henry Lawson*

Henry Lawson is an archetypal figure in Australian culture. In 1918 David McKee Wright named him 'the first articulate voice of the real Australian'.[1] Some years later, Vance Palmer wrote that Lawson was 'a portent' for the nation.[2] Portent he has been for formulators of the Australian tradition. Critics still argue, to the delight of press and public, about the significance of this man. In his best apocalyptic style, Manning Clark has warned that Australia is 'Lawson writ large . . . a forewarning to all of us of "wretched days to be" '.[3] Colin Roderick, faithful to the legend that is Lawson, has countered that Lawson remains our 'poet-prophet . . . for universal brotherhood', who held 'an ideal . . . up to mankind'.[4]

The complex character of Henry Lawson and the rich complexity of his stories appear to open unlimited options for interpreting the man and his work. He has become a cultural myth, a legend. And like all myths, the myth of Henry Lawson helps us to understand something about Australian culture while it also imposes that meaning upon us. It is not Henry Lawson himself, but the stories about 'Lawson' that have accumulated and been circulated through culture over time, which make him a legend. Layers of myths and interpretations have been built up around the writer and his works. The uses of Lawson, the social and political contexts into which he is put, and the interpretations produced through social practice but received as truth—these have made Lawson a cultural object. It is the cultural object, handed down to Australians through commentary and cultural practice, not the man himself, which will be the focus of this chapter.

David McKee Wright's preface to Lawson's *Selected Poems* published in 1918 gave substance and structure to the legendary view of Lawson as Australia's pioneering artist, the saint and not the sinner of the familiar dichotomy. The timing was sadly ironic. Publication coincided with a period in Lawson's life when his physical health and creative abilities were at their lowest ebb. The artist's reputation, however, has evolved not in the light of his actual circumstances, but through the layers of encoded knowledge about Lawson, such as that related in Wright's preface. But there is a common element which can be detected in Lawson's diffident constructions of himself in the autobiographical writings and in the ambivalent constructions of 'Henry Lawson' by critics and biographers throughout the twentieth century—that is, the naming of woman as the source and origin of man's (Lawson's and/or the national character's) failings. This can be demonstrated through an analysis of the discourse of Lawson-on-Lawson, and that reiterated by formulators of the Lawson industry, which has survived and flourishes to this day.

THE CONSTRUCTION OF HENRY LAWSON

By 1918 Henry Lawson was in decline. From the time of his final separation from his wife, Bertha, in 1903, his life had been one of slow but steady deterioration of both physical and creative energies. His bouts with alimony and alcohol resulted in several trips to gaol on charges of non-payment of support and abuse to his wife, and to the Convalescent Home for brief periods of drying-out and to the Mental Asylum at Darlinghurst, 'to escape from the damned lunatics outside',[5] as he wrote to a friend.

When Lawson searched for the source of his wretchedness, he settled on obstacles in the world outside. He blamed not the police, who were, after all, 'only doing their duty', nor his bohemian drinking mates, who stood with him at the pub's 'mystical communion rail', but women, whom he accused of 'sucking the life blood out of him and destroying his creative gifts'.[6] His anti-feminism can be detected in the poem 'One-Hundred-and-Three', written in 1908 and revised during this later period of despondency:

> The clever scoundrels are all outside, and the moneyless mugs in goal—
> Men do twelve months for a mad wife's lies or Life for a strumpet's tale.
> If the people knew what the warders know, and felt as the prisoners feel—
> If the people knew, they would storm the gaols as they stormed the old
> Bastille.[7]

These anti-feminist sentiments, like those in his essay, 'The She Devil', (1904), are a world apart from Lawson's idealization of women in his radical nationalist days of the early 1890s, when he was inclined to represent women as symbols of the revolutionary ferment of the times:

> Last night as I lay sleeping out a vision came to me:
> A girl with face as fair and grand as ever man might see—
> Her form was like the statues raised to Liberty in France,
> And in her hand a blood-red flag was wrapped about a lance.
> She shook the grand old colour loose, she smiled at me and said:
> 'Go bid your brothers gather for the Waving of the red'.
> > ('Waving of the Red', 1893)[8]

Those where the days when Lawson believed: 'We'll know the worth of a purer youth / When the women rule with men.'[9] As Lawson became more embittered, he began to blame women for the shortcomings he saw in himself and the world. The rhetorical fervour of early days, 'when the world was wide' and women would join the revolution with men toward an egalitarian republic, gradually eroded into the bitter recriminating verse and prose of a defeated man, who along with warders and gaolers, would lead a revolution within capitalism against women. The idea of Woman, idealized into a symbol of hope or objectified into a figure of failure, permeates Lawson's writing. It also affects the critical and biographical writings about Lawson-as-a-cultural-object. Critics in their commentaries on Lawson's personality and writing rely on masculine/feminine dichotomies to assess strengths and weaknesses in Lawson and the national character. There are common assumptions underlying the concepts of masculinity and femininity employed in the commentaries on Lawson which are shared by critics across a range of ideological perspectives.

So, in 1918, when Lawson was reduced to writing doggerel to provide advertising copy for Heenzo cough syrup as a means of supporting his considerable appetite for beer, his friends at the *Bulletin* were preparing a new edition of his selected verse. The preface to the volume, written by David McKee Wright, provides a legendary tribute to the poet and a fulsome assessment of his achievement which survives to this day. In the preface, Wright fused the idealized image of the noble bushman associated with Lawson's 1890s writings with a new idealized image of the soldier returned from the Great War. Here is what Wright had to say:

> Lawson has lived the life that he sings, and seen the places of which he writes; there is not one word in all his work which is not instantly recognised by his readers as honest Australian. The drover, the stockman, the shearer, the rider on the skyline, the girl waiting at the sliprails, the big bush funeral, the coach with flashing lamps passing at night along the ranges, the man to whom home is a bitter memory and his future a long despair; the troops marching to the beat of the drum, the coasting vessel struggling through blinding gales, the great grey plain, the wilderness of the Never Never—in long procession the pictures pass, and every picture is a true one because Henry Lawson has been there to see with his eyes and heart.[10]

This paragraph, which enumerates the themes in Lawson's writings, establishes his credentials as the authentic voice of Australia, which is the voice of the bush. It also registers the familiar themes of the bush adventurer, caught between hope and despair, measuring his grit against a threatening landscape, where women wait. And it sounds the drum of troops marching, linking the bushman with the soldier, an idea Wright expands in his next paragraph:

> When in April 1915, Australians made the historic landing at Gaba Tepe, the unexpectant world saw young soldiers from a peaceful Commonwealth bearing themselves in the stress of war like veterans of the older fighting nations. The spectacle arrested and surprised. But Lawson had sung of these things more than twenty years before. Nothing Australians did in Gallipoli, or later in the fields of France, was new or strange to those who remembered the bugle note of his early poems. With prophetic insight he had dreamed a people's dream— had felt in that soldier-heart of his early manhood the tremor of a coming tempest, though the world skies were then clear—and had foreknown with every fibre of his being the way in which men of the bush and the mountain and plain would respond to the battle-call.[11]

This paragraph links Lawson's radical, nationalist, republican sympathies of the 1890s with the conservative, Anglophile, imperialist demands of Empire in the Great War. Although the bush ideals embodied in the national character had been previously associated with the 'true' Australian, the manipulation of this image after the war indicates the ease through which the national character could be defined within the needs of Empire.[12] In the period between 1850 and 1890, which Lawson depicted in prose, Britain needed wool and wheat, which Australia supplied by taming the bush. In the 1914–1919 period, Britain needed soldiers, and the image of the bushman was transformed to suit the demands of a new era. The flag of revolution became the flag of Empire. Both conservative and socialist interests were served by the common image of the bushman-cum-digger. One doubt which had been expressed concerning the bush hero had been the question of his capacity for self-discipline (a question which, as we have noted, was registered in the writings of the Democratic Nationalists in relation to the gold-rush era as an adolescent phase of national maturity). Now at Gallipoli it seemed that the digger had proved himself. The idealized virtues of the bushman became manifest once again, this time in the figure of the digger as the archetypal Australian—and Wright's preface names Lawson as his prophet.

The preface then paints an intimate picture of Lawson, emphasizing his allegiance to the Australian common man:

> He lives his life in Australia still—a life very close to ours, yet remote and lonely as that of genius is wont to be. London called to him, and he left us for a while, but came back more Australian than he went away. You meet him in the street and are arrested by his eyes. Are there such eyes anywhere else under such a forehead? He has the softened speech of the deaf, but the eyes speak always more than the voice; and the grasp of his hand is brotherly. A great sense

of sympathy and human kindliness is always about him. You will not lightly forget your first meeting. A child will understand him better than a busy city man, for the child understands the eternal language of the heart written in the eye; and Australia, strong-thewed pioneer though she be, has enough of the child left in her to understand her son.[13]

Genius, gentleness, sincerity, brotherhood, innocence—all the romantic virtues of the pioneering Australian artist are here parcelled up for public consumption. They are attached to a man who at the time of writing had been in gaol five times (on charges of assault and non-payment of child support), where he spent 197 days, and had just returned from a convalescent home where friends, and Lawson himself, hoped he could emerge from the blur of alcoholism to 'polish up a few poems'.[14] Wright sympathetically invokes Lawson's presence by reference to his sensitive eyes, his softened speech, and his brotherly handshake. These attributes relate to events in Lawson's early life which are said to have marked his outward appearance and personality. He had been deaf from the age of nine, and shortly thereafter, was deeply affected by the death of his younger sister. In his youth the schoolchildren named him 'Barmy Harry', and chided him for his introversion and sensitivity. The outward signs of those debilitating events are romantically idealized in Wright's preface as hallmarks of his stature as Australia's pioneering creative artist. By 1918 the grasp of his hand was more shaky than brotherly; and his eyes, in which women had often read signs of vulnerability, spoke the language of defeat.

Critics variously interpret these personal attributes as indicative of feminine weakness or a poetic sensibility (which can of course amount to the same thing). That which is deemed 'weak' in Lawson's writings and in his personality is handled in one of three ways by his critics and commentators: it is muted, as in the case of David McKee Wright; it is attributed to heredity and blamed on the instability of his maternal ancestors; or it is attributed to his environment and traced to the unsympathetic attitudes of his mother and wife. These are some of the complex issues elided by Wright's fulsome praise; issues which would occupy the minds of critics for generations and make 'Henry Lawson' an industry in Australian culture.

Wright's preface, in these three short paragraphs, introduces a number of important issues of relevance to this study. Firstly, he locates in Lawson's writings a source of ideas about an authentic Australian culture through the selection of themes which become associated with the national identity. Secondly, Wright fuses the noble bushman and digger soldier into a common character type, a fusion which demonstrates how national identity as a construct can be moulded to suit the changing needs of dominant interest groups. Thirdly, he identifies Lawson as the founding subject, the origin of the voice of Australia, through the evocation of Lawson's personal presence in the text, a strategy which also will be reiterated through time to suit the values and beliefs of the dominant culture.

Despite changes in emphasis and attitude within the discourse on Lawson and the Australian tradition, a central and abiding issue for the critics is an interpretation of Lawson's character formulated with reference to masculine/feminine dichotomies. But the evolving discourse will establish academic reputations, foster critical debate and encourage scholarly adventurers. And although the 'idea' of Henry Lawson is an invention of writers, artists, critics and historians located mainly in the academy, it becomes a commodity widely circulated through the culture and put to social, political and economic uses. Still the competition to define the 'real' Henry Lawson, 'the first articulate voice of the real Australian', remains tied to the primary desire of Western man to name and thus master the illusory and undecidable construct called the self.

There is one final irony associated with the 1918 publication of Henry Lawson's *Selected Poems* to which Wright attached his influential preface, which Denton Prout has called an 'almost legendary vision'.[15] It appears that George Robertson, Lawson's publisher, was concerned about the uneven quality of much of the poet's verse. He wanted the poems revised for publication. After six months of apparently unsuccessful correspondence with Lawson, he turned the task over to David McKee Wright, who proceeded to 'improve' the poems by eliminating stanzas, rewriting lines, altering rhyme and diction.[16] The edition, which included forty-eight poems, 70 per cent of which had been written prior to 1900, resulted in a literary production of bowdlerized verse, the changes of which remained undetected until Angus and Robertson published Colin Roderick's memorial edition of Lawson's collected verse in 1967–8. And David McKee Wright, himself a poet born in Ireland, had a literary reputation for writing 'not like an Australian at all . . . but like an Irishman straight out'.[17] These facts add an extra dimension to the discussion of origins for a nationalistic culture detailed in Chapter Two and the statement that 'there is not a word in all his work which is not instantly recognised by his readers as honest Australian'.

Within four years of the publication of *Selected Poems* Henry Lawson would be dead. But the idea of Henry Lawson and the canon of his works had already been revived. Henry Lawson-as-cultural-object would be enlisted into the debates on the national character which continue through the twentieth century. Lawson becomes the code, the founding father, the voice of Australia. But the character of this voice will undergo dramatic changes as it is moulded to suit changing social, political and economic requirements. The focus of this study is the place of 'woman' in the Australian tradition. Lawson and the Australian character are decidedly masculine concepts. But identity-as-masculine-sameness defines both what it valorizes as male and represses as female. Wright's preface names Lawson as the authentic voice of the bush and of Australia. It locates in his writings the Australian character as common man who is nonetheless susceptible to a variety of forms of historical revision. It also, and at the same time, posits a reality intimately present in the man himself. The three emblematic paragraphs cited above refer to women only once and in the singular, as a character in Lawson's fiction, 'the girl who waits at the sliprails'. The text, however, maintains the metaphor of woman as (m)otherland. It personifies Australia as a mother to Lawson: 'strong-thewed pioneer though she be, [who] still has enough of the child in her to understand her son'. Although woman is muted, the preface still participates in a specifically Australian signification of the feminine, as do subsequent studies which reiterate these themes.

WOMEN IN LAWSON'S FICTION

In Lawson's stories and the poems which they parallel, women are constructed to represent a number of physical and psychological dilemmas for man in the bush. For example, they frequently appear as idealized symbols of hope or are objectified into figures of defeat. Their displacement into feminine metaphors for the bush follows a similar pattern—although, in both cases, instances of defeat far outnumber those of hope. In addition, woman's status, as well as that of the imagined landscape, is perceived in relation to men.

Titles of the stories in which women feature indicate the degree to which Lawson imagined women as appendages to men. For example, women are named in relation to men. The titles of his stories attest to this habit of thought, as in 'His Mother's Mate', 'The Drover's Wife', 'The Selector's Daughter', 'His Adopted Daughter', 'The Shanty-Keeper's Wife', 'Brighten's Sister-in-Law' and 'The Pretty Girl in the Army'. Or, women are signaled as curious objects on whose behalf men have the authority to speak, as in 'Mitchell on Women . . . on Matrimony . . . on the "Sex" and other "Problems" . . . on The Sex Problem Again'. Or, the title announces that men have the authority to speak for silenced or absent women, as in 'Telling Mrs Baker', 'She Wouldn't Speak', and 'No Place for a Woman'. Lawson's stories by title indicate that there is no question but that women 'belong' to men.

As characters in the fiction, women parallel man's dilemma in the bush, poised between hope and defeat. Occasionally, and primarily in Lawson's early writings, women are imagined as symbols of hope, which have a positive influence on men. The bush, as well, takes on these feminine attributes. The early explorers' visions of landscape, like that of Stokes who saw the Arcadian plains as 'Plains of Promise', are recognized in Lawson's early verse which imagines Australia as 'a garden full of promise', a 'common garden' for pastoralists and laborers alike, and an 'Eldorado . . . beneath the Southern skies' for the diggers in poems like 'Freedom on the Wallaby', 'Triumph of the People', 'The Southern Scout' and 'Roaring Days'.[18] But already lurking in the garden of Lawson's poetry is the snake of capitalist greed, which in another time had made of England a 'hell in Paradise'.[19] That snake in the garden will later be employed to signify the threat of (feminine) otherness, as in 'The Drover's Wife' and 'The Bush Undertaker'. In the poetry when bushmen's aspirations give way to actual experience, the land takes on harsh attributes, like those noted by Vance Palmer, of a cruel mother—'an enemy to be fought'. The funereal qualities of the vast waste land, recognized by Marcus Clarke, enter Lawson's verse in praise of pioneering settlement. In 'How the Land was Won', Lawson writes:

> The darkest land 'neath a blue sky's dome,
>   And the widest waste on earth;
> The strangest scenes and the least like home
>   In the lands of our fathers' birth;
> The loneliest land in the wide world then,
>   And away on the furthest seas,
> A land most barren of life for men—
>   And they won it by twos and threes.

He tells of the struggles of exploration and settlement and death and birth in desolate huts:

> That's how the first were born to bear
>   The brunt of the first man's curse![20]

The first man's curse, the curse of Eve, exists as a contrapuntal force throughout the poetry and prose. The curse, embodied metaphorically in women, is said to operate against man's attempts at heroism.

In Lawson's early stories and verse, written between 1891 and 1899, the idealized Arcadian bush of the past begins to give way to an experienced barren wilderness. Paradise erodes into Hell as the greed of the capitalist system infects the garden of republican hopes. Women are represented as its victims, but they function as foils for man's heroic actions. But both the bush and women are the raw materials on which men act and through which they attempt to realize their identity as bushmen. The female characters in Lawson's early stories mostly live in the city: 'a great city of shallow social sham, of hopeless, squalid poverty, of ignorant selfishness, cultured or brutish, and of noble endeavour frowned down or callously neglected'.[21] Women's victimization is measured against the harsh urban environment. As they move into the bush, they themselves, like the land, become an alien force against which man must struggle. Only now, the struggle is not against the greed of the city as an objective social force, but against the unspeakable subjective fears of melancholy, despair, defeat and madness, which the land and women represent discursively as threats to masculine identity.

In any season, the bush for Lawson is an annihilating force. His descriptions signify the maddening qualities of the landscape as imagined through the beleaguered eyes of the battling bushman. In the dry season it appears as 'barren', 'raw', 'parched' and 'sun baked' with 'hungry, wretched selections' and 'scenery that looks better when the darkness hides it'. In the wet season it can be even worse: 'general rain . . . and there began the long, long agony of scrub and wire fence . . . even more dismal than the funereal "timber" itself . . . everything damp, dark, and unspeakably dreary . . . all around suggested death . . . [with] naked white ring-barked trees standing in the water and haunting the ghostly surroundings.'[22]

Female characters personify the disintegrating influence in the bush. They become metaphors for defeat, succumbing to exhaustion, despair and death, as they mirror man's dilemma. 'The Selector's Daughter' introduces this theme. At seventeen, the girl, we are told, looks like an old woman in her 'faded dress' and 'ugly, old-fashioned hood'. 'Oh, if I could only go away from the bush!' she moans. Being a woman, she cannot escape the bush/her fate as easily as the males in her family have done. She keeps the house in order through her mother's long and fatal illness while her father spends long weeks away. He returns, drunk and abusive, with a stolen steer. After his arrest and that of her brother the daughter becomes 'nervously ill . . . nearly mad'. She is the girl who waits at the sliprails, to whom David McKee Wright referred in his preface to Lawson's poems. But she greets only a father returned with a new woman who beats the daughter in a drunken rage and sends her away—to suicide. The daughter, persecuted by her loneliness in the bush, her mother's death and a 'weak' father with his abusive new wife, jumps from a granite cliff into a deep but rocky waterhole.[23] She, rather than the bushman, succumbs to despair. Maggie in 'Babies in the Bush' is another crazed woman, driven insane by the disappearance of her children while her husband was away on a drinking spree.[24] The bush, it seems is 'no place for a woman'. In Lawson's fiction generally female rather than male characters go mad in the bush. Many bushmen succumb to madness or suicide offstage, so to speak, but generally they are mentioned only in passing. But there are two significant exceptions to this tendency which are worthy of note. One is Ratty Howlett, the crazed selector in the story actually named 'No Place for a Woman'. Ratty imagines that his wife is still with him, years after she has passed away—a victim of loneliness, isolation and death during an unattended childbirth. Ratty Howlett, as a mad bushman, is an interesting case. His name connects him to a series of signifiers in Lawson's bush stories. 'Ratty' is an Australian colloquialism for odd, eccentric, beyond the border of sanity. The name also associates him with the animal world, and on a lowly rung at that. His surname, 'Howlett', extends the signification of his mad dilemma and connects it with the landscape (as in the bush as 'a blasted, barren wilderness that doesn't even howl'). If the bush *could* speak, Lawson had suggested earlier in this description from 'Hungerford', it would howl. Ratty is a quiet man. But through his condition readers can imagine the threat the alien landscape poses to the native son. Another anomaly of Ratty Howlett's situation is that he lives alone—excluded from the masculine bush community of mates. His fate has occurred in a setting called 'no place for a woman' which actually becomes no place for a man (the place of madness beyond a rational order). But the phrase 'no place for a woman' takes another twist in the story. The narrator relates that he was surprised to hear that Ratty at one time had a wife, 'thought he was a hatter', he says. A 'hatter' is a bush eccentric, a man who lives and works alone, gradually becoming so shy of human company that he avoids it—isolated in his madness from the social order. Hatters, by definition, never marry. This, in turn, helps to explain their condition of eccentricity. These codes of meaning illustrate how women, or the feminine counterbalance necessary to masculine sameness, preserve the semblance of identity within a human community. 'Bushmen stand in awe of sickness and death' (and madness too, although the word remains unspoken), the narrator relates in this story.[25] To have become 'ratty' is indeed an awesome threat.

The other exception to the rule is the old shepherd in 'The Bush Undertaker'. He, too, lives alone, with the company of his dog, 'Five Bob', perhaps the archetypal hatter in Lawson's fiction. In a story long noted for its black humour, the shepherd discovers the dead remains of a man whom he imagines to be his lost mate, Brummy, while foraging in the bush on Christmas day. Identifying the corpse by the nearly full bottle of rum which lies at his side, the shepherd carts it home, all the time restless with unspoken fears provoked by the recurring presence of the 'great greasy black goanna' which reappears to disturb the 'weird and dismal' equilibrium of his erratic life in the bush. The goanna may be this story's threat of feminine otherness. It represents his disorientation from humanity in an absolute sense. There is not much hope for the bush undertaker. He is resigned to defeat. He murmurs to Brummy just before he delivers 'some sort o' sarmin' above the makeshift grave: "Brummy, . . . it's all over now; nothin matters now— nothin did ever matter, nor—nor don't. You uster say as how it 'ud be all right termorrer' (pause); 'termorrer's come, Brummy—come fur you—it ain't come fur me yet, but—it's a-comin." '[26] This story with its representation of disintegration, alienation, loneliness and acceptance of defeat, borne with stoic eccentricity, concludes with the famous epitaph for 'the grand Australian bush—the nurse and tutor of eccentric minds, the home of the weird, and of much that is different from things in other lands'.[27]

The central character in this story has no name save that of 'the Bush Undertaker', which locates him within the preserve of the dead. He, like Ratty Howlett, lives and works alone, outside the community of mates. Ratty Howlett and the bush undertaker are rare figures in Lawson's fiction. They are bush eccentrics, exiled to a life without companionship. But their plight gives definition to the general condition of madness, isolation and death outside the constraints of the Father's Law—the ultimate threat of the bush. Although the bush is 'no place for a woman', nonetheless, a woman in a man's life is seen to preserve his identity and protect him from disintegration. Thus, when female characters succumb to madness, their condition poses a direct threat for man/Man. His fragile armour in this battle against the bush is mateship. Harry Heseltine, commenting on the stories of mad women in the bush, writes that mateship is practised not for its positive qualities but as 'a last line of defence against an uninviting, even hostile frontier'.[28]

Within the tradition, however, women *are* the frontier. They stand on the border between sanity and madness, civilization and the wilderness. In each of these stories a relationship is established between the writer and audience. Together they form a bond against the threat of an alien and alienating environment. The primal fear that a mother might reject her child, or the bush might reject its inhabitants, is played out on the terrain of the feminine. Within a human community, women act out man's fears, becoming what Man is not (that is, insane, defeated or dead), what is not Man. The bond between teller and listener, like the bond of mateship between men in the bush, establishes a connection between men which mediates the alien threat. As readers, whether male or female, we enter that bond against the alterity of otherness imagined as a place beyond the Father's Law.

At the same time in Lawson's stories there is the sense that the fate of women lies in man's hands. He carries a burden of guilt for her inability to cope with the bush, which operates textually as a projection of his own. This is especially true in the sequence of stories concerning Joe Wilson. The stories tell of the courtship, marriage, gradual decline and eventual collapse of the union between Joe and Mary Wilson. As the stories progress, the ageing, disintegrating narrator attempts to understand the forces which destroyed the innocent, hopeful past. Brian Matthews details the sequence as one in which the characters move from alienation to disintegration within an indifferent, hostile and pitiless bush.[29] Mrs Spicer, in 'Water them Geraniums', stands at the edge of the frontier between sanity and madness. She is described as a 'gaunt and flat-chested' woman with a face 'burnt to a brick', 'wild looking eyes', and a 'lost groping-in-the-dark kind of voice'. Having coped with an absent and alcoholic husband, delinquent children, visiting swagmen who hang themselves, isolation and poverty, she has reached a stage 'past carin'. ' "I'm gettin' a bit ratty" ' (like Ratty?), she tells Joe, shortly before she dies, ' "like a broken down horse." ' But she leaves instructions to 'water them geraniums', thus clinging, even at death, to the last remnants of civilization.[30] And Joe is shocked by the recognition that Mary, growing weary and indifferent, could suffer the same fate. About Mrs Spicer Matthews writes:

> She is a warning, not just to Mary but to all women, that their very personalities may be distorted, their characteristic femininity denatured, as deprivation, inadequacy, makeshift and longing take their physical, mental and spiritual toll; and that they may pass into a limbo where existence is not that of a woman or man, but one of confused, dissociated sensations—pain, nostalgia, bitterness, despair.[31]

In a footnote he continues, 'Spicer is a warning for Joe: he exists only as a gloomy, moody and bitter shadow of what he once was'.[32] Matthews is a careful reader of Lawson from an existential perspective. He sees the stories as crises of consciousness. But he does not question where these constructs of 'characteristic femininity' come from. 'Nature' will suffice.

But masculinity and femininity are cultural constructs. Lawson's stories reinforce gender divisions with difficulty, not so much because women escape the categories (they seldom do) but because masculine identity is not secure. The bush threatens to reduce men to exhibiting characteristics which Western culture assumes are feminine: that is passivity, weakness, depression, despair and, finally, madness or death. These are threats to the human personality which can beset men, but in Lawson's stories they are more often projected on to and lived out in the lives of fictional women. The stories reveal the hardships of the bush on women who are confined to the home and family responsibilities which men can (and perhaps must) escape. The disintegration of women is a threat to men, quelled in the call to mateship.

Ratty Howlett and the nameless bush undertaker lost the community of mates in their battle with the bush. In their madness they 'become' women—tending house, making tea, entertaining their fantasies. Mrs Spicer's final words, 'Water them geraniums', which also form the title of the story, tether her as a woman, however precariously, to the masculine order of sanity. Madness is a condition named, explained and (necessarily) contained by phallocentric culture to protect and preserve the identity of the self. The mad man is robbed of his selfhood—reduced to playing the role of the woman. The mad woman is robbed of her femininity, 'denatured' according to Matthews, as masculine property.

The bush as a frontier which poses madness against sanity, or loss of control against mastery of the self, is realized textually in a number of stories. In 'Water them Geraniums' when Mary tells Joe that ' "I can't stand this life here. It will kill me!" ' Joe reflects, ' "If I don't make a stand now . . . I'll never be master. I gave up the reins when I got married, and I'll have to get them back again! . . . What women some men are!" '[33] Mary's sanity is juxtaposed against Joe's mastery of the situation. If Mary can be restored to the masculine economy, in response to Joe's desire, she will be 'saved' by the structures of reason. Her 'indifference' (a term used to describe both Mary and Mrs Spicer) makes her enigmatic, inaccessible, impenetrable—an intolerable state within the male economy. This brings us back to an earlier discussion of women in the bush—the bush is both no place for and the place of woman as she stands within and also challenges the required masculine representations of femininity. Women and men, when they disintegrate into madness, chaos or disorder on the landscape of the bush, become the bushman's enemy: the ultimate threat to his identity.

Lawson had addressed the threat of this sort of fragmentation before. In 'Mitchell on the "Sex" and other "Problems" ' (1898–9) two mates ponder over the complex social and economic problems of the day. Mitchell believes they all have their origin in man's first curse, the curse of Eve, or, the sex problem. I will quote the introductory remarks of his speech at length, italicizing the text to note the sliding signification of the pronouns 'we' and 'us' 'you' and 'they' which mark divisions between universal humanity, males and females and the categories of inclusion and exclusion assumed. Mitchell explains:

There's no problem, really, except Creation, and that's not our affair; *we* can't solve it, and *we've* no right to make a problem out of it for ourselves to *puzzle* over, and waste the little time that is given us about. It's *we* that make the problems, not Creation. *We* make 'em, and *they only smother us; they'll smother the world* in the end if we don't look out. Anything that can be argued, for and against, from half a dozen different points of view—and most things that men argue over can—and anything that has been argued about for thousands of years . . . is worse than profitless, it wastes the world's time and ours, *and often wrecks old mateships*. It seems to me the deeper you read, think, talk, or write about things that end in ism, the less satisfactory the result; the more likely *you are to get bushed* and dissatisfied with the world. And the more you *keep on the surface of plain things*, the plainer the sailing—the more comfortable for you and everybody else. We've always got to come to the surface to breathe, in the end, and in any case; we're meant to live on the surface, and we might as well stay there and look after it and ourselves for all the good we do diving down after *fish that aren't there, except in our imagination*. And some of 'em are very *dead fish* too—the 'Sex Problem', for instance . . . [emphases mine][34]

After this long, rambling, somewhat obscure introduction, Mitchell specifically mentions a few of the 'isms' of the day which divide 'us'. Socialism, capitalism, spiritualism and unionism are referred to. That is, everything but the central problem to which this passage and the story, 'Mitchell on the "Sex" and other "Problems" ', builds and which is clearly the main concern—feminism. Soon enough Mitchell mentions the culprit: the 'notoriety-hunters' who take men to court 'for maintenance and breach of promise cases', . . . 'the rotten "sex problem" sort of thing', which, he says, is 'the cause of it all; it poisons weak minds—and strong ones too sometimes'.[35] If we deconstruct this argument, what Mitchell is telling Joe, and the readers too, through a bond of 'mateship' which is the bond of masculine resemblance against the feminine other, is that sexual divisions are natural and ordained by God through Creation. God and Christian morality become the source and origin of Mitchell's authority. But the text reveals how sexual divisions exist in the logic of phallocentric discourse which names God as the source and origin of Truth and also makes possible Mitchell's position of authority over the 'problem' of women.

Who are the 'we's' to whom Mitchell refers? Let us trace the logic of the argument. We [men and women within the masculine economy] cannot solve the problem of sexual divisions (which is 'no problem, really'). But 'we' [men and women, but mostly women] have no right to make a problem over it for 'ourselves' [men and women, but mostly men]. It is worth pointing out here that the women who were being urged by Mitchell not to make a problem of sex differences could include Louisa Lawson, Henry's mother and founder of the first feminist newspaper, *The Dawn*, which brought 'the sex problem' to public notice, and Bertha Lawson, his wife, who persuaded Henry to enter the Inebriates Home for six weeks during the year this story was written and worried over debts to the landlord as she sat at home each night with two small children while Henry frequented the Dawn and Dusk Club with his bohemian mates. 'We' [men and women, but mostly women] make the problems, and 'they' [the problems, but also women] 'only smother us'. At this point in the argument, the problem becomes both 'sexual divisions' and 'women', as the spur of Mitchell's dilemma. Later, Mitchell will shift some of the blame to men, because they have allowed women to dominate. He says:

> It was Eve's fault in the first place—or Adam's rather, because it might be argued that *he should have been master*. Some men are *too lazy* to be masters in their own homes, and *run the show properly*; some are *too careless*, and some *too drunk* most of the time, and some *too weak*. If Adam and Eve hadn't tried to find out things there'd be no toil and trouble in the world today; there'd have been no bloated capitalists, and no horny-handed working men, and no politics, no free trade and protection— and no clothes. [emphases mine][36]

Therefore, the complex social, political and economic problems of the day in Mitchell's naive romanticized reasoning can all be traced back to Adam and Eve. And the worst effect is that 'the sex problem' (etc.) 'wrecks old mateships'. Ironically, and at the same time, mateship is the status which both promotes and protects the bushman from 'the sex problem', while it both makes possible and denies woman's position of authority in the home of the absent father.

Critics of Lawson are somewhat embarrassed by these harangues of Mitchell's and their misogynistic biases. But the assumptions which make this argument possible have been present in Lawson's writings and beyond them within the Australian tradition from the outset. The views, which are not necessarily Lawson's, operate within the logic of a masculine culture. When men fail 'to run the show properly', that is, within the assumptions of male dominance and female submission, they are judged to be and sometimes see themselves as 'weak', 'careless' and 'lazy'. That is, they become lesser males taking over attributes within the category of the feminine. They turn to their mates in the pub or the bush to create an illusion of power through male bonding.

As Mitchell continues his argument, he says that the more you [men and women, but mostly men] think on the problem the more likely you [men] are to get bushed. To get bushed, within the Australian tradition, is to lose one's bearings, to get lost in every sense, to fail to attain an identity against the landscape of the bush. The threats to identity, within the larger discourse, have been named as absorption, or resignation to melancholy, despair, madness, and/or death—'the terror at the basis of being'. The solution is to 'keep on the surface of plain things' (the logic of masculine sameness), and not dive down after 'fish that aren't there'. This latter phrase recalls the opening phrase 'there's no problem, really' which began this discourse on the evils of the world, reduced to evils of sexual division, or 'the sex problem (etc.)'. The problem, acknowledged through negation, becomes the imagined power of the controlling and castrating women. To stay on the surface is to exteriorise the self, that is, man, reason and speech in a 'proper', 'natural' order and to contain the threat which woman and the feminine pose to men and masculine selfhood of weakness or defeat in this 'unnatural' chaotic state in which 'men' can become 'women'.

All those mad women in Lawson's stories—the selector's daughter, Maggie Head, Brighten's sister-in-law and Mrs Spicer—exist as figures of defeat for man. But Mitchell's speech demonstrates that even the strong bush pioneer women, the drover's wife, for example, can pose a threat to man's identity through their dominance within the family. Although they preserve male authority within the domestic space, they also can and do become unified with the hostile environment against which man battles. Within different webs of signification the bush and bush women form a frontier for man between sanity and madness, unity and disintegration, proper and improper spheres, which man must solve by mastery. The final refuge, when both consciousness and the 'proper' social world have apparently broken down, is the authority of language, the symbolic order and the Father's Law. Discourse constitutes the self. The designation of male strength and female weakness, male dominance and female submission, male activity and female passivity, are constructions of a masculine symbolic order assumed to be natural facts or truths ordained by God. When this order is disrupted it is seen to be the fault of women. So, when Mitchell and his mates lament about their failures to master women, and therefore master themselves, their misogyny relies on the authority of 'God' or the 'natural order' as the context which frames the argument. Male dominance may fail in the individual case history; but its authority is upheld in the symbolic order.

When critics search through Lawson's works for the character who personifies the 'ideal' bushman, who battles bravely and does not succumb to the hostile, anti-human threat of the bush, they generally settle on Mitchell. Colin Roderick calls Mitchell the 'homespun philosopher' who comes closest to being Lawson's 'ideal projection'.[37] Manning Clark sums him up in the following way:

By the end of 1893 Mitchell had been launched on the world, at first as the man who was habitually one-up on all competitors. He was the man with whom Australians could identify, because Mitchell by his very Australianness always came out on top. In recognizing their self-image in Mitchell, Lawson was not only making Australians aware of themselves, but giving them a self-confidence. Mitchell was the larrikin streak in the Australian: in time Lawson would also fill in that part of the Australian bushman and bushwoman which had more in common with the saint. In time, too, Mitchell would be the medium through whom he would tell the world something of his vision of life, of how those who had endured the hardships of the Australian bush knew about 'the power and the glory' as well as shame and degradation.[38]

(All Australians? Who speaks, for whom, and by what authority?) There are many Mitchell stories. In them women are not always the alien other against which the bushmen must struggle—sometimes it is the boss, or the bush, or the city. But, always, the threat is subdued by what Clark calls one-upmanship. Mitchell's 'self-confidence' is won by boasting, by asserting the demands of the male-as-underdog against 'unnatural' threats which assault and challenge his deserved status. Often, as in 'Mitchell on the "Sex" and other "Problems" ', the source of his mastery of self-presence depends primarily on the phallocentric operations of language.

The bushwoman as saint, to whom Clark refers, must undoubtedly be the drover's wife. She is the woman to whom both Hancock and Clark refer in their histories of Australia as an authentic representation of women in the bush and whom Summers recognized as the classic 'coper', idealized as the bush Mum (discussed in Chapter Three). All Australians know her. As children they read her story in school. As adults they encounter it more often than any other story in anthologies of Australian prose. Lawson must have loved her, because she helped to make his reputation in England. Edward Garnett, the British critic, from whom Nettie Palmer took her lead in assessing Lawson as the 'voice of the continent', had this to say about 'The Drover's Wife': 'If this artless sketch be taken as the summary of a woman's life, giving its meaning in ten short pages, Maupassant has never done better.'[39] We can trace Lawson's literary reputation, as it changed to suit the needs and attitudes of the times, by reading what various critics have had to say about this literary figure.

LAWSON CRITICISM: THE USES OF THE FEMININE

In the early decades of the century, when Lawson's prose was deemed 'authentic' by sympathetic reviewers, his 'realistic' short stories were judged to be representative, photographic and sincere.[40] In the 1920s, Australia entered a conservative phase. As Richard White explains, 'the bush and the bohemians were sobered up, made respectable and reinterpreted to stand for the new bourgeois values associated with the new nation, for the new ideals which needed protection.'[41] For the most part, critics begin to challenge Lawson's bush as unrepresentative, morbid and brooding. But what they deem undesirable in the fiction, they attribute to failings in the personality of the artist. Further, the form of chastisement relies on an understanding of masculine/feminine dichotomies. Lawson is depicted as weak, womanish and unmanly when his writings no longer conform to the nation's dominant idea of itself. In 1922 A. G. Stephens wrote that Lawson saw the bush 'through the distorting glass of his own moody mind'. But Stephens blames what he sees as an idiosyncratic fault of the artist on Lawson's 'feminine' weakness. Stephens' quotation continues: ' "My aunts said I should have been a girl," he wrote. His womanish wail often needs a sturdy Australian backbone.'[42] The quote, taken from Lawson's autobiographical writings, illustrates how Lawson took on to himself the negative connotations of feminine sexual identity as an explanation for aspects of his personality which differed from the rigid masculine norms of his time.

The 1920s was an era when the concept of the purity of the race was enlisted to stand against the Yellow Peril. It was a time, according to White, when 'the bohemian image of the outback was reduced to wattle, sunshine and "White Australia"'.[43] Lawson-as-a-cultural-object became the site of an ideological battle among critics intent on bolstering the national image. The bush, through the symbol of the wattle, came to represent the land of joy and wholesomeness. Fred Davison, editor of the monthly journal *Australia*, complained that 'Lawson failed most abjectly to sense that joy and to give it expression.' He 'didn't know Australia—not the real Australia—and couldn't write about it'.[44] But, although critics severely chastise Lawson for his 'woeful' portrayal of bushmen, the drover's wife is spared.

After the Great War, the culture enlists Lawson into the cause of mature nationhood in terms echoing those of David McKee Wright's 'almost legendary' preface. The gold-rush digger, the noble bushman, the Anzac soldier fuse into a single image of manly strength, independence and courage. During this era the industrialists, with their international connections to the United States, actively competed with the pastoralists to sell a new image of a wholesome, sane, pure and innocent Australia in league with the West, against the threatening, divisive, unhealthy, decadent and impure non-Western world. Working-class interests became divisive to the 'national' interests of the nation's middle class.[45]

This ideological shift had several interesting effects on the cultural production of Australia. For example, films which depicted Australia's convict past and bushranging, as well as those which depicted drought, were banned from overseas distribution. In 1921 the Superintendent for Immigration appealed to travellers to monitor their speech while overseas. 'Such words as "drought" and "strike" and "rabbit" and "taxes" and "politics" should be thrown overboard as the vessels put to sea', he cautioned.[46] At the same time critics began to alter the image of Lawson. His bush becomes the terrain on which national pride is built. The drover's wife becomes a 'large and symbolic figure' who 'opened the eyes of other writers to what is really poignant and dramatic in the life around them'.[47] After both world wars, the image of manly toughness, 'born of the lean loins of the country itself', would unite the academic nationalists to their literary brothers of the 1890s.[48] And the drover's wife, though a woman, is seen to personify these traits.

With a shift of national interests away from the bush and towards the city, away from particular forms of working-class republicanism and towards a so-called universal middle-class culture, Lawson and the literature of the 1890s also underwent a reinterpretation. Harry Heseltine announced the new theme in his ironically titled essay, 'Henry Lawson: Our Apostle of Mateship'. He suggested that the popular vision of 'a happy band of brothers marching bravely forward to a political and social utopia, united in their hatred of tyranny, their love of beer, their rugged manliness and independence' is a façade which does justice to neither Lawson nor the Australian character.[49] He and critics who agreed with his modernist stance argued that the tradition as represented by the Democratic Nationalists was parochial, not universal; representative of the bush, not the city; the working class, and not the middle class; the ignorant common man, and not his educated brother; the raw experience of man, and not his metaphysical soul.[50] It is Heseltine who first notes the nihilistic tendencies in the tradition which Lawson fathered. He restated his case in the essay 'The Literary Heritage' (1962):

> The canon of our writing presents a façade of mateship, egalitarian democracy, landscape, nationalism, realistic toughness. But always behind the façade looms the fundamental concern of the Australian literary imagination. That concern, marked out by our national origins and given direction by geographic necessity, is to acknowledge the terror at the basis of being, to explore its uses, and to build defences against its dangers. It is that concern which gives Australia's literary heritage its special force and distinction, which guarantees its continuing modernity.[51]

Whereas earlier commentators had described the bush as a physical threat to man's identity, Heseltine imagined it as a moral, spiritual and existential threat. We traced this ideological shift from a nationalist to a modernist perspective in regard to landscape representation in Chapter Four. When this attitude was explored with reference to 'The Drover's Wife', as in Matthews' *The Receding Wave*, the story was described as one of 'ruthless pessimism' in which the woman confronts the bush as a 'common enemy' to men and women alike. Her life of hardships culminates in a 'sense of spiritual and emotional exhaustion'.[52]

Colin Roderick is one critic whose views on Lawson and 'The Drover's Wife' have changed over time. In the 1960s Roderick described her situation as that of 'the self-sacrificing lonely life of the bushwoman who in those days helped to lay the foundation of our prosperity'.[53] This position aligns the author with the attitudes of the Democratic Nationalists. But in his recent study, *The Real Henry Lawson*, Roderick shifts ground. He cites 'The Drover's Wife' as Lawson's 'first short story of high quality' and maintains that the dominant note is one of melancholy.

> The bush suffered a change which reflected his own fears and insecurity. Nothing attractive, nothing lovely, nothing of good to report entered his portrait of it: it was all sinister and destructive. It developed from a mere background into an active alien force against which human fortitude spent itself until it was crushed.[54]

(We note that reference to the drover's wife as a woman is curiously absent; for Roderick in this instance the story is one of the bush and 'human fortitude' which is crushed. Actually the *snake* is crushed in the story. An interesting elision.)

But Manning Clark has another story to tell. For him, 'The Drover's Wife' presents to Australians an awareness of both a surface heroism and a metaphysical terror. He explains that the surface story tells of a wife's heroism and her sacrifice for her children, but underneath it all she confronts and conquers all the fears of despair and defeat which 'touched him [Lawson] deeply'. He proclaims, 'Lawson knew that her heroism, the halo of glory with which he endowed this bush mum, was of a high order.'[55]

'The Drover's Wife', in the hands of the critics, has been a prized commodity for public consumption. The many interpretations which this story has received demonstrate both the evocative, symbolic richness of the text and the ways in which the story as a cultural object has been enlisted in the defence of dominant ideological perspectives concerning the nature of Australian culture. The commentators refer to 'The Drover's Wife' as a cultural entity in three ways. *As literature*, the story has grown from an artless sketch to a work of high quality. *As a figure*, the wife has been described as a tough dramatic individual symbolizing courage and hope and also one of crushed fortitude exhibiting emotional and spiritual exhaustion. *As an image of the Australian character*, her situation reflects the nation's prosperity and its pessimism. The former depictions belong to writers associated with the Democratic Nationalists who share a Whig view of progress which celebrates the country's prosperity and initiative. In their view, the literature of the 1890s is described as realistic, although their representations of the national character reveal an allegiance to social Darwinism with its emphasis on heredity. The tough stock of transplanted Britons whom the drover's wife personifies produce for them a national type which will lead the country to maturity as an independent, strong and resourceful nation. Women are pioneers. They function as symbols of hope.

The later depictions emerge out of the writings of critics associated with the bourgeois modernists, whose anti-Whig sympathies deny a faith in historical progress. Their construction of the literature of the 1890s emphasizes the nihilistic, violent and irrational dark side of the Australian tradition. Their representation of the national character arises out of a modern social theory which investigates the forces of the environment. They decry Australia as a static nation, tied to world-wide economic and political realities which limit future growth. Nationalism as a concept has grown both 'sour and barren'.[56] Women personify the national dilemma. They function symbolically as figures of defeat.

Whether referring to Lawson's story, the figure of the drover's wife as an historical entity, or the woman as a dimension of the national character, the two sides of the argument depend on a series of dichotomies within Western thought. The debate contrasts the objective with the subjective; optimism with pessimism; reason with doubt; realism with romanticism. The former qualities are desired, while the latter are feared; the former associated with the masculine, the latter with the feminine within the critical discourse on Lawson and the Australian tradition. However, both the Democratic Nationalists and the New Critics embrace 'The Drover's Wife' in their attempts to define and master the national character. Could it be that for critics, who otherwise take up a variety of disparate positions, this figure represents 'the people's dream' of a malleable, pliant, non-threatening but phallic bush/mother?

A RE-READING OF 'THE DROVER'S WIFE'

A central problem for nineteenth-century explorers and settlers who confronted the bush was the dilemma of absence where presence was desired. Finding only a void, a wasteland, they invested the bush with visions of cultivation, noble cities, fruitful terrains, sheep and illimitable grasslands— all marks of man's progressive mastery. It is not surprising, then, to discover presence and absence as a dichotomy around which 'The Drover's Wife' revolves. In this story the husband is absent. His central role in the family has been taken over by the wife. Her dilemma is that the woodheap is empty. Its absence has been filled in by the presence of a snake. So, from the outset, the woman and the snake take up the space of absence. But the story, through woman, will serve to secure man's place in the bush and the Australian tradition.

The story calls for a closer re-reading. 'The Drover's Wife' tells the story of a woman's courage and fortitude within carefully delineated parameters of masculine discourse.[57] Her husband has been away, droving, for six months. He had once been a squatter with resources sufficient to take his wife to the city (in the more costly sleeping compartment) and furnish the family with a buggy. But his fortunes have declined. The vision of the land as a paradise for the common man has faded, and the bush, described as a flat plain of 'stunted, rotten native *apple* trees' (emphasis mine) where only the she-oaks sigh, serves as a reminder of woman's association with nature and man's lost Arcadian dreams. As the story opens, the woman emerges from the kitchen (her 'proper' sphere), which is separated from the hut and 'larger than the house itself, verandah included', in response to her children's cries that a snake has entered the woodheap and slid under the house. The first words of dialogue read 'Snake! Mother, here's a snake!' The phrase provides a visual code for the reader to identify the Snake with the Mother, through the suggestive placement of the words side by side and the rhetorical device of their capitalization. This sets up a series of links between the woman and the snake which is extended later when the wife tries to tempt the snake into the kitchen with two small dishes of milk. This narrative detail underlines the mother's role as both Eve, the temptress in league with the snake, and Mary as nurturer, the giver of milk. When the confrontation with the snake finally occurs at the climax of the tale, the mother 'sits as one fascinated' as she watches Alligator, the dog, who 'shakes the snake as though he felt the original curse in common with mankind'. In effect, Alligator replaces the absent husband here, performing the role of Adam, the first man to restore order in a post-lapsarian paradise.

Although these associations set up a chain of signifiers which link the woman to the snake, sin and nature, that is, woman as Other, another and more dominant set of associations exist to link the woman to Man. In terms of Lawson's imaginary ordering of the world, evidenced in his early verse, the snake in the garden of promise, before being named as woman, was called greed. It is exhibited here in the character of the blackfellow. We recall that the woman had bargained with a 'stray blackfellow' on the previous day to collect wood for her, and she had rewarded his initiative with 'an extra fig of tobacco, and praised him for not being lazy.' But he had built the woodheap hollow. Woman as Man stands against the blackfellow, the snake, the world's greed and the threatening bush. Her position appears to be secure within the masculine economy. She is innocent of guilt as the drover's wife; the blackfellow, the snake and the bush beyond connote guilt, greed, sin and death emanating from realms of the natural, animal and racially alien human worlds.

There are several signifying chains in the story which link the alien other with the native blacks, although the natives function ambivalently as a source of both good (when identified with the white settler's hopes) and evil (when seen to act against them). On the negative side of signification, when the snake first appears, Tommy, the eldest son, wielding club in hand, yells, 'I'll have the beggar', thus linking the snake as beggar with the first beggar, the Aboriginal native. When Alligator, the dog, grips the snake and pulls it into the kitchen, the snake is described as 'a black brute, five feet long'. This description, which directly follows the discovery of the hollow woodheap, built by a blackfellow who 'was the last of his tribe and a King', metonymically links the black snake/beggar/native with the forces of threat to white civilization. On the other hand, when the wife's last two (female and unnamed) children were born in the bush, and on one occasion when she was left unattended and ill as the husband struggled to bring the drunken doctor back to attend her, 'God sent Black Mary'. But Black Mary, midwife and witness to God's curse on Eve that she bring forth children in pain and distress, was 'the "whitest" gin in all the land'. Lawson's prose reveals an ideology of white, male, Anglo-Saxon culture which is as ambivalent to blacks in this instance as it can be to female characters elsewhere.

The woman's heroism is established textually through a flashback reminiscence structured to build suspense as she maintains her all-night vigil awaiting the confrontation with the snake. She has overcome both natural and living threats: bushfires, floods, cattle disease, raging bullocks, greedy crows and malicious swagmen—all part of the alien otherness of the bush. In these activities she acts in a masculine role as the pioneering hero. She even dresses in her husband's overalls on occasion to further mark her (borrowed) masculine position. Her pleasures as a wife and mother have been few: Sunday walks with the children for which 'she takes as much care to make herself and the children look smart as she would if she were going to do the block in the city', and prepared welcomes for her absent husband. The omniscient narrator (objective/masculine) assures us that she is content with her lot, although the children think she's harsh, despite her love. 'Her surroundings are not favourable to the development of the "womanly" or sentimental side of nature.' But her words to the children, their Sunday behaviour, her sewing and her reading firmly establish her 'feminine respectability'. Thus, she is depicted as a woman of courage and fortitude within the domestic sphere who is also able to function in a masculine role when required. The point of view allows for no conflict between her 'self' and her maternal role. She is happy to protect the position of her husband, his property and the 'natural' social order of family life. The isolation of the bush, that 'everlasting, maddening sameness of the stunted trees' which 'makes a man want to break away', she handles with a mixture of laughter and tears.

There is, however, considerable tension between the signification of the woman as the drover's wife, that is, associated with the self, and the woman, signified as other who stands in an inferior relation to man. In the story she is identified both as Man and not-man; hero and victim; self and other. Every one of her heroic feats is mediated by her limitations. For example, she tends the sheep but her husband's brother kills them and brings provisions. She quells the bushfire but has Tommy working 'like a hero' by her side while the baby 'howled lustily'. In this action the text establishes the drover's wife in a variety of contradictory roles. Dressed in overalls, she is the husband; with blackened arms, she is (and is mistaken by the baby as) the blackfellow; working with Tommy as the hero, she is inferior to man; in response to the baby's cries, she is the maternal mother. Despite all this, the bushfire 'would have mastered her' had it not been for the help of four bushmen. She saves the hut (private sphere) from flood but she could not save the dam (public sphere). 'There are things that a bushwoman cannot do.' She takes the children for bush walks but has limited orienteering skills—only a bushman can fix a point. She confronts the snake with a 'green sapling club' while Tommy has a stick/club 'bigger than himself' (and he's eleven). She kills the snake, holding Tommy back with 'a grip of iron', with the help of Alligator who provides the family with the voice, growl, surveillance, courage and protective behaviours of a husband—'they couldn't afford to lose him'. After the crisis she soothes the dog to reduce his anger and agitation. And despite her bravery, she cries a lot. In only one instance is her fortitude and courage unqualified. This is when we are told of how she rode nineteen miles for assistance on horseback carrying her dead child. She can be phallic as long as she is also, and above all, a maternal woman. This is a carefully constructed character, capable of being man and woman, phallic and maternal, hero and victim, Eve and Mary and also standing in the symbolic space of the other—the snake, greed, original sin, the blackfellow, nature.

When the crisis has passed and Tommy sees tears rising in his mother's eyes, he hugs her and whispers a promise, ' "Mother, I won't never go drovin; blast me if I do!" ' Lawson leaves the mother and child coupled at the story's end. Together they watch as the 'sickly daylight breaks over the bush'. Her apparently manly sacrifice is rewarded by maternal love and domestic contentment. Order is restored out of chaos. Absence has been replaced by a plentitude called Woman.

It is difficult to comprehend how any commentator on 'The Drover's Wife' could have maintained that it was an 'artless sketch', or a 'realistic', 'photographic' depiction unless one accepts that the biblical primal scene, so enmeshed within the structure of the story, has become so 'real' for Western readers that its presence need not be acknowledged, and the sliding space of woman so naturalized that this fantastic creation can still seem convincingly real. The woman, the dog and the boy in this story all confront the 'common curse', Eve's curse, the curse of original sin—that which separates civilization from the wild and barren wilderness, the self from the alien other which can be discursively linked with the 'place' of the feminine. No wonder that the woman watches the snake 'as one fascinated'. But she confronts and conquers the alien threat, as a phallic mother, acting in the place of the (absent) father. And the son, already a 'larrikin' at age eleven, despite his promise (made through the discounting double negative that he 'won't never go drovin') undoubtedly will follow his father, as a means of escape from the 'maddening sameness' of the bush/woman.

In addition, the drover's wife, as Madonna (in the child's eyes) or God's police (in those of the wider society) preserves masculine authority, not only in the bush but for the nation. As long as she remains at home, tied to family but acting in both masculine and feminine roles, men can roam the bush where they often act like boys. In stories like 'Rats', 'The Shearing of the Cook's Dog', 'The Iron Bark Chip' and countless others, the men on the land regress into childlike behaviour, idealized into 'mateship', while their position of authority is protected by the loved and feared—but mostly feared—bush Mum. When we investigate the drover's wife as a cultural construction which comes to be seen as an authentic historical representation of women in the bush we can more fully understand how Manning Clark could maintain that her 'halo of glory . . . was of a high order'.[58]

'The Drover's Wife' is often compared (favourably) with Barbara Baynton's story, 'The Chosen Vessel', which will be examined in the next chapter. But 'The Drover's Wife' occupies a central position in the Australian tradition, while Baynton's story is labelled 'dissident'. The reasons are not hard to detect. As we have discovered, the Australian tradition involves a struggle for a national identity against the otherness of the bush. The drover's wife, as she confronts the danger of the snake, the blackfellow and the wilderness, stands on a terrain between sanity and madness, courage and defeat, physical strength and spiritual exhaustion. But she has an identity. She is the drover's *wife*. She stands in his place, quelling the threat of feminine other, archetypically present in the form of the snake, by means of her phallic attachment. Her conquest of the snake signals the victory of the white presence over the bush. In this she, too, is a pioneering hero of the Australian tradition. Yet she maintains the distinctive marks of femininity, occupying both (privileged) masculine and (inferior) feminine positions within the culture's gender order. This bush Mum, as an object in discourse, mediates the threats of feminine otherness for all readers, while at the same time preserving the space of the feminine other. She fulfills the people's dream of the perfect mother—powerful, yet capable of being mastered herself, without a struggle. The perfect Australian fantasy.

A SEARCH FOR ORIGINS

Critics of Lawson have spent a great deal of time attempting to determine the source and origin of the story 'The Drover's Wife'. There are many contenders. Perhaps this is in part symptomatic of the evocative force of the fantasy and the ongoing desire to possess the perfect mother in reality. Anne Summers reports that the story belongs to Mary Gilmore, who related it to Henry Lawson. The event had happened to *her* mother, when Mary was six years old. Summers reports that Gilmore recalls her brother making the promise to her mother to 'stay home and take care of you', a version of which Lawson uses to bring his tale to a close.[59] But Colin Roderick disagrees, claiming that Lawson said the story 'was modelled on the life of his aunt, Mrs. Job Falconer'.[60] Denton Prout, one of Lawson's literary biographers, maintains that the incident of the raging bullock which the drover's wife remembers having killed, had actually happened to Lawson's mother, Louisa.[61] Brian Matthews, commenting on the story in the light of previously unpublished autobiographical materials, suggests that the stories Louisa told to Henry as a child concerning her bush experiences, including the dangers of intrusive snakes and swagmen, provided the inspiration for the tale.[62] The physical description of the drover's wife is said to resemble extant descriptions of Henry's mother.[63] But the most startling discovery, for those who search for empirical evidence on which to ground reality, is that announced recently by E. J. Zinkhan.[64] Zinkhan has located a previously unacknowledged item in the Lawson canon—an article written by Louisa Lawson in 1889, three years before the publication of 'The Drover's Wife', called 'The Australian Bush-Woman'. The article appeared in both an English and an

American woman's magazine. Louisa's descriptions of the bush woman, her mode of life, her activities and her fear of madness bear a striking resemblance to her son's fictional representations. The critic recognizes that this discovery might pose a threat to the authority of Henry Lawson's tale. But she issues a caution: 'We must continue to be circumspect regarding the literary connection between mother and son, and particularly circumspect in our next question . . . Did Louisa provide an influence on Henry's use of language in "The Drover's Wife?" ' Textual comparisons between Louisa's essay and Henry's story reveal not only common themes but also 'recurring syntactical patterns' which the critic finds 'intriguing'.[65] There are differences, however, which Zinkhan delineates. The woman in Henry's story fears threats from the outside—the snake, the bush, the bushmen. But the bushwoman in Louisa's article can also fear her own husband who, if Australian, is likely to be lazy and domineering, and if European, violent and brutish.

There are a number of issues here. One, of course is the question of who speaks, for whom, and by what authority. Louisa speaks as the editor and feature writer of a feminist journal, *The Dawn*, to an international audience of women with whom she hopes to share an interest in women's rights. She ends her article with the following remarks: 'the iron strength of character, the patience, endurance and self-repression which the bush-women practised and developed, passing to a generation more enlightened and progressive, will give us a race of splendid women, fit to obtain what their mothers never dreamed of—women's rights.'[66] Henry speaks as a budding writer to a local audience of Australians with whom he hopes to share a belief in Democratic Nationalism. They have a different relation to their subject and audience and a different investment in the masculine economy. But both write from within a discursive network of meanings and ideological constraints which structure the debate on national identity. Louisa's text relies on the same Whig faith in progress and dependence on ideas adopted from social Darwinism regarding the strength of racial types, as do those of her son and the writers of the school of Democratic Nationalism he is said to father. But Louisa posits the nation's 'iron strength of character, . . . its endurance . . .' in the women who braved the hostile bush and contributed to the development of an enlightened and progressive society. She notes, however, that women had to practise 'self-repression' in the interest of national goals. Critics of Lawson will see these characteristics reflected in 'The Drover's Wife'. Within the Australian tradition, however, the drover's wife comes to represent not women's interests or strengths but those of a (masculine) national character. If men fail to exhibit the necessary characteristics desired for the country, then women can stand in their place, but at the expense of their difference within the masculine economy. They come to represent that economy. Louisa's article 'The Australian Bush-Woman' which contains a critique of the actions of men in the bush has been lost to history, while Henry's 'Drover's Wife' in which the benign husband is absent lives on.

Another issue is women's *access* to the tradition. Louisa's article, calling attention to attributes of the national character not entirely favorable to men, was published overseas. Despite considerable scholarly interest in all things Lawsonian, it remained undetected for nearly a century. The article which announces the discovery appears in the final 'Notes and Documents' section of *Australian Literary Studies*. The same edition announces the discovery of some previously unpublished manuscripts of Henry Lawson by Brian Kiernan. A month later, Kiernan's 'scoop' discovery would be announced to the nation in blazing headlines on the front page of metropolitan newspapers.[67] Kiernan's 'scoop' would sell newspapers, boost the profits of the publishing industry, enhance an academic reputation and reify the authority of Henry Lawson as 'the first articulate voice of the real Australian'. Kiernan's discovery serves the 'national interest', whereas Zinkhan's dissident voice, like that of Louisa Lawson and the short stories of Barbara Baynton, might be divisive. The speaker's relation to power continues to shape and determine the discourse on the Australian tradition.

Is this why 'we must continue to be circumspect' concerning the relation between Lawson and his mother, Louisa? To be circumspect is to look at an issue from all angles. The issue here is the source for 'The Drover's Wife'. The critics want to determine whether it arises out of Lawson's genius, which is what the fuss is about, or Mary Gilmore's ancedote, or that of his aunt, or Louisa's life as told to her children through reminiscences. Any of these answers might be acceptable within the Australian tradition because they preserve the reputation of the artist as one who creatively fuses the material of his life history and imagination into fiction. To suggest that Lawson may have borrowed the idea from an article of his mother's and copied its themes and syntax endangers the writer's reputation for originality. What is at stake, finally, is Henry's originality as the true voice of Australia. Cautious critical circumspection is, indeed, needed to protect the space of his presence. Louisa's article has been and continues to be a muted element in the debate. For, to uphold the tradition, it is imperative that 'The Drover's Wife' be satisfied with her lot and that she *belong* to Henry Lawson.

BIOGRAPHICAL STUDIES OF LAWSON'S PERSONALITY

Who is 'Henry Lawson'—this absent centre around which national identity takes form? In recent years a number of articles and biographical texts have been produced which tell the story (or rather stor*ies*) of the man and his work, the man whom Vance Palmer called a 'portent' for the nation. There are at least five book-length biographies of Lawson as compared to only one full-length analysis of his writing. It is Lawson-the-man, to a far greater degree than Lawson-the-writer, who has been the subject of interest for scholars and readers alike. The genealogical history of the Lawson family's presence in Australia presents a fund of material to stir the literary and historical imagination. The details can be and have been structured in a way that reproduces the outlines of the Australian legend.

The historical discourse represents the family history according to a common pattern. There seems to be agreement among historians as to the broad outlines of the Lawson family in Australia. The narrative is presented according to these general outlines. Henry's maternal ancestors, John and Ann Ralph Albury, emigrated to Australia in 1838 after having been evicted from their cottage in Kent, where John worked as a hop farmer. Ann, known for her dark piercing eyes, was said to be descended from the gypsies. Although a supposition, this detail is recounted with regularity in the historical narratives. It is assumed that Australia, for this couple, symbolized a new hope for the landless poor of rural England. Their son, Harry, became a shopkeeper on the goldfields, where he was known as an 'incessant disturber of the peace'.[68] He married Harriet Winn, the daughter of either an English clergyman or a commercial traveller (the facts are obscure) who emigrated to Australia with her sister in 1848, to become a domestic servant. She becomes one of the army of 'God's police' whom Caroline Chisholm believed would provide the 'nucleus for the formation of a good and great people'.[69] Louisa Albury, Henry's mother, was born of this union. As a child she appears to have exhibited a great talent for poetry and music, writing verse at school and home and singing to the diggers in the pubs (but also in church!) in a strong soprano voice. Neither her mother, represented as demure and respectable, nor her father, described as boorish and domineering, encouraged Louisa's interests. At eighteen in 1866 she married Neils Larsen, a Norwegian sailor and handyman who had deserted his ship at Melbourne in 1855, drawn to the diggings and the elusive lure of gold. Henry Lawson was reputedly born in a tent on the Grenfell goldfields in 1867 (an assumption which Manning Clark adheres to but Colin Roderick refutes).[70] By this telling, Lawson has a 'classic' Australian heritage.

These are the background facts of history about which there exists a consensus among Henry Lawson's biographers. How they will interpret these facts, in their constructions of Lawson and his personality, will vary. But like Lawson himself in later life, when they search for a scapegoat for Henry's failings, they tend to blame the women in his life. Brian Matthews' biographical study *Louisa* (1987) significantly shifts the tide of critical understanding towards a more sympathetic reading of her character. The text is, however, a study of Louisa, not Henry Lawson and thus does not alter the general critique forwarded here. Stephen Murray-Smith, in his short biography of Henry Lawson, is a rare exception.[71] He reports that Louisa, upon marriage to Peter (as he preferred to be known) was a curious, independent and sensitive girl, who grew gradually resentful and unhappy in the isolation and dreariness of the bush. When her second child was born, during one of Peter's frequent absences, when she was left alone with two-year-old Henry, she vowed to leave the bush. She took up sewing as a means of supporting her plans. But as there was no Married Woman's Property Act, Peter forbade her to separate from him and used the money to buy a selection, but with the intention to dig for gold, not to farm. Louisa battled against insanity, escaping briefly to Sydney during her difficult third pregnancy, returning to the goldfields, regaining her strength and vowing to establish a school to guarantee the education of her children. But she had to convince her husband to represent her interests in the children's education, since the school's organizing committee would not allow women to attend the meetings. Murray-Smith reports that Louisa listened to their negotiations through a crack in the door. At the age of thirteen Henry helped his father to build the school. With Louisa's encouragement he also began writing poetry, which his father burned. In 1883, Louisa left the bush, moving to Sydney where she joined republican social and political circles, began publishing *The Republican*, and later, *The Dawn*. She arranged the publication of Henry's first book of poetry in 1894. Of her life in Sydney, Murray-Smith writes:

> she fought for prison reform, against 'ragged' schools, against gambling and drunkenness and against every manifestation of that spurious masculinity which still makes Australia one of the few places in the world where the man who deserts his wife and family is accorded a tough and ready sympathy among the community of men.[72]

This is a rare portrait of Louisa. Murray-Smith renders a consistently sympathetic interpretation of Louisa as a woman of strength and integrity who gave the encouragement which made Henry's writing career possible. Concerning Henry's personality, Murray-Smith writes that he was a sensitive and introverted youth who 'needed [his mother] a hundred times more than he needed his father but he always wished with one side of his nature to escape from the obligation by the quickest and most convenient route: to forget'.[73] Murray-Smith speculates that Henry's inability to resolve his debt to and reliance on Louisa drove him to the companionship of his mates at the pub. This is a far cry from the dominant tradition which most often takes its clues about Lawson's childhood and relationship with his parents from his short story, 'A Child in the Dark, and a Foreign Father'. The story is a retrospective autobiographical account of Henry's childhood begun about 1902 after the collapse of his marriage when, critics agree, he was 'in a most pitiable state'.[74] The story recounts his early childhood in a way that pits a nervous, unstable and insensitive mother against a patient, long-suffering and obliging father. Murray-Smith cautions that the story also positions the reader against the mother in a projection of her personality which is without historical accuracy.[75]

But the tide of historical reconstruction would swamp the undercurrent of sympathy for Louisa which flows through Murray-Smith's biography. A majority of critics, including Desmond O'Grady, Denton Prout, Manning Clark and Colin Roderick, cite 'A Child in the Dark, and a Foreign Father' and Lawson's autobiographical reminiscences written between 1903 and 1922 as reliable, factual documents in their search for the 'real' Henry Lawson. All agree that there were strengths and weaknesses in Henry's character which would contribute to both his 'genius' and his disintegration. They attempt to reconstruct an essential personality, searching through the evidence selectively in order to explain his propensity for alcohol and slow decline. Some critics side with heredity, others with environment, as the source of the conflict—but all agree that the destructive influences on Lawson were feminine influences. Colin Roderick writes that Lawson had 'a brittle temperament . . . inherited from unstable maternal ancestors [which] led him, as it led his Norwegian grandfather, into the deceitful refuge of alcohol'.[76] Manning Clark, who imagines a link between Lawson and Henrik Ibsen, blames the 'sins of the father', presumably drinking and debauchery on the goldfields (we remember the character type from Chapter Four), for Lawson's sensitivity, which resulted in his deafness. But he writes, in a somewhat contradictory fashion, that Lawson had 'a feminine mind in a masculine body', and later, 'a violent destructive person inside the gentle Henry Lawson'.[77] Throughout the commentaries, the cultural categories of masculinity and femininity structure the arguments. Those characteristics found in Lawson's personality and deemed inappropriate for a man are called feminine and also blamed on actual women as their source. Clark's latest reminiscence appears in a thumbnail sketch of Lawson, commissioned for the coffee-table Christmas publication, *The Greats: the 50 Men and Women who Most Helped to Shape Modern Australia* (47 males and 3 females) which features an informal close-up photograph of Lawson on the dust-jacket.[78] In that article Clark again takes up the arguments concerning Lawson's weakness. He reiterates the opinion about Lawson that 'he should have been a girl' and adds other critical perspectives, including evidence of a repressed homosexuality, a spendthrift personality and the influence of British philistinism as reasons for his disintegration.

Critics who side with environment as the source of Henry's weakness generally begin with the marriage of Peter and Louisa. Desmond O'Grady represents Peter as a 'patient and kindly man', as he appears in 'A Child in the Dark , and a Foreign Father'. 'It was his misfortune', O'Grady continues, 'that his wife Louisa Albury was ambitious, intelligent, unaffectionate, interested in Spiritualism and potentially a crusading feminist.'[79] Life, he concludes, was Hell. Denton Prout reports that, 'Peter's dream of domestic bliss was shattered [when] he realised that his wife was a tartar, who had married not from affection but as a means of escape.'[80] Both Prout and Clark present a picture of Louisa Lawson as a domineering, manipulative, ambitious and unstable woman. She was 'impatient with the weak and foolish, that is, all those who opposed her', writes Prout.[81] 'She was one of those women who was endowed by nature with an incurable itch to take charge of the lives of everyone she met. Those who liked to surrender control over their lives admired and adored her', writes Clark[82] in the same vein. Embittered by a sense of deprivation, she was neither attentive nor affectionate to her children. Clark reports that 'this heightened [Henry's] native bent towards solitary brooding.'

The biographical accounts of O'Grady, Prout, Clark and Roderick all contain consistent harangues against Louisa, which are not only dependent on each other, but also, beyond the commentaries on Lawson, on stereotypic notions of woman as the source of the world's evil (that is, the deficiencies in men). And yet, these critics purport to be embarrassed by the misogynistic ravings of Mitchell in Lawson's stories. When they turn their attention to the marriage between Henry and Bertha Bredt they take their cues from the same pre-existent set of cultural assumptions. Only the stakes are larger—Henry's 'genius' is now the issue. Several critics report that George Robertson, Lawson's publisher, warned Bertha not to marry Henry. He cautioned, 'Henry Lawson is a genius and you know what geniuses are like—they never make a woman happy.'[83] It appears that everyone was against the marriage—and Bertha herself had her doubts.[84] But once she committed herself, this 'Gentlewoman', who 'was inclined to lay stress on gentility and the proper observation of etiquette',[85] persevered for six years with a man prone to instability, depression, drunkenness and abusive behaviour. Clark, who sardonically refers to both Bertha and Louisa, wife and mother, as 'fine flowers of puritanism' claims that she was deluded into thinking that 'her loving kindness and devotion could still the madness in his blood'. But, he chastises, 'She never paused to ask whether that would also destroy his genius.'[86] And Roderick, echoing O'Grady's theme and syntax in regard to the marriage of Henry's parents, concludes, 'It was unfortunate that his [Henry's] lot was to be linked with that of a woman who viewed her responsibility to her children as of prime importance. If Lawson were to fail as the family provider, she must be father and mother to them.'[87] (Why is it that the fictional drover's wife can be praised for these attributes while the historically constructed wife of Henry Lawson is damned for the same qualities? It seems that the deciding factor is the influence such behaviour is reputed to have on the husband.) Each of these critics in a variety of ways reads Lawson's character through assumed characteristics of Lawson's mother and wife which would be deemed appropriate, even praiseworthy, if found in a man. They then chastise the women for their 'faults' while absolving the men of blame. They conclude that the source of Lawson's weakness, even failure, was paradoxically the strength of the women in his life.

It only remains for the biographical critics to turn to Lawson's stories (but not 'The Drover's Wife') for reinforcement of the views. O'Grady proclaims that the central male characters in Lawson's fiction have all been *betrayed by women:*

> Mitchell, Steelman, and the Oracle have all been betrayed by women . . . the paradise of earlier days is lost; something fatally crippling had happened to the typical lonely figure of Lawson's Bush . . . The trouble in each man's past was caused by a woman; and thus has affected their outlook and in turn the form of their stories.[88]

The flaws critics see in Lawson are also those which they attribute to his potentially noble bushmen characters. Paradise is lost, paralysis has set in. And, consistently, the source of man's failure is women. The supposed betrayals by women are cited as justification for the failures and inadequacies of men. These textual strategies, or phallic fictions as Lita Barrie calls them, parallel the sense of betrayal felt by men and blamed on the bush when it failed to answer man's needs and desires, which was registered in the last chapter.

What has happened to Henry Lawson, the poet-prophet who dreamed the people's dream? The terms of debate within the discourse on Lawson and the national identity have changed. One of the manifestations of this change can be registered with regard to conceptions about the role of the artist. The Democratic Nationalists construct the artist as a man of the people who authentically reflects their reality. Critics like Hancock, Ward, Palmer and Wright assumed in Lawson a strength which they saw depicted in the fictional struggles against an alien landscape. But for the New Critics, the artist is a genius, detached from society, who projects in his fiction the inner fears of man on to a metaphysical reality. Critics like Heseltine and Matthews and biographers like O'Grady and Clark assume that Lawson's bush is a psychological projection of his own idiosyncracies; his bushmen represent the sinister and destructive forces of modern man. But in both cases, 'Henry Lawson' serves to confirm their view of life. In their Lawson (or the author function they substitute for the man) the critics find their cultural and ideological beliefs confirmed. In every case the idea of 'the feminine' is enlisted as a threat which at the same time upholds the cause of masculine identity.

When Lawson's biographers trace his personal and creative decline, his unmanly weakness, they describe him not as representative, but unique. The difference can be registered in two essays by A. A. Phillips on Lawson. The first, written in 1948 and revised as the leading essay in the 1958 publication of *The Australian Tradition*, 'Henry Lawson as Craftsman', was the first critical essay to deal seriously with Lawson's talent as a writer. Phillips praises his 'developed technique'. In opposition to the prevalent critical view of Lawson as an 'artless', intuitive writer, Phillips asserts, 'his practice was too consistent, too closely allied to his artistic purpose, to be the fruit of happy accident or unguided intuition.'[89] But once Lawson's credentials as a craftsman are established, Phillips concludes that Lawson's highest value is that 'he could set down fairly what every bushman back of Bourke knew to be the truth'.[90]

By 1966, with the intervening ascendancy of the New Critics and the biographical reinterpretations of Lawson's personality, Phillips modified his views. In 'Lawson Revisited' he writes, 'Lawson was not merely objectively delineating the New South Wales plains: he was projecting on to them the landscape of his own soul.'[91] Far from representing the robust rebelliousness of the national spirit, Lawson's prose reflects the guilty sense of 'a defeated man's dark melancholy'.[92] The problem, once again, is interpreted as women. Lawson could not resolve women's rejection of him (has Phillips been reading Desmond O'Grady, perhaps?) and the resultant alienation from his wife and mother. Failing to master the alien other, he succumbs to feminine weakness. Phillips writes, 'Furphy was right when he said that Lawson was *too feminine* . . . [M]oreover . . . Lawson was *indifferent* to the *virilities* of human response—too *indifferent* to achieve a *balanced* view of life' (emphases mine).[93] Eighty years of critical commentaries on Lawson and the national character reproduce the same tautological contradictions which plagued Lawson's own life. Man fails to attain an identity; his defeat leaves him with feelings of guilt. But Woman is the *source* of the guilt. If she (or the signifying force of the feminine) can be mastered, she could also be the source of man's redemption, but only by standing in an inferior or idealized relation to him. Lawson in the hands of his biographers is an effect of masculine/feminine categories.

When Henry Lawson began to slip into decline, his writings also blamed women and his 'feminine' personality for his personal and artistic failures. As we have seen in this chapter, the feminine, as a signifier of lack within the discourse on the Australian tradition, parallels the significance of the concept for Lawson. In Lawson's writings, as long as the alien other is a physical force, located 'out there', in the greed of the city, the boss and the natives, women stand as symbols of hope for man's conquest, through which he will attain a noble identity. But when the alien other is perceived as a psychological force, 'inside' in the form of melancholy, despair, defeat or madness, women stand as figures of defeat who personify what man fears—that he will not attain authority, difference, self-presence, that is, identity. The bush as a garden full of hope which contains a snake to be crushed, becomes a barren, howling wilderness which contains the melancholy of a defeated man.

The critics of Lawson, depending on the social, economic and political requirements of the age and the speaker's relation to the dominant discourse of the day, have found in his writings evidence of manly strength and feminine weakness, national prosperity and supranational pessimism. The ideas take on an Australian specificity with regard to the national's colonial history. 'The Drover's Wife' can be seen as a symbol of freedom and progress, or constriction and defeat, depending on the requirements of the age and the critic's ideological ties to the 'national interest'.

The biographical reproduction of 'Henry Lawson' as a cultural object gives substance and weight to the assumption that *the man*, and not the discourse on the man, is the founding subject of the Australian tradition. But the man of the critical commentaries is a fiction. He is an impossible subject, constructed through the discourse and the interpretative formulations of the texts on Lawson. The discourse creates a myth of origin for national identity, located in Lawson, but capable of being moulded to suit changing needs. Critics posit an identity for Lawson and/or the national character, define its complexities and then construct imagined divisions within his assumed personality to mediate the strengths and weaknesses in Lawson and the national character. In the discourse Lawson's strengths represent Australia; his weaknesses are idiosyncratic.

Further, the commentaries foster a homogeneous tradition by reference to the idea of Lawson as an integrated personality, a national type. In addition, the discourse on Lawson and the national character establishes a bond between writer and audience which functions to stabilize and solidify the construction of a masculine identity (even if Lawson is a 'poor' example; even if the cultural categories masculine/feminine contributed to his own self-doubts and gradual disintegration). This bond of masculine resemblance locates woman within the same masculine economy, but as different from man, what he is not. Contradictions, states of ambivalence and plural possibilities which challenge discursive mastery and might pose a threat to the stability of this order are repressed. Lawson's stories as well as his personality are mastered (but in a variety of ways) as entities within the discourse on national identity.

In Lawson's lifetime, the writings of Barbara Baynton attempted to destabilize received systems of meaning. Her stories mime the bush tradition with irony. But they, like Louisa's Lawson's article and Murray-Smith's biography, have been veiled behind later constructions of the 1890s, Lawson and the national character. I will turn to Baynton's writings now, to register her dissidence as another site of radical resistance existing within, but muted by, the tradition.

CHAPTER 6

BARBARA BAYNTON: A DISSIDENT VOICE
FROM THE BUSH

A woman is a perpetual dissident as regards the social and political consensus
. . . woman is here to shake up, to disturb, to deflate masculine values, and not
to espouse them.

Julia Kristeva, *Polylogues*

When critics like A. A. Phillips speak of the Australian tradition in terms of its 'fervent celebration of a robust nationalism' represented by the fiction of Democratic Nationalism in the 1890s, they seldom think of the writings of women. Phillips, however, in his 1966 revised edition of *The Australian Tradition*, included a new chapter on Barbara Baynton, author of *Bush Studies* (1902).[1] The inclusion of Baynton in the revised edition is significant. It brings to the attention of readers and students of the Australian tradition a writer whose fierce but short-lived talent had been overlooked and all but lost. Phillips applies the label 'dissidence' to the character of Baynton's writing, along with that of Miles Franklin's *My Brilliant Career*, Norman Lindsay's *Redheap*, Arthur Adams' poem 'The Australian' and some of the short stories of Henry Lawson, like 'The Union Buries its Dead'. He writes that they exhibit an 'undercurrent of revolt against the barbaric fate of being an Australian'.[2] The issue is not woman's fate, but that of 'being an Australian'. Nonetheless, the manner in which this so-called dissidence is approached has relevance in the light of contemporary theoretical questions concerning the relationship between culture, writing and gender. Phillips' remark concerning Baynton's dissidence is relevant to both the production of 'woman's place' in the annals of Australian literature and to the processes of naming through critical exegesis.

All of the examples which Phillips cites thematically defy the mood of cheery optimism which the Democratic Nationalists assert as central to the Australian tradition. They treat with irony the code of egalitarian democracy built on the doctrine of mateship. Critics like Harry Heseltine have argued that the pessimism inherent in these writings, which emphasize the physical and psychic horrors of outback life, represent the other side of the coin which bears the imprint of the national character. Nowhere are the horrors of outback life more powerfully represented than in the short stories of Barbara

Baynton. Baynton's dissidence, however, can be registered on a number of levels. Phillips calls her a dissident writer because her short stories defy the tradition which he would assert. But feminists can claim her as a dissident in Kristeva's sense of the term. She writes of the bush and woman's place in a way that poses a challenge to received notions concerning both 'woman' and the national character. Her writings shake up, disturb and deflate masculine values. When read against the grain of established masculine critical standards, Baynton's fiction provides a superbly ironic critique of the Australian tradition and the impossible position of Woman as she has been constructed and repressed within it.

As this study has indicated, the Australian tradition takes male identity as its theme. The experience of actual women as historical figures is muted. The idea of the feminine, however, is embedded in metaphors of landscape and has been noted as an absent presence in the metonymic relations of man to the land and to mateship, the bush, freedom and egalitarian democracy. Woman within the tradition has been displaced as an object which man fears and desires. The principal form of displacement has been in terms of the landscape. The bush—variously represented as funereal, absorbing, pliant, passively resistant, actively destructive, barren, cruel, wretched, a wilderness, a wasteland—has been the alien and alienating other against which man has struggled to forge an identity. Female characters, like those in the short stories of Henry Lawson, embody man's fears of isolation, loneliness, despair and madness in his confrontation with the bush. They mirror his dilemma.

Female difference has been constructed in terms of oppositions. Woman is man's opposite, marked with an inferior status. Within this symbolic order there is no room to explore what woman, or beyond her the category of the feminine, might be as absolute difference beyond reference to the established system of representations. The categories of masculinity/femininity, embedded within the discourse on the Australian tradition, establish relational differences between the sexes. The woman is man's double, what he fears in himself. She is caught in his representations, as his Other. Thus, Woman becomes the source and origin of man's failure. His fears of inadequacy can be blamed on her imagined betrayal.

These dimensions of the literature, muted in the critical discourse, become central concerns in the short stories of Barbara Baynton. In her stories, women are depicted as the innocent victims of men in the bush. But they are also the victims of language—named by the masculine economy; appropriated to positions of inferiority within the discourses of religion, politics and mythology; and sacrificed through their dispersement to the dominant symbolic order. Thus, Baynton's writings can be seen as both an examination of woman's place in history and the symbolic order and at the same time as a refusal to accept that place. Although as a writer she must submit to the dominant discourse which makes her writing possible, she also presents through irony an unsettling challenge to masculine authority.

THE CONSTRUCTION OF BARBARA BAYNTON

Through the years critics have found it difficult to deal with both the character of Barbara Baynton and the vision of the bush which her stories project. The woman herself is an enigma. Her grandson, H. B. Gullett, in a memoir to Baynton which introduces the Angus and Robertson edition of *Bush Studies*, reports that 'She was a highly imaginative woman with no strict regard for truth. She told her children many conflicting stories of her early years and of her parents, and it rather seems as if the truth to her was what she chose to believe it ought to be at any given moment, and of course it would vary with her moods.'[3] One might expect that a woman who delighted in 'stories' rather than 'truth' would be hard to pin down. Her life as well as her stories of the bush have defied critical mastery.

Critics who have attempted to explain why her vision of the bush should contain depictions of 'the harshest, ugliest, cruellest aspects of primitive outback life'[4] generally surmise that Baynton, who was thrice married, must have suffered at the hands of her first husband, a bush selector, who left her for one of her cousins while her three children were quite young.[5] A. A. Phillips, John McLaren, H. M. Green, Sally Krimmer and Alan Lawson all mention 'revenge' as a possible motive of the writer behind Baynton's texts.[6] H. M. Green, for example, suspects that the author took 'grim and masochistic pleasure' in her depictions of 'unrelieved, uncalled-for misery' in the lives of women who suffered at the hands of cruel and vicious men on the hostile landscape of the bush.

The facts, however, are obscure. Critical interpretations of the alleged facts of Baynton's life have served to excuse the bush, and the Australian tradition of which Baynton is a part, for the excesses of her fiction. They uphold the tradition which her stories defy. Those stories have much in common, however, with the account of bush life which Louisa Lawson presents in her article, 'The Australian Bush-Woman', discussed in the last chapter, and the evidence from personal diaries and letters of bush women which Lucy Frost presents in her study of women in the bush, *No Place for a Nervous Lady*.[7]

All that is known of Baynton and her fiction could serve as a model for women's transgression of the Father's Law. Details of her birth, her age, her self-proclaimed illegitimacy, her father's occupation, her parents' names, her schooling, her Presbyterian upbringing, her life before her marriage to Dr

Thomas Baynton, and her retreat from the bush to Sydney and later to London, where she gained fame and high social standing, are clouded in mystery. Sally Krimmer's historical research, a summary of which is included in the Introduction to the Portable Australian Authors edition of *Barbara Baynton*, verifies some of the details. Krimmer sets right Baynton's 'true identity' in terms of official records of her legitimate birth and family history. Why Baynton chose to fabricate a story of a dubious past remains 'inexplicable'. If mystery surrounds the stories of Baynton's life it is also a characteristic mark of her fiction, although critics have failed to acknowledge this. They assert, to the contrary, 'a single-minded vision . . . a consistent style . . . a consistent vision' in her fiction.[8] The deconstructive reading which I will attempt in this chapter offers an alternative to that critical perspective.

WOMEN IN BAYNTON'S FICTION

Barbara Baynton's known literary production consists of six short stories which were first published in England in 1902 and revised for publication in the 1917 edition of *Bush Studies*, plus two additional stories and an unfinished novel, *Human Toil* which are included in Krimmer and Lawson (eds) *Barbara Baynton*, Portable Australian Author Series (1980). None received favourable critical acclaim at the time of their publication. Baynton herself appears to have been innocent about the vagaries of the publishing industry. Yet she possessed a rare talent which has only begun to attract the attention of a renewed contemporary audience.

Four of the six short stories which appeared in the original edition of *Bush Studies* contain women as their central characters. They are 'Billie Skywonkie', 'Squeaker's Mate', 'A Dreamer', and 'The Chosen Vessel'. In each story the woman appears as a vulnerable figure who is often nameless, and desired only in the crudest of sexual terms. Male characters are portrayed as brutal, vulgar, selfish and crude specimens of humanity who scratch for a living from the arid land on small selections. But Baynton's texts can also be read as stories which exhibit a wry detachment from the concerns of male identity and survival, although this perspective has received scant notice. Krimmer and Lawson, for example, have this to say about Baynton's stories:

> Here is found no noble sentiment but rather a savageness man has retained from his beginnings to enable him to cope with his brutal surroundings. But the land takes its toll, its 'revenge' as Henry Handel Richardson put it. Always the sun is greedy, sucking any nourishment from the barren land. When man likewise becomes a predatory being, it can be seen that the landscape has moulded him into its own image.[9]

This critique cites the landscape, recalling Richardson's evocation of the earth as vengeful mother, for the deficiencies of the men. It is seen to shape them in its image. But the short story 'Billy Skywonkie' which gives rise to this description does not depict the land in such terms. It is true that the bush is described as a hostile force. But the source of the problem is the 'greedy sun' which sucks the life from the land and results in the 'barren shelterless plains'.[10] Billy Skywonkie, the character whose name is used for the title of the story, is associated by his patronym with the sky, not the land. When the female, whom Billy transports across the plains to the selection where she is to be housekeeper, is introduced to his friend, the Konk, we are told that his monkeyish face 'blotted the landscape and dwarfed all perspective'. If one reads through the inversions of the text it is not the land but man's presence on the land which 'dwarfed all perspective'. He names it and the women who inhabit it in his grotesque image. In 'Billy Skywonkie' the men are given names, but the sole woman remains an anonymous sex object. Billy, who goes to meet her, the new housekeeper, at the train, expects 'a young "piece" from Sydney'. The would-be housekeeper, when confronted with the male arrogance associated with life in the bush, feels that 'she had lost her mental balance'. By the end of the story she is equated with the sheep which lies passively waiting for slaughter at the hands of the bushmen.

'The Chosen Vessel' is the story which has drawn most attention from the critics. They concur that it demonstrates Baynton's strength in depicting the value of the maternal instinct, the 'one quality which cannot be overwhelmed'.[11] The story is often compared with Lawson's 'The Drover's Wife'. H. M. Green writes that 'all her powers are focussed in this terrible little story'.[12] Other critics, including Phillips, Krimmer and Lawson, agree with Green's assessment. But the critics deal with this story, as with the others, within a narrow frame of thematic content. They describe what is said in terms of man's cruelty and women's vulnerability juxtaposed with the power of the maternal instinct. But if one reads *how* the story is constructed, one can detect the same deconstructive elements, present here as in her other stories, which unsettle attempts at interpretation. If one reads the story from a post-structuralist position, the woman is an empty signifier whose place is filled by the codes which name woman in the discourses of mythology, religion and politics in which woman is denied her difference outside of the patriarchal order.

An examination of 'The Chosen Vessel', an abridged version of which originally appeared in the *Bulletin* in 1896 under A. G. Stephen's chosen title, 'The Tramp', and its reception by the critics, will serve to illustrate the nature of the problem. Focusing on the place of woman as sign in the short story and critical commentaries, keeping in mind the question of woman's dissidence, I will trace the ambiguities of meaning within the original text and its more singular 'truth' as represented by the critical tradition. I begin with an abbreviated summary of narrative events for readers unfamiliar with the story. Then I discuss its reception by the critics, and, in particular, the essay by A. A. Phillips which introduces *Bush Studies*. The essay is significant because it has served as Baynton's preface, granting her entry into the Australian tradition for a generation of modern readers. It constructs her place and serves as a reference point for later critics and readers of her work. Finally, I return to the short story and attempt a deconstructive re-reading of the text.

'THE CHOSEN VESSEL'—AND THE CRITICS

Baynton's unabridged manuscript, revised slightly for publication in 1917, presents, in five parts, the story of a beseiged bush woman.[13] Part One introduces a woman and baby alone in the bush. When the story opens, the woman is tethering a calf to prevent its wandering with the cow during the night. She is vaguely restless, unhappy with her lot, the isolation of the bush, her responsibility for the farm and a small child and her unsatisfactory relationship with her husband. As she works, she reflects on her fear of the cow, whose protests she has been taught to curb with a stick, and her husband's deprecation of her fears of both cow and bush. In anger at her fear, he has called her . . . 'the noun was cur'. She wonders if the enemy who is her husband would run as does her enemy the cow if threatened by a stick, 'but she was not one to provoke skirmishes even with the cow'.

A swagman has been by earlier in the day looking for food, money and something more, by the look of his eyes as he gazed upon the mother with babe at her breast. In expectation of his return, the woman leaves some food and her mother's brooch, 'the only thing of value that she had', on the kitchen table. She then retires with her child to the barricaded house for the night. The sound of the returning swagman wakes her and she listens intently, careful not to wake the sleeping baby in her arms. In mounting terror, she watches his shadow circle the hut as he seeks a place of entry. When he is about to gain access through a fallen slab, the woman hears the sounds of horsehooves approaching and she runs from the hut, babe in arms, shrieking to the horseman for salvation. But she falls into the arms of the intruder as the horseman rides away, with curlews picking up her final cry of 'Murder' as they fly above his head.

Part Two details the discovery of the dead mother and her child by a boundary rider who initially misinterprets the scene as that of a lamb and ewe murdered by a dingo. 'By God!' and then, 'Jesus Christ!' he utters as he cuts away the infant's gown from the dead mother's grip.

Part Three recounts the story of the horseman, Peter Hennessey, who passed the woman and child without stopping to help them. A devout if superstitious Catholic, he had been riding that night to a nearby voting district to cast his ballot for a candidate of his own political persuasions and not for the squatter candidate supported by the priest. He contemplates his revolt, which 'had over-ridden superstition' as well as his mother's pleas for his salvation, when the mother and child appear to him, calling 'For Christ's sake!' Peter misinterprets the scene as a holy vision sent to redeem him in answer to his mother's prayers. He proceeds to cast his vote for the priest's squatter candidate and only learns the 'true' nature of his vision when he returns to the priest to confess of his revolt and redemption.

Part Four depicts the swagman and his dog at the waterhole. The dog faithfully runs to return the swaggie's hat from the water but will not allow the man to wash the blood of sheep from its mouth and throat—blood which makes the swagman tremble. The original story and the 1917 final revision ends with the comment, 'But the dog also was guilty.' (This sentence has been omitted from the Angus and Robertson editions of *Bush Studies*. Krimmer and Lawson restore it to their edition of *Barbara Baynton*.)

If one accepts the opening as a distinct element in the story, what emerges is a five-part structure which includes:

opening: mother, called 'cur' (or worse)—isolated, fearful but passively resigned to the bush;

action: her rape and murder by a nondescript swagman-as-everyman;

discovery: by the boundary rider who functions to link the different levels of meaning—natural (lamb and ewe), human (mother and child), and supernatural ('By God!' 'Jesus Christ!');

action: redeeming vision of the horseman which quells his revolt;

ending: guilty swagman and his loyal dog.

This was the only story by Barbara Baynton to appear in the *Bulletin* (December 1896). A. G. Stephens, editor of the Red Page, thought her work 'too outspoken' for an Australian audience, but praised it for its realism.[14] Six of her stories, including 'The Chosen Vessel', were first published in England under the title *Bush Studies* in 1902. Like 'The Chosen Vessel', all convey a hostile image of the bush as perceived by its victims—the old, the weak, the women. But the stories have been read in terms of the way in which they reflect or challenge the Australian tradition. Censorship of the stories to fit their assumed context began with first publication. Stephens edited the story for first publication in the *Bulletin*, cutting the entire third section concerning the Catholic voter/horseman. He retitled the story 'The Tramp', possibly even changing Baynton's 'universal' pronouns for the bushman as 'he' into 'the tramp'.[15] Baynton offered the title 'What the Curlews Cried', but it was rejected. Thus, from the outset, the religious theme of Part Three, which fuses the sexual with the symbolic, the bush mother with the Virgin Mother, the silenced with the spoken theme, is censored. In addition, Stephens' change of title had several immediate effects. It shifted reader interest away from the woman's murder (for that is 'what the curlews cried'), and on to the character of the murderer, called a 'tramp'—*not* bushman or swagman— by Stephens. It also allowed the reader to question the woman's character— perhaps she, too, is 'the tramp'?

When A. A. Phillips wrote of the story he commented that Stephens' judgements were 'sound' in these matters and suggested that even more could have been peeled away.[16] He cites the opening episode, in which the text evokes a harsh image of the husband (not to mention the wife), as unnecessary as well. We need only to know, he says, that the husband was absent. The extra details are examples of Baynton's 'subjective obsession' about man's cruelty forcing its way into the incidental details of the story. Phillips is one of the few critics to take an active interest in the works of Barbara Baynton. His major essay on her work, and on 'The Chosen Vessel' in particular, has been republished with slight revisions no fewer than seven times between 1961 and 1980.[17] Until 1980, Phillips' critique was the major and most accessible essay on Baynton available to readers. The essay provides a space for Baynton within the Australian tradition. But her place is established within the codes of meaning for femininity which we have traced in the earlier chapters. A re-reading of the essay will demonstrate how the woman, in this case Barbara Baynton, becomes an effect of the discourse.

Phillips, like Stephens before him, explicates and situates the text on another terrain. He makes it meaningful on *his* terms. This involves a chopping and changing, a literal cutting up of the text, in the name of 'objective' literary and critical standards. The story by his interpretation is not about the murder of a woman at all, but about the bush legend. Once the critic has pared away the superfluous details of the story and reduced it to the interaction between the mother and the tramp, he can interpret it in terms of the Australian tradition, the 'rock [upon which] the Australian pride is ultimately based'.[18] Within this frame, Baynton is a 'dissident' because her writings pose a threat to that tradition. The critic's task becomes one of restoring the reader's faith in the legend by distinguishing between tramps and true bushmen and then ridding the bush of its tramps, both literal and figurative.

An analysis of Phillips' essay on Baynton reveals myriad ways in which the discourse is blind to women as writers and as characters except as they reflect or challenge the bush ideal. The category 'woman' is empty and filled by shifting significations which mirror the place of woman in what might be called the Australian Imaginary (in the Lacanian sense of what we take to be real but is imagined with reference to patriarchal symbolic order). Phillips wrote the essay. But the various codes of meaning through which we come to know the Australian tradition, the bush ethos and woman's place preceded and made possible Phillips' discourse. He is a spokesman for the tradition. The tradition gives him the clues necessary to interpret and delimit Baynton's dissidence.[19] A certain blindness to women can be detected even in Phillips' explication of the story's theme. In that explication the woman herself does not exist; she is absent from the discourse.

Themes in Baynton's Work

When Phillips delineates what he sees as Baynton's major themes, he says that they convey 'the most intense effect . . . of the image of a lonely bush hut besieged by a terrifying figure who is also a terrified figure'. In 'The Chosen Vessel' it would be more accurate to say that it is not the hut, but the woman in the hut, who is besieged. And the terrifying figure is certainly not 'also the terrified figure'. Here Phillips repeats Stephens' manoeuvre of shifting emphasis from victim to attacker. He suggests that 'The Chosen Vessel' is a story about the hut and its attacker, not the woman.

The second theme Phillips mentions is the 'fierce power of the maternal instinct'. Still, there is no mention of the woman who possesses it. But later the text reads: 'The possessor of the maternal instinct is usually the victim of evil, which wreaks a terrible destruction'. The evil, we are assured, is 'essentially weak', while the maternal force 'has lasting strength'. So the woman, as a central character, motif or theme in Baynton's fiction has thus far been displaced as: (1) the bush hut, (2) the terrifying figure of her attacker, (3) the maternal force, (4) the possessor of the maternal force, (5) the victim of evil and (6) the survivor (child or dog) which endures as the maternal representative. Where is the woman? Absent. How is she portrayed? Idealised into the unproblematical motif of 'the maternal'. This treatment is hardly justified given both of the author's designated titles: 'What the Curlews Cried' (that is, 'Murder!'), and 'The Chosen Vessel', that is, the maternal mother/Virgin Mother ironically fused and thus destroyed.

Phillips' analysis aligns the maternal force in Baynton's stories with 'a bitter insistence on man's brutality to women'. He writes, 'One feels, perhaps without logical justification, that the two themes beat together in the pulse of

Barbara Baynton's intuitions'. In this sentence the reader can detect the workings of what might be called Phillips' imaginary in his juxtaposition of the logical with the intuitive. 'Perhaps without logical justification' for whom?

Critical Judgements

Phillips seems to be suggesting that *he* (the objective critic) has no logical justification for linking the two themes in her work. But as the sentence reads metonymically, he is also saying that perhaps *she* has none, that is, that there is no logical justification for linking the maternal instinct with man's brutality to woman. This introduces a confusion between critic and writer, logic and intuition, objective truths and subjective obsessions, male and female. A battle, which is both sexual and textual, surfaces in the text.

From this point on, the polarities between critic and writer, analysis and its object, vie for mastery. The substance of the argument has more to do with woman's place in patriarchal discourse than with the content of Baynton's fiction or the discerning views of the critic. In Phillips' critique there is a metonymic displacement of effect from the Australian tradition as a discursive formation onto the short story. In addition, the metaphor of the land as cruel mother finds its way into the commentary where both the land of Baynton's imagination and the writer (Baynton) of Phillips' imagination take on attributes of the cruel mother. The essay illustrates the power of discourse to reproduce the significations for woman-as-sign which take on the air of objective validity for writers and readers alike.

A strategy the critic employs in his analysis to deal with Baynton as a troublesome writer of dissident texts is alternately to praise and then to condemn her writing by use of his categories, which are also *our* categories for establishing differences between the masculine and feminine within the symbolic order of language. For example, Phillips concedes that Baynton is a powerful writer who conveys a sense of bush realism. In this she is 'one of the breed' of Australian (realist) writers. But, her 'nightmare visions' threaten to place her in the camp of melodramatic writers of 'popular genres of the period'. Her work is located on the border of nightmare visions and objective realism. Melodrama, as an inferior genre to the realist bush story, is still an appropriate genre for a woman writer. The assessment of Baynton as an inferior writer of sentimental and/or melodramatic tales is one reiterated by Adrian Mitchell in his treatment of the writer in *The Oxford History of Australian Literature*.[20]

What Phillips and a host of other critics who succeed him find it hard to deal with in Baynton's fiction is her compulsion to detail man's cruelty to woman ('perhaps without logical justification . . .'). For this she is labelled 'obsessional', 'subjective', in the country of the Freudian subconscious. That is, the author is seen as a possibly neurotic, avenging female, writing to assuage some emotional pain of her past. But if that (personal) theme is her weakness, which locates her among 'popular' writers, her strength, which locates her among Australian realists of the nineties, is her style. Her style is described as having a 'bread and butter directness' and a 'concrete detail' for 'life-as-it-is'. Phillips isolates the 'spare muscularity' of her prose, the power of her visualization, and lastly, the 'austere directness' of her 'pouncing feminine accuracy' as aspects of the fiction which mark her writings as 'masterly' works of 'thorough and effective craftsmanship'. One could apply these attributes ascribed to the prose to the character of the bush pioneer woman and the land which frames her existence: sparse, spare, muscular, austere. We have traversed this territory before.

Phillips is caught in the dilemma of trying to characterize a woman writer as an Australian writer of merit, without overt regard to her sex—in fact, with what often appears to be a deliberate suppression of the possible significance of her sex—and yet the analysis bristles with real and repressed gender-marked confusions. There appears to be a difficulty in viewing Baynton as a writer, and a good one, who is at the same time not male. The arguments proceed, leaving a trail of unspoken assumptions concerning the differences between good and bad writers, differences which sound suspiciously like naive critical assumptions concerning writers and woman writers. Consider the dichotomies invoked in the essay under the unspoken but culturally relevant categories of writers (that is, presumably male writers) and women writers:

Writers	*Women writers*
superior	inferior
objective	subjective
masterly	obsessional
logical	intuitive
dominance of reason	dominance of feeling
bush realism	melodrama/nightmare vision
Australian short story	popular genre

Where to locate 'Phillips' and 'Baynton' within these dichotomies is a repressed question in the essay. Although the critic might place himself on the left side of the polarities we often find him identifying with the attributes on the right. As the essay progresses, the critic continues to substitute *his* intuitions and feelings for an analysis of Baynton's logic and craft. He becomes his object's other.

In relation to point-of-view, for example Phillips writes: 'The reader is forced to sit behind her eyes and see with their pouncing feminine accuracy.' He then corrects himself, writing that, in fact, Baynton never writes from an 'uninventive' first-person narration. The reader follows her text through the vision of her characters. So, the critic denies what might be (but is not) a fault in the fiction by calling attention to it as if it were present in the stories. This tendency links Baynton's style to the attributes of an inferior, one might say 'female' fiction—the melodramatic, the subjective—making her guilty by association, and then shifting emphasis to praise her work for its superior, dramatic, symbolic and carefully controlled craftsmanship which marks her as 'one of the breed'.

Once Phillips has made a case for the power of Baynton's stories, he concludes with the following remarks:

> Yet, *despite evidence* of alert and considered workmanship, I doubt if she *deliberately* chose the method of viewing the action through the character's eyes. *It seems more likely* that it grew *naturally* from her strong sense of actuality, her *intuitive* assumption that the essence of a story's effect lay in the reader's sense of involvement in the event [emphases mine].

In the end, the carefully controlled craftsmanship of the stories becomes the happy result of accidental circumstances. Her power is reduced to the intuitive, the natural, while his intuitions take on the air of critical logic. It is interesting to compare this assessment of Baynton with that of Lawson discussed in the last chapter. In the Lawson essay, 'The Craftsmanship of Lawson', which is the leading essay of *The Australian Tradition*, Phillips for the first time defends Lawson's complex style and polished technique against those critics who chastised him for his artlessness.[21] The critical commentary on Baynton is all the more curious in this context.

Baynton's Bush

What kind of bush does Baynton evoke for Phillips? There appear to be at least two possible answers to this question: one logical and related to his conception of the Australian tradition, the other intuitive and tied to the male imaginary of woman's place. The logical answer is that Baynton is a dissident writer who helps us to define the Australian tradition by pointing out the harsh and violent elements in the bush, what should not be there—cruel men, 'tramps', less than ideal bushmen. This is her value and achievement as an 'outspoken' writer of the nineties.

The problem is that the brutal man *is* there, in the bush, and his presence threatens the legend. How can this be explained? Phillips has an answer, although he admits that he came upon it only through 'subtle' means of detection. He suggests that Baynton's male characters are not bushmen at all, but the 'peasant element' who are more clearly defined in her satiric stories. They include 'selectors of the dry country . . . the near descendants of the convicts . . . the Irish migrants'. Thus, there are two sorts of men in the bush, true bushmen and peasants. True bushmen, like peasants, confesses Phillips, 'lust after money and women', but peasants are violent in their pursuit. These categories bear no explicit relation to the actual stories and their descriptions. But they are directly related to Phillips' own discussion of bushmen as opposed to selectors in his 'Democratic Theme' essay in *The Australian Tradition*, the text which also includes the essay on Baynton. This is his logical solution to the problem of Baynton's dissidence. She is not describing bushmen at all but selectors, against whose negative image the true bushman forms an ideal identity. Thus, 'truth' has its origins in the woman's text, but her text must be displaced, and his text/sex/identity substituted, for it to emerge. The ambiguity of her text is silenced to produce the logical truth of the critic's making.

The second answer to 'What kind of bush does Baynton evoke for Phillips?' is subjective and intuitive. 'Something that emanates from the land itself.' But the land just might be 'Freudian country'—a terrain of metaphoric condensation and metonymic displacements. In Phillips' final section of the essay, textual and sexual processes, the origins of literature and life, the connections between critical discourse and erotic imaginings come together. The critic shifts attention away from the 'real' bush to its metaphysical counterpart. He writes of the 'something else' of the bush in Baynton's fiction:

> A sense of spiritual darkness emanating from the land itself, a feeling of primeval cruelty fed by the sunlight which glares instead of glowing, by the grey of the bush which some Europeanism in us insists should be green, and, more deeply, by the guilty sense that Man has forced his will upon the earth without the hallowing of ritual.

What do we make of this passage in terms of the schema of an Australian imaginary herein reproduced as a family romance of father sky, mother earth and the native son? The land as earth mother is the dark spiritual emanation of the eternal feminine; she is primevally cruel and unable to nourish properly. We remember precisely this evocation of the bush in the gold-rush trilogy of Henry Handel Richardson which was reiterated by Manning Clark in his five-volume history (see Chapter Four). It is the mythical bush as cruel mother. Father sun, or by metaphoric extension, English culture, civilization and the state, emits sunlight which glares instead of glowing. The union of the dark and glaring sun produces a bush that is grey, not green, parched not pastoral, native not English, and not 'near enough'. All of this is reader effect, and more specifically, the effect of the discourse on Australian identity through which Phillips reads Baynton. He finds and brings to life these imagined elements in her text which then echo back to the critic and through the critic to the readers as an emanation of Australia.

The trauma of a primal scene is encountered here: one that has never taken place, but is continually played out through imagined Oedipal relations and repressions. The last section of the passage cited above makes these inevitable erotic connections: 'a sense . . . a feeling . . . the guilty sense' (finally located in Man's guilt—in caps) for forcing his will on woman, displaced as mother earth. Again we are reminded of the close association of this construction with that of earlier commentators who represented the Australian native son as a guilty adolescent. The digger for Hancock, Palmer, Ward and Clark forced his passions upon mother earth and went away with feelings of guilt. Phillips, when sutured into Baynton's text, becomes another native son.

What has happened to the dual impulses, the logical and the intuitive, in Phillips' essay? It appears, if we consider the conflicting tendencies in the discourse, that the brutal masculine domination over women in Baynton's fiction, which Phillips identifies as that of the peasant/selector type by logical inference, turns out to be a feared impulse which has been censored and repressed, but powerfully present, in the author's intuitions about himself, and by implication the 'real' Australian bushman, all along.

Textual/Sexual Strategies

This turn of the essay takes us back to the earlier discussion about national identity and the place of woman in the Australian imaginary as well as the impossibility of locating woman's difference outside of the representations of the symbolic order, which creates the identity of both that which is excluded and that which remains. The construction of Baynton as a cruel, stern, vengeful mother/wife bears a striking resemblance to her bush as represented by Phillips. In the image of both the Australian character senses his own failure. In his desire for mastery over the bush and woman, he uses her incestuously, without the hallowing of ritual, that is, the respect due to woman within the Father's Law. The guilt is felt in relation to the Father.

It is a function of desire, according to Lacan, to mediate relations among men. But the regulation is in accordance with the Father's Law, in which woman is exchanged. The concept 'woman' is an empty signifier. In Phillips' text it has been filled in with an image of the woman writer as a vengeful wife and mother whose prose evokes a landscape of primeval cruelty. Ultimately both objects coalesce into one projection of the other—that which man fears in himself and creates through his fears, the place of woman as scapegoat. She is not only produced but her production is a prelude to the systems of signification which define woman as lack in relation to man.

In Phillip's commentary the Big Dichotomies break down as the critic finds in himself that which he projects on to the land as other. Baynton's text dissolves into his text and the twin themes of the power of the maternal instinct and man's cruelty to women are repeated in the textual/sexual process of exegesis. Her text becomes his reading of her text. If explication places the text in the position of a cruel mother, then the critic functions as the native son.

Phillips creates his object by means of cutting textual contents, selecting details, manipulating themes and repressing the woman. What he finds is a writer who defies the Australian tradition of ideal bushmen and must be put in her place. But what if her place is his place? Phillips' discourse masters the text as the child masters mother, culture masters nature. He projects an image of the cruel phallic mother onto Baynton, as the imagined palimpsest beneath her work, and then displaces this image on to mother earth, which is blamed for the deficiencies of her children (grey bush, brutal men, evoked as *effects* of maternal power, or lack thereof). But on a deeper level this 'Literary Gent' knows that he is implicated in his textuality/sexuality.

I want to make it clear that I am not blaming Phillips in what might be seen as an over-long analysis of his essay. He brings to the text an understanding of social and cultural experience already available through codes of meaning established within the cultural discourse. The essay effectively demonstrates the ways in which the dominant system of signification, which gives rise to the Australian tradition, operates to name and place women, the bush and native sons within it. Readers and critics alike participate in the generation of meaning. One's understanding of what it means to be an Australian is caught in the same web of signification which supports Phillips' essay on Baynton.

Phillips is not alone in his interpretation of Baynton's work. A majority of critics, including her more recent commentators, Sally Krimmer and Alan Lawson, assess the strength of her achievement in terms of her evocation of women, men, the bush and 'the maternal'. Krimmer and Lawson, although more generous to Baynton and less concerned with her place in the Australian tradition, write that in her stories the 'malevolent landscape' is linked to a 'man/woman confrontation where women, without choice, become acquiescent victims of men, largely without realizing it'.[22] They continue: 'the woman is shown as maternal, loving and peaceful while man is portrayed as brutally sexual.' They refer at length to 'The Chosen Vessel' as a representative piece which shows 'motherhood as a hope for humanity'. They conclude that 'the supreme example of woman's instinctive desire to protect her young is found in 'The Chosen Vessel', where motherhood is presented as being the one quality which cannot be overwhelmed.'[23]

A RE-READING OF 'THE CHOSEN VESSEL'

Is there not something ironic about the title 'The Chosen Vessel', which in this case refers to a woman who is brutally raped and murdered but at the same time refers to the appellation for Mary, the Mother of God? Is the concept of the 'maternal' which defines and thus denies the 'real' woman not problematic in its fusion of literal and figurative levels of textuality? Is the woman 'without choice' on both levels, or can we separate the two? Only when we do separate them can we register Baynton's irony in saying that what confers the power of the maternal as a concept, also demands the denial of the mother as a person. Baynton does not allow an unproblematic concept of 'the maternal' to dominate her text, the critics do. In fact, one could argue that it is the ironic handling of this concept which operates as a deconstructive force on the text. Krimmer and Lawson avoid these ambiguities in relation to both the theme and form of her work. They do, however, represent the woman in 'The Chosen Vessel' as one possessed and dominated by a series of power relationships within the culture. Their approach here differs in a significant way from that of Phillips. Their introduction concludes, however, with a few brief comments on Baynton's style reminiscent of the earlier work. They characterize her fiction as having a 'terrible logic', a 'singlemindedness', which renders her theme through a 'consistent style . . . a consistent vision . . . [and] a careful ordering'.[24]

Perhaps we need to look again at the text. Beginning with the ironic title and continuing through the development of what is taken to be the realistic theme there are several contradictory messages. One relates to the significance of the maternal function; another is the question of the woman's innocence or guilt. In 'The Chosen Vessel' there is a conflation of the mother with the maternal. The literal and the figurative meanings exist together. They cannot be separated. The 'maternal' is that which saves a child but kills a mother. But the mother is, inescapably, the maternal. The woman is an empty signifier which as living mother/symbolic Mother stands for both sacrifice *and* redemption. It is not filled by woman, who can be absent in an absolute sense, but by religion, mythology and politics in the discourses of the symbolic order.

On the question of the woman's fate, Krimmer and Lawson and a host of other commentators maintain that the woman is innocent and has no choice. But the text reads ambiguously. Read thematically, with reference to metonymic associations conveyed through the narrative, one could conclude that the woman is implicated in the guilt which results from her murder. The problem with this reading is that there is no direct thematic evidence, aside from the final and disputed sentence, to support this conclusion. The woman does nothing 'wrong' . She is apparently guilty of no crime. She does not 'deserve' her fate. And yet, she is murdered while the swagman goes free. These events set up a problem in the text which critical interpretations attempt to resolve.

How is her guilt established textually? One recalls that the woman has no name except that which her husband has given her—'the noun was cur'—in relation to her fear of the cow. The nature of this naming relates to other networks of meaning in the text which work in at least two contrary directions. One linking chain of signifiers establishes a relation between the woman and the dog. As the attacker approaches the house, the woman hears a 'thud of something striking the dog's ribs, and the long flying strides of the animal as it howled and ran'. Violence to the dog (heard) precedes violence to the house (heard and felt, as if on the body of a woman): 'She heard his jerked breathing as it kept time with the cuts of the knife, and the brush of his clothes as he rubbed the wall in his movements, for she was so still and quiet, that she did not even tremble.' This violence to the house precedes the woman's own struggle with the attacker and describes by metonymic substitution her violent rape and murder, which is neither seen nor heard but represented by the cry 'Murder!' which is picked up and carried across the plains by the shrieks of the curlews which fly with the horseman. These connections echo back to the 'long flying strides of the animal [dog, now woman] as it howled and ran'. The final evocation of the dog occurs at the end of the story, which depicts the dog's unswerving loyalty to the man who has been its and the woman's attacker.

The final sentence, which as we have seen appeared in the first and in 1917 revised edition of the story, reads, 'But the dog also was guilty.' Having registered the various links between dog and woman from the opening to the conclusion, the reader is forced to rethink the message of the text. Why divert attention, in the final sentence, from murderer to victim, from man to dog? In practice the dog is guilty of killing sheep (it has blood on its mouth and throat which makes the man tremble); but one normally assumes that the action arises out of instinct, to which no blame is attached. Perhaps it might be said that on a moral level the dog is guilty by association with the man to whom it is loyal; but loyalty is usually taken to be a virtue, not a fault. The woman exhibits both these characteristics: the 'instinct' of a mother to protect her child and the 'loyalty' to a man who abuses her. In this she is like the dog; but unlike the dog, she is a human agent, capable of making decisions for herself and thus culpable in the creation of her situation. In other words, if one accepts moral arguments concerning the agency of the human will for which there is some textual evidence, she had choice. She could have left the house and her vulnerable situation in the isolated bush and returned to her former home in the town. Her passive acceptance of the situation makes her an accomplice in her fate.

On the other hand, if one traces the links set up between the woman and the cow—the fear of which earned her the appellation 'cur' (or worse), one comes to quite a different set of conclusions. The cow, in its relation to the calf (as the ewe in relation to the lamb, later) figuratively represents the maternal instinct. The cow bellows whenever the woman tries to tether its calf and she fears that it might turn on her. She 'was afraid of the cow [that is, the maternal] but she did not want the cow to know it'. This suggests that she fears something in herself, that which is called the maternal and the demands of its authority over her existence. The woman does not impose demands. She is content to let the animals run free. Her husband insists on their control. His authority is represented (no doubt ironically) by the slight stick which he has given her to brandish at the cow and thus subdue the 'enemy'. Why must she do this if not to protect his property? Thus, the imposition of rules from which there is no effective escape and the repressed impulse toward revolt are two contradictory directions in the text which are opened up in the first paragraph and yoked together throughout the tale. Although never made explicit in the text, by metonymic links and metaphoric referents, the woman paradoxically *is* what she fears. She embodies 'the maternal' in the symbolic order. She belongs to the same economy which brings about her murder.

The Father's law limits the otherwise unlimited relationships between cow and calf, mother and child. It severs a 'natural' relationship, making the mother the enemy of the maternal even as it transforms her into its agent. The first sentence reads: 'She laid the stick and her baby on the grass.' The stick symbolizes the Father's Law; her baby symbolizes her entrance into that law as the maternal, as defined by the symbolic order. This opening sets up a series of relationships between the actors and the acted upon, the dominant and the dependent, those who have the power to name and to act, and those to whom such power is denied. As the story progresses this dimension is conveyed through a conjunction of the so-called literal and figurative signs for the mother and the Maternal. It is never possible to separate the literal from the figurative meanings. In Baynton's fiction it is most difficult for the reader even to imagine a one-to-one equivalence between the word and what it represents. Her attention is finely tuned to questions of female identity. To paraphrase Lacan, the images and the symbols of the woman cannot be separated from the images and symbols in the woman. She is constituted by the patronym which binds her existence to the name-of-the-Father.

The patronym by which the woman as chosen vessel is constituted and possessed extends well beyond the actual domain of the husband. A series of influences 'act' upon the woman. They effectively deny her herself, that is, her difference outside of a relation to Man in the symbolic order she inhabits with him. These influences subdue her and locate her in a relational place. Firstly, there is the 'natural' order of calves and cows, lambs and ewes, dogs and masters; then, by order of appearance, there is the husband whose verbal abuse establishes the law and the woman's inferior relation to it. 'Needn't flatter yourself . . . nobody'ud want ter run away with you', he tells her ironically. Then there is the swagman who steals 'the only thing she had of value', referring specifically to her mother's brooch, prefiguring the loss of her sexuality and ultimately her life, that is, her legacy from her mother. Then, the horseman acts upon the woman by confusing her actual presence with an imagined vision of the Madonna and Child. Lastly, the priest acts upon the woman. His religious doctrines translate the mother and child into an image which offers redemption and salvation for Man, but only by a displacement of woman into a religious mythology of the sacred Mother. She is sacred because she nurtures and protects the Child and guarantees the succession of authority from father to son, God to Christ, priest to Peter. This final evocation of the woman as Madonna represents the ultimate denial of woman outside the patriarchal order. In the story this final evocation also marks a shift in what is signified by the appellation 'the chosen vessel'. Peter stands before the painting in the priest's study and prays, 'My Lord and my God, and hast Thou chosen me?' Ultimately, after the death of the woman, he becomes the Chosen Vessel, thus marking for man the full and ultimate possession of the woman in all her disguises within the symbolic order.

It is important to note that the text links the sacred to the profane through the effect of the male gaze, that is, on the level of the imaginary. When the swagman first approaches the woman to ask for tucker, we are told, 'She feared more from the look in his eyes, and the gleam of his teeth, as he watched her newly awakened baby beat its impatient fists upon her covered breasts, than from the knife that was sheathed in the belt at his waist.' The man first possesses the woman with his gaze. The specular appropriation of the woman-as-mother by the swagman, who captures her as an object of desire, contains the image of both Virgin and whore. It links male incestuous desires to the castrating image of the mother as corrupted, that is, tainted by her sexual relation to the father. In the imaginary, with its links to the Oedipal triangle, endemic to Western culture, the mother is not only guilty, but the source of the crime. She is to blame for having been desired. She becomes the cause of his crimes against her. The sublimation of mother as Madonna and Virgin, freed from sexual taint, acts as a powerful defence against that which has been repressed. In 'The Chosen Vessel', the priest and Peter represent these dynamics of repression, and in each case the operations are effected through the gaze. Peter imagines a vision of the Madonna and Child as he rides out his attempted revolt against paternal authority. He confesses his assumed crime (revolt against the priest) under a painting of the Mother and Child which beams down on him in the priest's study. 'Her eyes seemed to beam with the forgiveness of an earthly mother for her erring but beloved child.' Thus, the 'woman', read at once as mother/Madonna, is not only the source of the crime(s), actual or imagined, but also the agent, spiritual and physical, for forgiveness. Peter lives on as the manifestation of the paternal order.

The religious connections which link the multiple levels of the story in relation to the mother/Madonna, given the 'reality' to which they refer, become heretical. Each prayer spoken in the text becomes a profanation. And Peter, the horseman who does not stop to help the screaming woman, is the only character to have a name, a signature within the text. What is his importance? Like the biblical Peter, he, too, sins in a denial which saves himself. We recall that he is on his way to cast his ballot for a candidate the priest does not support. His revolt against the priest's authority is played out under the 'glorified sky of earliest spring',. that is, according to biblical referents textually invoked, Easter. The dialogue he imagines as he rides through the night invokes the presence of Mary as the mediatrix between father and son. He recalls his mother's praying 'Mary, Mother of Christ, save my son', at the same time as he hears the woman 'calling loudly in despairing accents, "For Christ's sake! Christ's sake! Christ's sake!"' He interprets the image of the real woman as a vision conjured up by a pre-existent and preordained vision of woman which literally blinds him to the real. He sees her not; she is no-thing to him and yet she is the source of his 'blessed vision'. He returns to relate his redeeming vision to the priest as the curlews pick up the mother's cry of 'Murder!' We are reminded of Peter the Apostle's denial of Christ before the cock crowed thrice. Both Peters are forgiven, and both Christ and the child retain their authority. But a woman has been violently murdered. She is 'murdered' not only by the swagman, but by the various levels of signification which deny her existence—the 'natural' world of ewes and lambs, the domestic world of male dominance and female submission, the religious world of the Madonna and Child. The evocation of 'the maternal' also causes the death of woman by negating any sense of her difference from man's law. Peter is forgiven, but the woman is dead. Nevertheless, or by the same stroke, 'order' is restored. Yet the woman, like the Virgin Mary, bears the hallowed title 'The Chosen Vessel'. We recall that Mary was a 'vessel' because she received the spiritual semen of the Holy Spirit (i.e., Jesus). The woman in Baynton's story becomes the 'vessel' of the swagman's semen. His possession effects her death; she becomes Everywoman.

The conflation of referents for the woman, which deny as they seem to uphold the 'fierce power of the maternal', exist together at every point of text. But they work most explicitly with reference to Part Three—that which both A. G. Stephens and A. A. Phillips deemed unnecessary to the unity of plot, character and action. In Part Three a doubling takes place. The main action is repeated in a way that transforms murder into redemption, revolt into acquiescence, the absence of woman into the insistence of the maternal power, the transference of the literal into the figurative, the imaginary into the symbolic. If one reads through the contradictions, woman is not guilty at all—she is wholly absent. She takes no part in the actions of the story except to represent male desire as either Virgin or whore. Her 'lack', disguised as maternal power, enables 'him' (husband, son, horseman, priest) to attain or maintain an identity. She has been named, captured, controlled, appropriated, violated, raped and murdered, *and then* reverenced through the signifying practices of the text. And these contradictory practices through which the 'woman' is dispersed in the text are possible by her very absence from the symbolic order except by reference to her phallic repossession by Man. Baynton's text, in its deliberate inversion, calls attention to these facts while it calls into question the idealization of the bushman as the embodiment of the Australian personality.

The story, as our 'chosen vessel', comes to contain these contradictions. In its subversive textuality, it functions to deconstruct the 'place' of women in the (male) imaginary. The writer mimes the role imposed upon women by pointing to it from the stance of a dissident, speaking to a tradition from its dangerous margins. But critics like Phillips, Krimmer and Lawson, by reducing the text to determinate meanings and singular visions, reiterate what the text deconstructs. The critics therefore reify a foreknown law—whether it be Phillips' bush ideal, the bedrock principle on which the Australian legend has been built, or Krimmer and Lawson's ideal of motherhood as the hope for humanity. One critique works through repression, the other through sublimation—both deny differences. They censor and repress the very aspects which Baynton's text calls to our attention. A deconstructive reading also establishes a critical position. But it challenges interpretations which would posit 'a truth'. It insists that texts disseminate meaning which can never be reduced or determined, given the rich referentiality of language. The text calls attention to the complex constitution of woman in patriarchy through the discursive practices of language which name her as other in relation to man. By analysing the text as a *question*, by asking *how* it means by way of its constitution of the place of woman through its discursive practices, we can also begin to represent what has been unrepresentable all along. That is, woman not as other (in relation) but as otherness itself in her radical resistance to all her specular representations to which the text calls our attention: the non-sense of the unspoken, the unrepresented, the absence whose place is filled by the phallic mother who can be at once our damned whore and God's police woman, our good and bad bush Mum.

Through this examination of Baynton's text as it attempts to deconstruct the place of woman we can register her dissidence, not only as interpreted by A. A. Phillips as that which denies the legend, but also, and more fundamentally, as imagined by Julia Kristeva in her insistence that woman is the perpetual dissident. Kristeva writes:

A woman is a perpetual dissident as regards the social and political consensus; she is an exile from power and thus always singular, divided, devilish, a witch . . . Woman is here to shake up, to disturb, to deflate masculine values, and not to espouse them. Her role is to maintain differences by pointing to them, by giving them life, by putting them into play against one another.[25]

Critics may mute Baynton's radical difference by placing her within the Australian tradition as an intensely subjective writer of nightmare visions, but her texts can be read otherwise. The deconstructive irony which can be detected in all of Baynton's fiction, but particularly in 'The Chosen Vessel', mark her as a dissident in her radical resistance to the social and political consensus regarding woman's place within the Australian tradition. 'The Chosen Vessel', as represented here in its multiplicity of referential and rhetorical meanings, may help to restore to the vessel (which is woman in the Australian tradition) a richness and diversity which have been lost through repeated critical attempts at phallic mastery.

If Henry Lawson's Drover's Wife represents the dream of the perfect mother, powerful yet capable of being subdued and mastered without a struggle, Barbara Baynton's Chosen Vessel dispels the fantasy. The Drover's

Wife belongs to Lawson and the critical tradition, which mark her sacrifice with a halo of glory which was of a high order. But the Chosen Vessel ultimately belongs to no one. Within the Father's Law she has been created and destroyed. But Baynton's story traces the outlines of a radical resistance within the discourse. It represents, if one will excuse the excessive intertextual rhetoric, the barbaric fate of being named woman within the Australian tradition.

CHAPTER 7

CONCLUSION

> We have been destined to reproduce that sameness in which, for centuries, we have been other. . . . If we continue to speak this sameness, if we speak to each other as men have spoken for centuries, as they taught us to speak, we will fail each other. Again . . .
>
> Luce Irigaray, 'When our Lips Speak Together'

I taped the above statement to the wall above my computer when I began this book. Whenever I have been seduced into the operations of discourse, and constrained, by the very demands of writing, to structure and order a logically consistent, unified, 'masterly' argument, whenever I have been tempted to reinterpret rather than deconstruct the data, to set in place new 'truths' rather than to decentre the old ones, I have turned to Irigaray's caution and thought again. In this study I have been concerned with the myths of Australian culture as they have been encoded into history, literature, film, critical commentary and everyday life. I have attempted to show how those myths create a reality they appear to describe. And I have gestured towards a recognition of difference, of multiplicity, of plurality within meaning and subjectivity which the master discourses have disguised. I hope that, occasionally, I have managed to speak 'differently' in offering a critique of cultural representations and patriarchial presumptions. I hope that (yes, mother, your question is with me still) 'ordinary' readers will have taken some pleasure from the text. (I would associate the 'ordinary' reader with anyone interested in questions of meaning, of national identity and of gender representation, whether or not attracted to the discourses of post-modernism. This might not be quite what mother had in mind; nonetheless her advice has had its effect.)

The audience I have imagined on the other side of the computer monitor has been in the main a feminist one. I imagined us speaking to each other. But as I finish the text I recognize that *a* feminist audience does not exist. My 'ideal' audience (that is, the one I would choose if I could, given the concerns and implications of the text) may well be a plural audience—of women and men, from Australian and non-Australian backgrounds, ranging across a wide band of political perspectives and ideological positions, who recognize the problems of marginalization within the culture. It is we who need to speak together, to evolve a pluralist discourse from multiple positions of difference.

The study has been made possible by events taking place beyond its borders, by what is sometimes described as the post-modern dilemma. The phrase refers to a world-wide crisis of authority signalled by the demise of the power of the West. An epistemological crisis brews as well. No longer are we assured that scientific rationality and human will are the keys to understanding and, thus, controlling knowledge of the world. While the scientific community ponders the future of a new science in the light of Heisenberg's principle of indeterminacy, post-modern critics ponder the future of culture beyond representation. The post-modern feminist critique of patriarchy, which includes a critique of science, puts the issue of sexual difference high on the agenda of the post-modern debate. But we do not yet have a quorum. A majority of male critiques from a post-modern perspective ignore, reject, neglect or repress feminist critiques of culture and language. And most scientific critiques ignore, reject, neglect or repress the work of their fellow post-modern critics.[1] Every discourse has its margins, defined and maintained with reference to its Other, even when, as Craig Owens has written, 'the reassuring stability of the mastering subject is breaking down'.[2]

In Australia, cultural unity is said to emerge in the decade of the 1890s—a decade preceding Federation when Australia became an independent nation within the Commonwealth. Paradoxically, the Bicentenary celebrates the birthday of what is historically (nearly) the youngest Western democracy in (perhaps) the oldest prehistoric human-inhabited continent; one of the last outposts of British colonialism in the South Pacific. In addition, the country at the present time boasts of being the most multicultural nation in the world, with a higher percentage population of non-native-born residents from a greater number of foreign countries than any other Western nation. Yet it may also be the most homogeneous culture in the world. Clearly, it is time for dissident voices from all quarters to speak up, to be heard, and to listen to each other.

My theme is difference, sexual difference, and the history of its representation as the country has attempted to find a national identity. Language assumes that national identity is masculine. 'The feminine' is used in discourse as a token for all sorts of difference and positions of marginality, as I alluded to briefly in terms of representation of the Aborigines, Chinese and migrant populations in Australian history in Chapter Four. At the same time the idea of a natural or essential woman suppresses all sorts of differences between women by class, race, age, sexual preference and the like. Political discourse performs a similar operation on feminism and feminist critique when it utilizes the term 'feminism' to suggest a unified movement which disguises the plurality of perspectives within feminism (liberal, socialist, separatist, Marxist, psychoanalytic, matriarchal, semiotic, and so on). Women are trapped within the webs of discourse, unable to speak what we might be or to locate a place for woman's absolute difference beyond the constraining sentence of patriarchy. If we are to go beyond the white male mastery of the past, we also need to go beyond the boundaries of inclusion and exclusion which we use and are used by others to divide our positions, one from another.

SPECULATIONS

As I proceded through the study I could not suppress a number of questions the work brought to mind—questions which might be thought improper, or out of place in an academic study (another category of exclusion). I decided to save them for the Conclusion, where writers are allowed to break the rules. For the most part the questions have concerned my speculations on the effects of linguistic operations on everyday life, both past and present. I could not help thinking of the limitations which discourse must have placed on people's lives—of opportunities foreclosed by self-doubt, or guilt or defensiveness—and the subsequent loss of potential for various people and for the nation. I know 'what if's' are dangerous and impossible constructions. But what if Henry Lawson, with his abundant creative talent and complex sensitive temperament had not been labelled 'feminine' and taken the meaning onto himself? Surely the cursed suggestion 'that [he] should have been a girl' made a difference to his life, and that of his suffering family. In another, less misogynistic place, what might have become of him and his writing between 1903 and 1922; would we now have the Joe Wilson novel that never was completed? How would the outlines of the legend that is Lawson, and perhaps the nation's tolerance for alcohol and absent fathers, have been affected?

What could have become of Louisa Lawson's talent for politics and temperament for action had she not been excluded by law, custom and male authority from the public world of the bush? How was her professional life in Sydney aided and also limited by past oppressions? To what degree was her insistence on an all-female printing shop at *The Dawn*, which defied union dictates and broke new ground for female employment, a response to and also a rebuke of male authority? In another place, how might her life and our history have changed had she not been labelled 'masculine' and loathed for her strength?

What of Lindy Chamberlain? If her baby had disappeared while on holiday in another country would her testimony have been received differently? If she had not been a member of a minority religious group would the police and public have been able to fasten such fantastic fabrications about her demonic personality upon her? If the culture's constructions of femininity inscribed by bush representations of woman as a cruel, avenging mother had been otherwise, could she have avoided being branded as guilty before going to trial and perhaps have received a more sympathetic hearing by the courts, press and public?

What stories might we tell of Daisy Bates and Caroline Chisholm and a host of other pioneering women if they were not 'God's police'? What of convict women if not 'damned whores'? What of the bush if not 'harsh'; of national identity if not lost to the land?

THE PRESENCE OF THE PAST: NEW FICTIONS

These questions were not foreclosed by history. The doubts circulate along with the certainties. Occasionally, a commentary appears which notifies us of the complex and contradictory ways in which Australian myths confound the experience of cultural life. A new novel by Howard Jacobson makes this attempt. Jacobson, a Manchester-born Jew who arrived in Sydney to lecture in the 1960s and now alternates residence between England and Australia, reports that he 'wanted to write an acute and true book about what Australians are like'.[3] *Redback* is the product of this desire. Jacobson twists the myths with the stylus of satire. The book has activated some raw nerves on the psyche of Australia. Kristin Williamson, in a *National Times on Sunday* feature article entitled 'Setting a Redback on our Psyche', agrees that Jacobson's desire was achieved for her. She quotes with approval what he writes about women, mateship and the Australian character. His views and her gender-specific critical response have relevance for this study. We are all inscribed by the myths of culture. But men and women, insiders and outsiders read the meanings differently. On sexual relationships within the culture Jacobson writes: 'I came to realise that the Australian male was everywhere in hiding from the Australian woman rampant, in awe of her assurance, in fear of her quick tongue and vast vocabulary, in mortal terror of her rampaging wit.' *Redback* is the title of his text. It is also the name of an variety of Australian spider known for its fatal bite. In addition, it reminds the writer of a violent argument he once had with his Australian girlfriend which ended when she bit him on the nose. In the novel, the bite occurs in a more private but no less sensitive part of the body. Jacobson plays with the plurality of meanings. But in the quoted passage, the spider/bite/woman is evoked through her signifiers 'rampant' and 'rampaging'. Here is woman the heraldic beast, standing on hind legs, ready to act furiously. The indigenous spider is fused with the Scottish lion. Is she related to Phillips' Baynton, who writes with 'pouncing feminine accuracy'? The codes of meaning circulate. They can be read in a variety of ways.

Jacobson turns to mateship. He explains that

mateship has a misleading, robust ring to it, evoking booze and brawls and broads. Whereas, what actually happens whenever two or more Australian men are congregated is more sentimental and lachrymose. . . . [which] is not so much to do with the profound melancholy of the Australian outback as with alcohol.

In her review Williamson cautions that 'Australians are likely to be defensive.'

The defensive character of Australians is an attribute which I have registered on a variety of occasions in my teaching. The first instance I remember occurred while introducing students to psychoanalytic critical perspectives through a reading of Robert Frost's poem 'The Mending Wall'. The poem begins with the line 'Something there is that doesn't love a wall.' It offers several levels of textual meaning to the idea of a wall—beginning with the stone boundary which separates the narrator/farmer's apple orchard from his neighbour's pines and extending to other walls and boundaries which separate id from superego, emotion from reason, nature from culture, and, finally, infants from mothers—the first boundary which projects the child into the symbolic order. Students listen politely but they do not like the poem. One of them asks 'What does he *mean* "something there is that doesn't love a wall"'? In Australia we like walls. We need them. They are necessary.' I think of all the corrugated-iron fencing that separates one suburban household from another. I ask 'Why do you need those fences? What purpose do they serve?'

'To protect us from dingoes', comes a quick reply.

'In Adelaide?'

But the students are sure that walls are necessary. They like neither the poem nor the psychoanalytic approach. The two judgements may be related.

Another instance of defensiveness occurred during a term when I taught a course on Australian literature to a mixed group of Australian and American exchange students. In order to utilize the resources of the whole group and to begin to register the specificity of an Australian cultural heritage I asked the students to draw up two separate lists of Australian and American heroes. I suggested they think of explorers and pioneers, sportsmen, politicians, writers (and women). Neither Australian nor American students had any trouble filling in the American side of the list. Australian categories came more slowly. Burke and Wills went up next to Daniel Boone; the Man from Snowy River next to Paul Bunyan; Whitlam next to Kennedy; Don Bradman next to Willy Mays; Lawson next to Twain; the Drover's Wife next to Wonder Woman (with some laughter). Then, the class went cold. Defensiveness set in. Australian students not only had difficulty locating their heroes, they apologized for them as well. 'Well, ours aren't as good as yours, but . . .' The irrepressible Americans ignored the breach. They continued to laud their heroes until I had to stop the discussion, sending all the students to the library to research Australian culture. Through the week I consulted with the students, cautioning Americans to curb their exuberance and Australians to moderate their unnecessarily defensive posturing. Things improved. But it was hard work.

Defensiveness is a dominant theme in a new book of short stories, *Night Animals*, by Bruce Pascoe.[4] Pascoe is an Australian writer, likened to Henry Lawson. A recent review commented that Pascoe tells 'something of Lawson's feeling for the corrosive loneliness of bush life and for the ways in which the emptiness of the outback magnifies character traits to dangerous proportions'. He, also, is 'interested in certain essences of the Australian character'. Graham Burns, in a critique similar to that Heseltine applied to Lawson, writes that the stories 'deal with the possibilities of defeat caused by silent psychic forces beyond their control'. But Pascoe shifts his focus from gloom to the theme of *happiness* in one story, 'happiness [which] may attack with the apparent arbitrariness of a primal event'. As the narrator explains, 'You never expect it; it's like being eaten by a shark.' This is an Australian variety of happiness, a battler's happiness—one which evokes the reader's laughter in recognition of its absurd impossibility.

THE BUSH AND WOMEN: SOME ENDURING FICTIONS

Australian attitudes to the bush and to women continue to be shaped by the narratives of national identity, often irrationally and with negative consequences. I often hear stories which convince me that this is so. A colleague who teaches Environmental Studies at Adelaide University reminds me that throughout settlement history Australian pastoralists have attempted to deny desert conditions and to denigrate the drought characteristics of outback regions. Farmers call upon overseas experts to explain why droughts occur. Unsatisfied with the advice that droughts are an expected consequence of arid land farming, farmers sometimes express indignant surprise, as if the drought were a punishment for wrongdoing and could be avoided.

Conversely, when coastal city dwellers move to Alice Springs, they frequently arrive with hostile attitudes to the outback. They take the bush of Lawson's stories with them. Friends at the Conservation Commission in Alice Springs report that it takes a good six months for some newcomers to relinquish their initial prejudices and fears about the 'dead'/'red' centre. Most white Australians have great difficulty accommodating themselves to the unique and sustaining qualities of the outback. Bush bashing, apathy about ecological concerns, lack of interest in or appreciation for native flora and media denigration of 'the greenies' all flow from the assumption that the bush is a hostile environment. Only with the recent rise of the tourist industry has this attitude begun to change.

The construction of the bush as cruel mother, compounded by the stereotype of women as God's police, continues to affect the culture's consciousness of women. I think it relates to another incident which occurred while I was researching this book. I remember accidentally meeting a friend in the Adelaide Central Market a few years ago. She was visibly upset. We went for coffee. My friend had been a teacher and was at the time of our meeting a third-year law student as well as a student of mine in the Graduate Diploma in Women's Studies. She had been balloted for jury service on a rape trial and had just completed sitting for the fourth day. The jury was due to retire the next day to consider their verdict. I remember the drawn lines of concern on her face as she told me 'If this woman's story is not accepted, then none of us are safe.' Although possibly risking charges of contempt of court, my friend told me of the incredible events which were taking place in the jury room, events which she has since written about in the *Legal Service Bulletin*. Two aspects disturbed her in particular. One was that because she indicated that she believed the woman's story that the accused had broken into her flat by a bathroom window and had raped her against her will, my friend was labelled by the man who became jury foreman as untrustworthy. 'I didn't think we'd have to debate the merits of the case with an irrational feminist,' he declared. This led to a majority of jury members, and especially the six other women, to isolate her opinions from their deliberations.

The second aspect of real concern was that the jury members resorted to fantasies which bore no relation to the evidence presented in the case. They surmised that the victim (a separated woman in her forties who lived alone with her young daughter) and the accused (a youth who gave no indication that he knew the woman prior to the event) were having an affair. They suggested that the woman had brought the charges against the young man out of a motive of revenge possibly resulting from blackmail or the guilt of an erring wife or a lover's tiff. They believed the unsworn statement of the accused that the woman had consented to intercourse, having awakened at 3 a.m. to find him naked next to her bed and holding her hand. She then must have constructed the evidence of a break-in through her bathroom window. All of this was fabrication resulting from pre-existent opinions about woman's sexuality and temperament which bore no relation to the evidence of the case. When discussing the consequences of finding the accused guilty, one of the jury members had commented that the woman had lost nothing of value, but the young man could lose several good years of his life.

As my friend and I talked in the coffee shop, I suggested that she begin to consider ways of channelling her anger and frustration into some kind of public action which might alter a future, if not the present, situation. She highlighted the need for a review of the rape laws and court procedures, particularly the use of the unsworn statement; greater public awareness of the irrational but widespread hostility to women and the suspicion of female vindictiveness which can affect jury deliberations; concern about public understanding of the term 'consent' in rape cases; and a need to support the plaintiff regardless of the outcome of the trial. The next day the jury passed in its verdict. They voted 11–1 for acquittal. My friend was the only one convinced that this decision was wrong.

Fortunately, the story does not end there. My friend made contact with the victim shortly after the trial. Together they approached the Attorney-General's office and the Office of the Women's Advisor to voice their concerns about the case. They wrote to every politician in South Australia. They organized a public meeting for victims of crime at the university where both women spoke of the trial experience. Mounting public pressure led to an inquiry into rape laws and the abolition of the unsworn statement. Along the way the public became more aware of hostile and suspicious community attitudes towards women. And the alleged rape victim, although seriously affected by the psychological scars of the hearing, gained strength from the support of my friend and the larger community.

The accused rapist, although acquitted of this charge, never left gaol. Although the jury did not know, he was in prison awaiting trial for the abduction, gang rape and murder of another woman at the time of the rape case. The second jury found him and his four companions guilty of charges relating to the rape and murder. He is presently serving out his sentence.

My friend's story affected me deeply. It convinced me that our subjectivities are inscribed by the myths of women and sexuality which circulate in the culture. These myths mitigate against values for which the culture expresses belief: reason, justice, respect for women, protection from prejudice and the like. But the story also convinced me that women are more than their representation. We can and do take action which confounds the cultural codes, transforms attitudes toward sexuality and women and begins to articulate a new place for women within society.

READING THE CULTURAL CODES

Another adjunct to the work has been a heightened sense of awareness of the signs of contemporary culture. I register daily an increasing number of instances which demonstrate repetitions and transformations of cultural codes. We live in a time when Australia is becoming a mixed stock commodity in the world's signifying market. The increase in overseas visitors arriving for the Grand Prix, the America's Cup, the Bicentenary, outback holidays, or just to witness the West's 'last frontier' have brought about a great deal of traveller's commentary on Australia and Australians and local responses. I want to look at a few contemporary representations of the national character, the bush and women to register the ongoing vitality of the cultural codes, some possible effects and the signs of change.

The National Character

There are signs that Australians are still looking for the national character and not really wanting to find it. Australians are an inordinately defensive species. Overseas visitors comment and locals agree that the one thing that will not be tolerated by Australians is for an outsider to knock the culture—but then it is not necessary, the insiders do it better than anyone else could imagine. The cultural cringe that A. A. Phillips lamented in the 1950s is still a dominant posture, and one acknowledged regularly in and by the media. For example, in a recent book review concerning the republication of P. R. Stephensen's *Foundations of Culture in Australia* (1959) in the *National Times on Sunday* the reviewer, D. J. O'Hearn, writes:

> There is little doubt that the 'inferiority complex' still informs our culture and those who make decisions that affect that culture. It is inferiority that takes refuge in the 'ocker' image rather than celebrating the wit and anti-conformist individualism of the larrikin tradition. It is inferiority that compels our artistic entrepreneurs to import mediocre overseas performers and performances rather than risk the indigenous . . . the inferiority complex is still too widespread and embedded in our public life. The foundations of our culture certainly are in place but are overgrown with weeds. The edifice? Well, it is still in need of construction.[5]

I have kept a clippings file over the past few months. On an average weekend I can find with ease at least three or four featured items which knock the culture through a reiteration of old textual strategies, and at least three or four more which mute the criticism through a celebration of worn-out myths. The above excerpt actually does both. It knocks the culture with its attention to the inferiority complex evoked by the 'ocker' image and celebrates it with the suggestion that the image might be mediated with recourse to the larrikin tradition. The codes of masculinity and femininity are reproduced in the excerpt by the assumption that 'we' are male ('ockers' and larrikins). The gender codes are muted in the final reference to nature (the foundations, overgrown with weeds) versus culture (the edifice yet to be constructed). Further, the threat to identity is located on the outside, in mediocre overseas imports.

The terms of the debate appear not to have changed greatly since the 1950s, or perhaps the 1920s. Compare the above critique with that which David Walker makes in his 'introduction' to *Australian Popular Culture* (1979) concerning the image of Australia in the 1890s as compared with the 1920s. Walker is concerned with the issue of Australian identity in relation to the importation of foreign cultural artifacts (as is O'Hearn in the book review just cited). He discusses reasons why Australian commentators have seen the literature and events of the 1890s as culturally significant. He reiterates the familiar idea that the 1890s must be seen 'in retrospect' as the founding decade of Australia's national life, 'the only decade which can be regarded with any plausibility as post-colonial yet pre-modern'.[6] The phrase 'in retrospect' reminds us that the significance of the 1890s (seen as a 'culturally superior decade') lies not in the decade itself, but in the representation of the decade within the discourse on the Australian tradition.

Walker explains that the writers of the 1930s (Hancock, *et al.*) could recognize the cultural significance of the 1890s as 'post-colonial', that is, distinctly different in its production of cultural materials from prior colonial and Empire-identified models; and 'pre-modern', that is, pre-dating the influx of overseas imports, largely American, which flooded the country in the wake of World War I and gave popular culture a distinctively American taint. To make his point, Walker provides the reader with a comparison of ideas concerning the reputation of 'Australia' in the 1890s and the 1920s. Walker writes:

> Whereas the 1890's are commonly regarded as original manly, youthful, creative and essentially rural in inspiration, the 1920's are often dismissed as derivative, female, sterile and urban. The change in language summarises what was considered to be a regrettable shift from an Australian culture with a basis in folk art to an essentially imported culture designed for mass consumption. The move from cultural innovation to passivity is often associated with the

eclipse of the male in the cultural life of the community and the emergence of what was thought to be a superficial, feminised culture.[7] Like O'Hearn, Walker assumes the importance and the possibility of an indigenous, original culture. He reiterates (in this instance explicit) sexual dichotomies to define the 'real' masculine product from its artificial feminine contrivance. And he locates the threat to identity on the outside—in American cultural artifacts. Walker concludes that the links 'between women and cultural passivity' remain constant, despite shifts in emphasis concerning the nature of male identity. That which is masculine is linked to the bush and the folk art of the 1890s. That which is feminine is linked to the derivative, corrupting influences associated with city life. The feminine is marked as passive. But, in the text its imagined links with the foreign and corrupting influences in culture mark it as an *active* threat to Australian masculine cultural dominance. For 'masculine', read the self, the national character; for 'feminine', read the other, the not-me, the superficial, feminized culture. The feminine is seen to eclipse the masculine in cultural life as the bush was seen to absorb its inhabitants. But what is this passive, superficial feminine aspect of culture which is such a feared force? Both articles refer to overseas imports. Their target is the entertainment industry. But we live in a global village. Surely there is more to this threat whose weeds appear to choke the first breath upon the edifice of national life. The commentaries proceed as if cultural imperialism could be reduced to the importation of 'Sesame Street'.

David Walker refers specifically to woman's inferior status in Australian cultural life. He suggests that woman in Australia, whenever she is seen to challenge her assigned domestic role, is treated with anger and hostility. This was the case stated by Miriam Dixson in *The Real Matilda*. It was the case evidenced by the public denunciations of Lindy Chamberlain. In the Spearitt and Walker anthology, *Australian Popular Culture*, there is a number of articles which demonstrate this assertion with regard to the construction of manhood and sexuality.[8] They combine to contribute to the crudest of national sexual stereotypes, the 'Ocker' image, which some speakers within the culture condemn as a 'noxious pest' and others defend as a 'protected species'.[9] He can turn off the telly, and escape to the pub when the beer runs out, but can he buy back the farm? Has national identity actually been 'his' to claim?

The tendency to resort to woman as scapegoat for doubts about the nature of the native son's authority in the land appears too often, the strategy is too repetitive, the explanation too easy. There is something else in this tradition, something that may not emanate from the land/the bush/woman itself. If the syntax sounds familiar, it is. I mime Phillips to invert one cultural code and

allow it to interpenetrate with another. The 'something else' caught in the web
of the debate circulates around the ongoing question of identity. It surfaced
clearly during the time of the sacking of Prime Minister Gough Whitlam when
the Governor-General, Sir John Kerr, asserted the political authority of the
Queen. (Gough, perhaps taking his cue from Barbara Baynton's dissidence,
called the newly appointed Prime Minister, Malcolm Fraser, a name—the
noun was cur/Kerr.) This event as cultural myth is referred to in my recent
clippings as well. In a review of *Australia: Spirit of a Nation* by Michael
Cannon, David Greason[10] chastises the historian for his banal treatment of the
Whitlam era, one which the reviewer claims embodies the classic Australian
myth: that is, 'game little battlers who get shafted by the British establishment
while trying to buy back the farm'. But who owns the farm? Who ever has
owned it?

The concerns about British dominance in the affairs of state and American
dominance in popular culture jostle uncomfortably with the desire for a
unique national identity. The issue of authority, as coded within the Australian tradition, frames the news and acts as an interpretative framework for
individual action, sweeping larger economic and political complications into
the woodheap. Take, for example, the dilemma of possible administrative
mismanagement at the Canberra War Memorial which surfaced in the news
in 1987. The management principles of the then director were brought under
scrutiny. An independent inquiry, the Queen's counsel and the Solicitor-
General have concurred that 'there is a case of misbehaviour'. The counsel
called for the director's resignation, which was refused. The story of these
developments in the news carries the heading 'War Memorial Dog Fight'. It
begins: 'This is a story about an old digger, a Federal Minister, the Governor-
General, and a humble war memorial.'[11] ('Humble'? In another place it would
be an idealized edifice of a national cuture. It can be read another way.
Perhaps it is an ironic signifier.) The 'old digger' is the War Memorial
director, an Air Vice-Marshal and Korean war veteran, who 'has shown a
fighting spirit and a hard-nosed defiance characteristic of his digger
colleagues'. The federal Minister for the Labor government is transposed into
the representative of State power, which 'may have to wheel out one of its
biggest guns' (the Governor-General) to sack the little Aussie battler. The text
presents the dilemma through the 'little Aussie battler' code—which its
referents both transgress and confirm. The complexities of government
control, administrative mismanagement, political allegiance, power relationships and legal processes are all poured into the mythic mould of the digger
and the swells. But Manning Clark was right: sometimes you cannot tell them
apart.

We are inscribed in representation, but we are more than it can express. Behind representation is a system of power relations which authorize certain meanings and block, deny or prohibit others. The discourse on national identity preserves the place of the national character as an original, authentic Australian presence. To work effectively it must disguise the operations of power.

When the Australian character looks in the cultural mirror, the image he sees is a mis-recognition, an illusion. When the Australian woman looks, she sees a redoubled illusion—not only her image but also his image of her. Australian women have already begun to turn their backs on the mirror, or turn the mirror to the wall. They know that theirs is an otherness of another order. The question is 'Where do we go from here?' Can we decode the old myths and reinscribe into Australian culture a new plurality of meanings?

I am moved by a voice in the room. It is the voice of A-Luce, a different voice, epigrammatic. It calls to me from the wall, barely perceptible, just behind the computer monitor. I listen: 'you're nearly done', she whispers. 'Leave this task. Play a game of a different order.'

'I can't, now. Have to finish . . .'

'Stop looking in the mirror. Come through to the other side. We are clever girls; we won't get hurt. We'll play with the reflections and then . . .'

'I don't know . . .', I falter, gazing fatally in the direction of the mirror. 'It's improper.'

'I know', she echoes, pulling me closer.

A GAME OF A-LUCE THROUGH THE LOOKING GLASS; OR 'WOMAN' THROUGH THE AUSTRALIAN BUSH TRADITION

'Mirror, mirror, on the wall . . . Who's the littlest Aussie battler of them all?'

' "Harry Butler is today", A-Luce and Kay.'

'Harry Butler, the Northern Territory's Commissioner for Conservation and "the biggest greenie of them all"? Harry Butler, the CBE and "Australian of the Year"? Harry Butler, the only man in Australia to have an animal species named after him . . . even if it is a mouse? What is he battling now?'

'*That* Harry Butler is battling with *this* Harry Butler. The one who's been sacked by the Bicentennial Authority and banned from scheduled TV promotions. The Harry Butler, hero of Australian flora and fauna, who is now a consultant for Peko-Walsend Mining. The Harry Butler who opposed the government plan to register Kakadu National Park on the World Heritage List. The Harry Butler who ignored federal government direction, made a controversial film and took it to Unesco in Paris.'

'A film? What film? Reproduction of the image interests me.'

But the mirror is still. It gives no further response. I have asked one too many questions.

Butler's image appears in the mirror. Bushman's hat, corks around the band, trimmed beard, hair curling down over the edges of his open-necked shirt. Trees behind him. He's in the outback—Kakadu: Crocodile Dundee country.

'Good one! Boy from the Bush. Protector of the environment. "If you find something in the bush, always put it back", he used to tell my girls as they watched his show *In the Wild* on the telly.'

'All is not what it seems', A-Luce says, reaching for her speculum.

Startled, I drop my 'Women and the bush' clippings. Headlines spill out: 'riches beneath an Ancient Land' . . . 'A treasure chest buried under a national park' . . . 'Kakadu, Stage 2: clapped-out buffalo country, says Harry Butler'. I see his face among the words. It must be a trick of her devising. It's the same as the image in the mirror. There are lot of them actually. He always looks the same. His image reproduced against headings like 'Turning Wild about Harry' and ('what's this?') 'Harry Butler: I'm not a turncoat.'

The room is a blur of words and images. I clear my head. Pull myself together. 'Oh, look A-Luce, this one should interest you. Here's a photo of the mound called "Coronation Hill". It's at the centre of the controversy over Kakadu. Where the minerals are buried. In the press photo it looks like a Sidney Nolan painting of Central Australia. "The Australian Sublime." It's in shadow so you can't make out the scars from mining operations.' I reach for another clipping. It takes up a full quarter-page. A vicious crocodile, jaws extended and teeth bared, lumbers menacingly towards the viewer while pelicans gently glide on the Alligator River. 'Kakadu; Australia's best-kept secret', it announces.

She's not paying attention. Not interested in images. In words between quotation marks. Language as quotation. She's looking through the speculum. Two rounds of concave and convex glass. An ellipse. A tool for turning the inside out. Bringing the dark recesses to light. The mirror shudders. Images dance around the room, deflected by the speculum's conical shape. The surface of the mirror expands and contracts. Butler's looking strange. His bandied knees grow long. They curve and flow into a beer-barrel chest and wide, flat head. His body distorts as if in a hall of mirrors. His face transparent through refracted light. The image of another blending from behind it. Mid-western American chin distorting the lines of his beard. Like a carnival. Delighted, I nearly forget my task. The book. The words. My armour. My dress.

I try again. 'Here's something you'll like: The Minister for Minerals and

Energy says that Kakadu is "hardly a virgin wilderness". He explained to newsmen, "I wouldn't go so far as saying it is a tatty old tart. But it gets pretty close to it." Then there's this description of its "wonderfully secret place . . . 'Kakadu: The wet season cuts much of it off, and in doing so, guards like a chastity belt its innermost secrets.' " '.

She hears. The room erupts with laughter. A-Luce moves through the glass. Her motion pulls me forward, but I stop to recover my Kakadu clippings. It's three months' reading! Luckily the paper clips have held the 37 pro-mining and 7 pro-conservation clippings in separate bundles. The to-be-decided bunch has come asunder. I gather the items headed 'Greenies see Red' and 'The Greening of Labor'; 'Hawke in a Green Mode' and 'Government Caves In'. They don't need analysis. I clip them with others in the pro-mining bunch.

I look up. The image of Harry Butler is stable now. He blocks my way. Eyeing me with curiosity. My clothes are intact but his gaze penetrates. Makes me feel naked. Even my nakedness, his costume. This is not a friendly place. I feel bereft, lost, alone in this other world. Challenged by the image in the mirror. I call to A-Luce to come back. Don't leave me. Let me read you my clippings.

Her voice whispers. Leave them behind. I've heard them before. Their words make me laugh. I can not be still. My motion shakes up their world. Their mirrors. Their ice. They think we are indifferent. You/me. We who change places with every exchange. You have been still in their world. You are now still in their world. With their earth. Their mother. Careful not to shake things up too much. You have worked too long in the house of the Father. How can I touch you if you aren't here? Come with me. Use our tools to stretch the light. Come through the shadows in the glass. Leave your familiar room, your computer, your worn-out myths, your language of sameness.

My back aches. My eyes are weary. I have a sore throat. So sore I have not been able to speak for three days. So many words. To look at. To appraise. To correct. To re-type. I'm not ready. Let me work a while longer. For just a little time now. I have to type the footnotes. Print out the chapter. Proofread. Make corrections. Finish the bibliography. Then I'll be ready. Like dressing the girls for school. Find their shoes. Comb their hair. Pack their lunch. Clean away the milk and cereal at the kitchen counter. Sponge the sink. Drive them to school. Come back. Bring in the milk. Feed the cat. Boil some tea. Then I can be ready. Then there is time for me.

You are tethered to their world. A well-chosen vessel. The Father's. Put down your stick. Their stick. Take off your watch. Their time. Disconnect the computer. Their technology. Shake off the tether and come over to me. The time is now. Loosen your armour. Take off your dress, your academic disguise. Move away. Forget the footnotes. Dead ends. Giving everyone his due. Your debt to the fathers. As if you haven't paid enough. Proper names, titles. Ownership of ideas. You authorize their speech, their writing. Life in their world. We have lost the ability to speak except as they have taught us. Your throat constricted with their words. Your eyes weakened by their vision. A mirage.

Harry Butler glares at me. A film strip hangs from his pocket. I am reminded of his film. I want to know its name. Let me check one last detail before I go . . . A-Luce?

She is silent. I am exiled from her, from the voice that is several at once. My task divides me from her. I am not accustomed to her delights. When we speak one to another, another to one, together, we move beyond their boundaries. Closed and open, neither excluding the other. She will not think to dominate me. There is no push to her touch. No demand to her gaze. I can do as I like. What do I like? Am I swimming or drowning in the Father's pool?

I reach for the film strip. Harry Butler smiles. His eyes meet mine. He is pleased with my interest, my desire. I am caught in his reflection again. The mirror is crowded now. There are many figures circling his form. Paul Hogan as Crocodile Dundee watches me carefully. The latest 'typical Australian' cut to Russel Ward's mould. They tell me I am desired. They tell me Aussie girls don't have to be sheilas any more. They shift aside. Dundee's girlfriend peers over his shoulder. They nod their approval. A journalist, notepad in hand. The mirror is full of men. They gather around the girl, the woman. Ward, Phillips, Lawson, Heseltine, Clark. A few old blokes in the distance. Leichhardt, Mitchell, Eyre, Stuart. They have all been here. Are here now. Explorers, cartographers, mapmakers, botanists, geographers. They want to tell her their stories.

For distraction, I pick up the speculum. An ellipse. Elliptical. It indicates an omission; in speech, a suppression of letters and words. In the body, it brings the darkness to light. Turns the inside out. I hold it up to the mirror. Images stretch, elastic. Shapes move between the gaps of light. Other women surface on the glass. Louisa Lawson, Richardson, Dark, Prichard. They have been there all along. The gaps in the mirror are not empty. The women interrupt the stories the men are telling the girl. Dundee's girl. They mime her gestures, deliberately. The sound of their laughter marks the distance.

A-Luce . . . there are women in the mirror. Shall I address them? Invite them to play our game? The game I move towards even as I defer? The women in the distance nod. They know the game. I try to catch the journalist's attention. She is eclipsed by the men. Standing in their shadows. She opens her notepad. Records names, addresses, dates, titles, publications. She is deadly serious. Her pen divides the page into parts. Separates, underlines, catalogues, binds. She will take home a book of notes in which our names do not appear. Along with him. Back to America. A new story begins. A retelling. They will call it the 'Aussification' of America. And believe it.

Captain Phillip took an Aborigine back to England. They say he was proud to go. Put on the Father's dress. The Father's mannerisms. He was desired. Their desire was his death. He brought them the promised land. They saw him as barbarian, infidel, noble savage. His place in their world. They know no other. What of his world? Left behind. Layered over with the veneer of the master's words, explanations, histories, truth.

Butler offers me the film. His film. Made to represent the land of man's desire. 'Take it', his eyes say. Men can be generous. Friendly. Supportive. Even Australian men. Nice blokes really. Good sense of humour. They get bad press. Even little Aussie battlers. Didn't Dundee give her space? Respect? Protection when it counted? Sometimes you need a man with a knife. Like at Kakadu. Like in New York City. I reckon the Drover's Wife would have killed for one. A good knife. But there are some things even she could not do. I wonder if tackling hoods in the city was one of them?

She has a ladder in her stocking. I think of her dimpled thighs. Cellulite. The Yanks response to the girl they thought they lost. Exchanged. 'She wasn't so hot, she had dimpled legs.' Their eyes looking, appraising, levelling. They parcel out the pieces of her flesh. Measure to their standards of perfection. But Hoges. They can live with him. A new species. He brings them a gift. The promise of a new frontier. She will be its midwife. The mediator of a rival exchange between men.

The film falls to the floor before the mirror. The title visible. The last detail. It's a mystery. Detective fiction. With a classic title. Harry Butler made a film called 'What the Butler Saw'. His vision of Kakadu as clapped-out buffalo country. The men want me to take it. Have a look. To be complicit in the solution to their mystery. I go pale. Frigid. Angry. My pleasure, my desire caught in their system. My questions fused with their dilemma. My place a space of assurance for them. A guarantor of their identity. We know what the butler saw. Spy in the house of the Father. Who slipped in when the Prime Minister wasn't looking. Off on one of his trips. They think the mother is fickle. At it again. We just read the book. Saw the film. We know she wasn't there. Only their image of her. Their doubt. There are some things that only a woman can know.

I call to A-Luce. There is no sound. The men beckon. They want me to feel guilty for not finishing their story. A sigh. A sigh-n. She is here. Not gone away. Fluid. Not rigid like my anger. Present without words. Known without sight. Porous through the spaces concealed by the mirror. She expands to embrace me. I can feel her filling me with warmth. Her energies fuse with mine. Her laughter blends with other voices. We are multiple. I can leave the study. The site of their desire. Blood pulses through my fingers. The swelling pads of flesh float above the keyboard. Text appears. Words come. From another place. Like letters on a ouija board.

For three nights now I have been awakened at 3 a.m. The time my body knows best for birthing. I wake. I gasp. My breath becomes a cough. My cough a groan. Again and again. Erupting. Coming from everywhere at once. Turning my body inside out. Liquid seeps from eyes, ears, nose. The noise disturbs the household. No one sleeps. When will it stop? The house is alive with the sounds of my pain. A revolution in process. This is not a fantasy.

With her now. We travel through spaces hidden by the mirror. It is dark, hazy, mysterious. We neither see nor speak. We follow the uneasy rhythms of the body. We are pulled towards the woman. The women we were from the start. We didn't need to be invented by them. Given a name that was not our name. A place in which we were possessed. We have been displaced in their reflections, their stories, their categories, their territory which was our exile. It doesn't have to be like this. Entangled in their webs. Chained to their words that choke and gag the throat.

Wait. Their words are emptying out. Our lips are becoming red again. Full, moist, stirring. Awaiting exchange. We attend our bodies. Skin porous, open. It takes in and breathes out air. Tears and sweat mingle. With the air. The water. Between us. Blood envelops and nurtures our bodies. Circulates. We flow together, senses fusing. There is no competition between us. Space expands. Depth without chasm. Fusion without separation.

We are in the land called Kakadu. The land down under. Where their secrets are. Girdled, veiled and unveiled, again and again. To feed their hunger. To supplement but never satisfy their desire. Kakadu. No longer their virgin. Penetrated, transgressed, possessed. A reserve for explorations, consummations, exploitations. Theirs—and strangers from other lands. America. Asia. The world. Kakadu divided into three stages. Three seasons. This is the summer of their desire. Not of ours.

The rains pour over our bodies. The land. The wet. Limitless expanse. The air swells with mist. Streams flow with no fixed banks. Rivers merge with no division to the sea. No solid ground is visible. We sense its contours. There is no hardness, but density. No chasms but depth. No boundaries between earth and sea. Sea and sky. We have no need to imagine them. Names peel away in layers. Ranger, Coronation Hill, Gimbat, Goodparla, Alligator River, Kakadu, Gudjewg. The land re-leased from England, Commonwealth, nation. There before the arrival of Leichhardt, Gregory, Stuart, England, Australia, the Northern Territory, the World Heritage Foundation, the multinationals, Peko-Walsend. Abundant space etched with endless scratchings on the map of Western desire. Before them, others. The place to which the first boat people came. The Bugis to meet the Aborigines. Where the spirit of Namandjolg and his sister, moving in Crocodile and Rainbow Serpent, performed the first acts of creation on the landscape. The Dreamtime. For a culture with another way of knowing.

I can let go of my words, my names, my guide cards, my memory. It held their stories which were never ours. I am shedding my disguise. My dress, my skin. Peeling away the layers. There is so much to take off. Soon I will be down to my skin. It peels away. I am shed of the past. Reproductions. Images. Appearances. I feel differently now. Expanding without limits or borders.

My body is moved, moving. I want to speak . . . what? . . . will come. To invent a language to express all of us. You/me—with me. All. Not original and copy. Not master and reproduction. Resemblance without semblance. To find words which have no privilege, no price, no value. Wherein everything is exchanged. Words flowing like honey. Healing the soreness. The now of a new body. Becoming. Never finished. The face never completed. The lips never opening or closing on a truth. What would it be to whisper the sounds of the shapes we have found?

We have arrived at my point of departure. Dissolving without madness. Dispersed without fear. Are you with me mother?

NOTES

CHAPTER 1

[1]Richard White, *Inventing Australia: Images and Identity 1688–1980*, viii.

[2]Norman MacKenzie, *Women in Australia*, ix. MacKenzie's argument has been supported not only by feminist commentators, whose work is examined in Chapter Three, but also by humanist social critics in Australia. See below, note 6.

[3]G.A. Wilkes, *The Stockyard and the Croquet Lawn: Literary Evidence for Australia's Cultural Development.*

[4]Wilkes, 4.

[5]Marian Aveling, 'Taking Women's History out of the Ghetto,' Unpublished paper delivered to the Australian Historical Association Conference (Adelaide, 1986), 1.

[6]See for example, Ronald Conway, *The Great Australian Stupor*; Max Harris, *The Angry Eye*; Craig McGregor, *Profile of Australia*; and Sol Encel, Norman MacKenzie and Margaret Tebbutt, *Women and Society : An Australian Study.*

[7]Miriam Dixson, *The Real Matilda*, 22.

[8]Dixson, 188. See also 'The Case Stated', 21-56.

[9]See Anne Summers, *Damned Whores and God's Police*, 31-55.

[10]Delys Bird, 'Australian Woman: A National Joke?', *Australian Journal of Cultural Studies*, 1, 1 (May 1983), 111-14.

[11]See Jacques Lacan, 'The Mirror Phase', *New Left Review*, 51 (1968), 71-7.

[12]See Hélène Cixous, 'The Laugh of the Medusa', *Signs*, 1, 4 (Summer 1976), 879 and 'Castration or Decapitation?', *Signs*, 7, 1 (Autumn 1981), 45.

[13]See Michel Foucault, 'The Discourse on Language', trans. by Rupert Swyer, *The Archeology of Knowledge*, Appendix.

[14]See A. A. Phillips, Preface to the second edition, *The Australian Tradition: Studies in a Colonial Culture*, vii-xii.

[15]White, *Inventing Australia*. See Introduction, viii-x.

[16]John Docker, *In a Critical Condition*. See 34-8, 46-9, 63, 86-92.

[17]Graeme Turner, *National Fictions: Literature, Film and the Construction of Australian Narrative*, 8.

[18]Roland Barthes, *Mythologies*, trans. by Annette Lavers, 109.

[19]Raymond Williams, *Culture*, 13.

[20]Russel Ward, *The Australian Legend*, 1-2.

[21]Paul Taylor in 'A Culture of Temporary Culture', *Art and Text*, 16 (1984-5), 94-108, comments that the diversity and discontinuities of Australian culture have been muted to produce a unified, if artificial, image. Constantly reproduced in the stories of our past, present and future, they present a culture of effects separated from causes. He concludes that Australia seems to be becoming aware of its 'otherness' from Europe and America through an assertion of difference against overseas cultural imperialism. At the same time, we look to Europe and America for affirmation of ourselves as exotic, alien—an identity of 'otherness'.

[22]See Meaghan Morris, 'Two Types of Phototographic Criticism located in relation to Lynn Silverman's Series', *Art and Text*, 6 (1982), 63-4. On the continent and the burden of metaphor see Peter Botsman, 'From Deserts Structuralists Come', *Foreign Bodies Papers*, 39-53. Botsman traces the desert image through the discourses of history, politics and literature. He concludes that barrenness has become a metaphor for Australian culture. Writers who resist what they see as a dry, barren, cultural wasteland circulate the idea of Australia in terms of the cultural cringe, the great lack, the world distanced from itself and assert a culture in need of salvation from without—from Europe.

[23]Turner, 49.

[24]Vance Palmer, *Legend of the Nineties*, 20.

[25]Jacques Lacan, 'Guiding Remarks for a Congress on Feminine Sexuality', cited and discussed in *Feminine Sexuality: Jacques Lacan and the École Freudienne*, ed. by Juliet Mitchell and Jacqueline Rose, 43.

[26]Palmer, 1, 4.

[27]See Rosalind Coward, *Female Desire*, 16.

[28]On the explorers, see, for example, Ross Gibson, *The Diminishing Paradise: Changing Literary Perceptions of Australia*; Robert Dixon, *The Course of Empire: Neo-Classical Culture in New South Wales, 1788-1860*; Paul Carter, *The Road to Botany Bay: An Essay in Spatial History*; and Lenore Coltheart, 'Australian Misère: The Northern Territory in the Nineteenth Century', Ph.D. dissertation, Griffith University, Brisbane, Queensland, 1982. On the Australian tradition, see Ward, Palmer, Phillips, Summers and Dixson, previously cited. On ideological perspectives informing a nationalist tradition see Tim Rowse, *Australian Liberalism and National Character*, and John Docker, previously cited. On constructions of national identity see Richard White and Graeme Turner, previously cited.

[29]Julia Kristeva, trans. by Josette Féral, 'The Powers of Difference' in Hester Eisenstein and Alice Jardine (eds), *The Future of Difference*, 92-3.

[30]Luce Irigaray, 'The Power of Discourse', in *This Sex Which is not One*, trans. by Catherine Porter, 76.

CHAPTER 2

[1]Nettie Palmer, *Modern Australian Literature*; W. K. Hancock, *Australia*; Vance Palmer, *Legend of the Nineties*; Russel Ward, *The Australian Legend*.

[2]Anne Summers, *Damned Whores and God's Police*; Miriam Dixson, *The Real Matilda*.

[3]Meaghan Morris, 'Aspects of French Feminist Literary Criticism', *Hecate*, 5, 2 (1979), 66.

[4]The title of an anonymous review of Lawson's anthology, *While the Billy Boils*, which appeared in the *Sydney Morning Herald*, 29 Aug. 1896. The title was also chosen by Manning Clark for his 1978 address on Lawson to an Adelaide Festival of Arts Writer's Week forum.

[5]See Graeme Davison, 'Sydney and the Bush: An Urban Context for the Australian Legend', *Historical Studies*, 17, 71 (Oct. 1978), 191-209.

[6]David Walker, 'The Getting of Manhood', in Peter Spearitt and David Walker (eds), *Australian Popular Culture*, 124.

[7]Walker, 124.

[8]I am indebted to Patricia Grimshaw, 'Women in History: Reconstructing the Past' in Jacqueline Goodnow and Carole Pateman (eds), *Women, Social Policy and the State*, 42, for calling attention to this element in McQueen's text.

[9]Jacques Derrida, *Of Grammatology*, intro. and trans. by Gayatri Chakravorty Spivak, 170.

[10]See A. D. Hope, 'Standards in Australian Literature', *Current Affairs Bulletin* (Nov. 1956) reprinted in Grahame Johnston (ed.), *Australian Literary Criticism*; H. P. Heseltine, 'The Literary Heritage', *Meanjin* 1 (1962) rpt in C. B. Christesen (ed.), *On Native Grounds*, 3-15; Vincent Buckley, 'Utopianism and Vitalism', *Quadrant*, 3, 2 (1958-9), rpt in Johnston, 16-29, for divergent academic opinions concerning the literary worth and aesthetic value of the literature of the 1890s.

[11]See C. M. H. Clark, *A History of Australia* and Humphrey McQueen, *A New Britannia?*

[12]See Colin Roderick (ed.), *Henry Lawson Criticism*.

[13]Derrida, *Of Grammatology*, 170.

[14]Derrida, 'Structure, Sign and Play in the Discourse of the Human Sciences,' trans. by Alan Bass in *Writing and Difference*, 278.

[15]Michel Foucault, 'The Discourse on Language', trans. by Rupert Swyer in *The Archeology of Knowledge*, 221.

[16]Foucault, 224.

[17]Michel Foucault, *Language, Counter-Memory, Practice*, trans. by Donald Bouchard and Sherry Simon, 142.

[18]Elizabeth Webby, 'Parents Rather than Critics: Some Early Reviews of Australian Literature', in Leon Cantrell (ed.), *Bards, Bohemians,and Bookmen*, 19.

[19]*Sydney Gazette*, 1 Nov. 1826, review of Charles Thompson's *Wild Notes from the Lyre of a Native Minstrel*, quoted in Webby, 20.

[20]Brian Kiernan, 'Literature, History, and Literary History: Perspectives on the Nineteenth Century in Australia', in Cantrell (ed.), *Bards*, 405.

[21]Paul deMan, *Blindness and Insight*, 105.

[22]Nettie Palmer, 7.

[23]Nettie Palmer, 57.

[24]Hancock, 256.

[25]Hancock, 256.

[26]Hancock, 257.

[27]Kiernan, 'Literature . . .', 10.

[28]John Docker, 'Australian Literature of the 1890's', in C. D. Narasimhaiah (ed.), *An Introduction to Australian Literature*, 9.

[29]McQueen, 104.

[30]Henry Lawson, 'Hungerford', *While the Billy Boils*, 27.

[31]Henry Lawson, 'The Bush Undertaker', *While the Billy Boils*, 146.

[32]Palmer, *Legend*, 11.

[33]See Colin Roderick, *The Real Henry Lawson* and Brian Kiernan, *The Essential Henry Lawson: The Best Works of Australia's Greatest Writer*.

[34]See Janet Hawley, 'The Lost Works of Henry Lawson', *Advertiser* (Adelaide), 4 Dec. 1982, and Lawson's prose works published on 4–6 Dec. 1982. For a review of the controversy see the review article by Brian Matthews, 'Lawson scholars—The Sparks Fly', *Advertiser*, 5 Mar. 1983.

[35]Cecil Hadgraft, *The Australian Short Story Before Lawson*, introduction.

[36]Mary Lord, 'Retrieving the Baby', *Australian Book Review*, 83 (Aug. 1986), 13-14.

[37]See Edward Said on Foucault in 'The Problem of Textuality: Two Exemplary Positions,' *Critical Inquiry* 4 (Summer 1978), 709.

[38]This comment was taken from John Barnes, 'Australian Fiction to 1920' in Geoffrey Dutton (ed.), *The Literature of Australia*, 160.

[39]Sylvia Lawson, *The Archibald Paradox*, 260.

[40]Sylvia Lawson, 178, 179.

[45]Richard White, *Inventing Australia: Images and Identity 1688-1980*, vii.

[46]White, see 97-109.

[47]White, ix.

[48]Graeme Turner, *National Fictions*, 96-7.

[49]Dixson, 23.

CHAPTER 3

[1]Francis Adams, *The Australian* (London, 1893) quoted in Vance Palmer, *The Legend of the Nineties*, 47.

[2]The title of a short story by Henry Lawson, and a common refrain.

[3]Adams, in Palmer, 47.

[4]Andrew Pike and Ross Cooper, *Australian Film, 1900-1977: A Guide to Feature Film Production*, 367.

[5]Laura Mulvey, 'Visual Pleasure and Narrative Cinema', *Screen*, 16, 3 (Autumn 1975), 206, and 'Afterthoughts on "Visual Pleasure and Narrative Cinema" inspired by *Duel in the Sun*', *Framework* 15/16/17 (1981), 12-15.

[6]Mulvey, 'Visual Pleasure', 209.

[7]For a description of primal fears and fantasies with reference to masculine identity and feminine lack see Robert Con Davis, 'The Discourse of the Father', in Robert Con Davis (ed.), *The Fictional Father: Lacanian Readings of the Text*, 1-26. Davis discusses the 'maelstrom' of maternal need outside of the articulation of the Father's Law in precisely these terms.

[8]Christian Metz, *Film Language: A Semiotics of the Cinema*, trans. by Michael Taylor, 5, 23. Veronica Brady in a review of Graeme Turner's *National Fictions* calls attention to this dimension of the film as text as well. See her review in *Westerly*, 3 (Sept. 1987), 91, 92.

[9]See Teresa deLauretis, *Alice Doesn't: Feminism, Semiotics, Cinema*, 116-21.

[10]In one scene in the film *Picnic at Hanging Rock* viewers glimpse through a magnifying glass a newspaper account of the disappearance of the girls which is headed 'College Mystery Deepens: Four Still Missing' over an oval school photo of Miranda. The *Sunday Mail* article with its heading, layout, pictorials and narrative re-invokes this scene from the film.

[11]Peter Haran, 'Missing Boys: Mystery Deepens', *Sunday Mail* (Adelaide), 4 Jan. 1987, 3.

[12]'My Son Is Dead: Mother,' *Advertiser*, 4 July 1987, 2.

[13]Des Colquhoun, 'Realities of a harsh land no joke,' *Advertiser*, 1 April 1987, 1.

[14]Sidney Smith, cited in Bernard Smith, *European Vision and the South Pacific 1768-1850: A Study in the History of Art and Ideas*, 170.

[15]Peter Cunningham, *Two Years in New South Wales* (London, 1927), cited in Richard White, *Inventing Australia: Images and Identity 1688-1980*, 8.

[16]T. Crofton Croker (ed.), *Memoirs of Joseph Holt, General of the Irish Rebels, in 1798* (London, 1838), cited in White, 17.

[17]Letter of King to Portland (1 March 1802), cited in Miriam Dixson, *The Real Matilda*, 124-5.

[18]Marcus Clarke, *His Natural Life* quoted in L. T. Hergenhan (ed.), *A Colonial City: High and Low Life—Selected Journalism of Marcus Clarke*, 362-4.

[19]Marcus Clarke, *The Australian Landscape: Comments on Two Paintings*, revised and reprinted as the Preface to A. L. Gordon, *Sea Spray and Smoke Drift*. (Melbourne: Clarson, Massina, 1876). Both versions are reprinted and compared in Hergenhan, 467.

[20]Henry Lawson, 'Hungerford' in Colin Roderick (ed.), *Henry Lawson: Short Stories and Sketches, 1888-1922*, 106.

[21]Thomas Mitchell, *Journal of an Exhibition into the Interior of Tropical Australia, in Search of a Route from Sydney to the Gulf of Carpentaria* (1848), quoted in Ross Gibson, *The Diminishing Paradise: Changing Literary Perceptions of Australia*, 119-20. See Gibson, Chap. 4, 'Experience in Purgatory' for an explication of the mythic elements in the narratives of exploration. Gibson does not attend specifically to the feminine signification of landscape in this study. He does make the metaphors explicit in his superb short film 'Camera Natura.'

[22]Charles Sturt, *Narrative of an Exploration in to Central Australia* (London, 1849), II, 2 quoted in Gibson, 126-7.

[23]Edward John Eyre, *Journals of Expeditions of Discovery in Central Australia and Overland from Adelaide to King George's Sound, in the years 1839-41*, ((London, 1845), 1, 23 quoted in Gibson, 127-8.

[24]See Lenore Coltheart, 'Australia Misère: the Northern Territory in the Nineteenth Century', Ph.D. dissertation, Griffith University, Brisbane, Queensland, 1982, xv. Coltheart identifies the terms: 'progress, development, growing, expanding, thriving, discovery and conquest' found in the narratives of NT land exploration as those derived from the four stages assumptions; the terms 'hostile, harsh, obstructive, fickle, impoverished, deceitful, and raw' as those which define the land with reference to an Arcadian ideal, and 'empty, sleeping, desolate, and forsaken' as coming from an Arcadian frame of reference but with the deliberate exclusion of the Aboriginal natives. I am grateful to Lenore for generously sharing her work and her enthusiasm for my project with me.

[25]Henry Lawson, 'The Drover's Wife', in Roderick (ed.), *Henry Lawson*, 50.

[26]W. K. Hancock, *Australia*.

[27]Palmer, *Legend*, 20.

[28]Miriam Dixson, *The Real Matilda*, 23.

[29]Meaghan Morris, 'Two Types of Photographic Criticism Located in Relation to Lynn Silverman's Series', *Art and Text*, 6 (1982), 68-9.

[30]Teresa deLauretis, *Alice Doesn't: Feminism, Semiotics, Cinema*, 121. deLauretis is discussing the work of Jurij Lotman in this passage and appropriating his discussion of the relationships between psychoanalysis, narrative and meaning to her feminist analysis.

[31]See Barbara Creed, 'Horror and the Monstrous Feminine: An Imaginary Abjection', *Screen*, 27, 1 (Feb. 1986), 44-71 for a discussion of the idea of the monstrous feminine in the work of Lacan and Kristeva which has relevance to the present study.

[32]Anne Summers, *Damned Whores and God's Police*, prologue.

[33]Luce Irigaray, 'Commodities on Their Own', trans. by Claudia Reeder in Elaine Marks and Isabelle de Courtivron (eds), *New French Feminisms, An Anthology*, 108.

[34]Henry Lawson engages the reader in this construction of the bad mother in his autobiographical story 'A Child in the Dark, and a Foreign Father'. See Roderick (ed.), *Henry Lawson*, 680-5. Almost without exception, critics have accepted the narrative as truth and employed it as evidence to prove that the faults in Lawson's personality and writings can be attributed to Louisa, his mother. I discuss this further in Chapter Five, pages 139-46.

[35]A. N. Maiden, 'Witch-Hunt: How the Chamberlain Case Touched a Nation's Inner Fears', *Time (Australia)*, 24 (15 June 1987), 33.

[36]For documentary texts see Kay Daniels, Mary Murnane and Anne Picot, *Women in Australia: An Annotated Guide to the Records*, 2 vols; Anne Summers and Margaret Bettison, *Her Story: Australian Women in Print, 1788-1975*; and Janet Read and Kathleen Oates, *Women in Australian Society, 1901-1945: A Guide to the Holdings of Australian Archives*. For subsequent documentary anthologies see Ruth Teale (ed.), *Colonial Eve: Sources on Women in Australia,1799-1914*; Beverly Kingston (ed.), *The World Moves Slowly: A Documentary History of Australian Women*; and Kay Daniels and Mary Murnane (eds), *Uphill all the Way: A Documentary History of Women in Australia*.

[37]See Jill Julius Matthews, *Good and Mad Women: The Historical Construction of Femininity in Twentieth Century Australia* and Kereen Reiger, *The Disenchantment of the Home: Modernizing the Australian Family 1880-1940*. For an overview of issues in feminist historiography which includes a discussion of current methodological problems see Patricia Grimshaw, 'Women in History: Reconstructing the Past' in Jacqueline Goodnow and Carole Pateman (eds), *Women, Social Science and Public Policy*, 32-56.

[38]Dixson, 60.

[39]Dixson, 32.

[40]Summers, 238, 21.

[41]Summers, 97.

[42]Summers, 200.

[43]C. M. H. Clark, *A History of Australia*, vol. III, 272, quoted in Summers, 311-12.

[44]See Summers, 'A Colonized Sex', 197-266.

[45]Summers, 311-12.

[46]Manning Clark, *In Search of Henry Lawson*, 52.

[47]Susan Sheridan, 'Review of *Who is She?: Images of Women in Australian Fiction*'. Ed. by Shirley Walker (St. Lucia, Qld: University of Queensland Press, 1983), *Australian Literary Studies*, 11, 9 (1984), 546-52.

[48]Susan Sheridan, ' "Temper Romantic; Bias, Offensively Feminine": Australian Women Writers and Literary Nationalism', *Kunapipi*, 7, 2 and 3 (1985), 49-58.

[49]See Graeme Davison, 'Sydney and the Bush: An Urban Context for the Australian Legend', *Historical Studies*, 17, 71 (Oct. 1978), 191-209. Richard White, John Docker, Sylvian Lawson, Susan Sheridan and others who have examined the legend from the perspective of the 1980s have accepted Davison's contention that the legend 'was not the transmission to the city of values nurtured on the bush frontier, so much as the projection onto the outback of values revered by an alienated urban intelligentsia' (208).

[50]See Susan Sheridan, 'Women Writers', Chapter 20, in L. T. Hergenhan (ed.), *A New Literary History of Australia.*

[51]Bronwen Levy, 'Constructing the Woman Writer', in Carole Ferrier (ed.), *Gender, Politics and Fiction*, 179-99.

[52]Sneja Gunew, 'Migrant Women Writers: Who's on Whose Margins?', in Ferrier (ed.), 163-78.

[53]Sneja Gunew, 'Framing Marginality', *Southern Review*, 18, 2 (July 1985), 142-57.

[54]Patricia Grimshaw, 'Women in History: Reconstructing the Past' in Goodnow and Pateman (eds), 32-55.

[55]Marilyn Lake, 'The Politics of Respectability: Identifying the Masculinist Context', *Historical Studies*, 22 (1986), 116-31.

[56]Lake, 122.

[57]Judith Allen, 'Evidence and Silence: Feminism and the Limits of History' in Carole Pateman and Elizabeth Gross (eds), *Feminist Challenges*, 173-204.

[58]Allen, 188-9.

[59]See articles by Genevieve Lloyd, 'Selfhood, war and masculinity', 63-77; Moira Gatens, 'Feminism, Philosophy and Riddles without Answers', 13-29; and Elizabeth Grosz, 'Philosophy, Subjectivity and the Body', 125-43, in Pateman and Grosz (eds).

CHAPTER 4

[1]W. K. Hancock, *Australia*, 1.

[2]Luce Irigaray, 'This Sex Which is Not One', trans. by Claudia Reeder in Elaine Marks and Isabelle de Courtivron (eds), *New French Feminisms*, 105.

[3]Tim Rowse, *Australian Liberalism and National Character*, 1-20.

[4]R. W. Connell, 'Images of Australia', *Quadrant*, 52 (March-April, 1968), 15.

[5]Anne Summers, *Danmed Whores and God's Police*, 58.

[6]For an exception to the rule, see Susan Gardner 'My Brilliant Career – Portrait of the Artist as a Wild Colonial Girl' in Carol Ferrier (ed.), *Gender, Politics and Fiction*, 42-3. Gardner examines women's writing in terms of Anglo-American feminist archetypal criticism. She acknowledges that colonial writing evokes the feminine metaphor for the land and examines significant differences between male and female writers with particular reference to Miles Franklin's two novels, *My Brilliant Career* and *Childhood at Brindabella*.

[7]Tzvetan Todorov, *The Conquest of America*, trans. by Richard Howe, 157.

[8]Roland Barthes, *The Pleasure of the Text*, trans. by Richard Miller, 37.

[9]Michel Foucault, *The History of Sexuality*, vol. 1: *An Introduction*, trans. by Robert Hurley, 100-1.

[10]Michel Foucault, 'Nietzsche, Genealogy, History', in *Language, Counter-Memory, Practice*, trans. by Donald F. Bouchard and Sherry Simon, 139-64.

[11]William Dampier, *A Continuation of a Voyage to New Holland*, quoted in Ross Gibson, *The Diminishing Paradise*, 10.

[12]John Locke, *Second Treatise on Government* (London, 1689), Section 35 in Peter Laslett (ed.), *John Locke: Two Treatises on Government*, 310. Prime Minister Billy Hughes reiterated this moral imperative to settle and cultivate the land in his justification of the Commonwealth's acquisition of the Northern Territory and the post-World War I soldier resettlement schemes. He said, 'God had never intended us to retain the Territory unless we were able to use it. We must either settle the country . . . or allow someone else to do so'. (*Australian Public Documents*, 1926, (112), 419, cited in R. L. Heathcote, 'Images of a desert? Perceptions of Arid Australia', *Australian Geographic Studies*, 25 (Apr.1987), 6.

[13]Lenore Coltheart, 'Australian Misère: The Northern Territory in the Nineteenth Century', Ph.D. Thesis, Griffith University, Brisbane, Queensland, Dec. 1982, 65-6.

[14]John Lort Stokes, *Discoveries in Australia: with an account of the coasts and rivers explored and surveyed during the voyage of H.M.S. Beagle, in the years 1837-43 . . .* 2 vols (London, 1846), quoted in Coltheart, 47.

[15]Stokes, *Discoveries . . .*, quoted in Coltheart, 43.

[16]*Sydney Morning Herald* (28 March 1845), quoted in Coltheart, 53.

[17]James Collier, *The Pastoral Age in Australia*, 95.

[18]William Harcus (ed.), *South Australia: Its History, Resources and Productions* (London, 1876), quoted in Coltheart, 71.

[19]J. G. Knight (ed.), *The Northern Territory of South Australia* (Adelaide, 1880), quoted in Coltheart, 71.

[20]Hancock, 51.

[21]Hancock, 1.

[22]Hancock, 21.

[23]Hancock, 9.

[24]Hancock, 23.

[25]See J. B. Hirst, 'The Pioneering Legend', *Historical Studies*, 17, 71 (Oct. 1978), 316.

[26]H. P. Heseltine, 'The Literary Heritage', in C.B. Christesen (ed.), *On Native Grounds*, 12.

[27]Heseltine, 10.

[28]Heseltine, 10.

[29]Heseltine, 30.

[30]Humphrey McQueen, *A New Britannia ?*, 17.

[31]Wentworth, quoted in McQueen, 'Foreword'.

[32]Harpur, quoted in McQueen, 'Foreword'.

[33]McQueen, 11.

[34]McQueen, 14.

[35]See C. M. H. Clark, *A History of Australia*, vol. IV, 50.

[36]Samuel Sidney, quoted in J. M. Powell, *Mirrors of the New World: Images and Image-Makers in the Settlement Process*, 73.

[37]Hancock, 45.

[38]Hancock, 35.

[39]Hancock, 36.

[40]Hancock, 36.

[41]Hancock, 40-1.

[42]Collier, 129-130.

[43]Collier, 95.

[44]Vance Palmer, *The Legend of the Nineties*, 38.

[45]Palmer, 38.

[46]Russel Ward, *The Australian Legend*, 121. For a fuller discussion of the history of the Chinese presence on the goldfields see Clark, *History*, IV, 113-18, and C. F. Yong, *The New Gold Mountain: The Chinese in Australia*, 171-89.

[47]Hancock, 244.

[48]For a fuller discussion see Tim Rowse, 'The Production of Hancock's *Australia*', in *Australian Liberalism and National Character*, 89-94. It is interesting to note the differences between the depiction of sexual relations between the women at the goldfields and Australian diggers as compared to American women and the California goldminers. In the Australian tradition there is no equivalent to Miss

Kitty of 'Gunsmoke' fame or 'the Unsinkable Molly Brown'—both mythic embodiments of the American 'whore with the heart of gold'. Metaphors for the land within the American tradition parallel those through which women are represented. Annette Kolodny studies feminine metaphors in colonial American landscape representation in her book *The Lady of the Land* (Chapel Hill, N. C.: University of North Carolina Press, 1975). Although she does not treat the gold rush, her analysis of colonial landscape metaphors makes an interesting comparison with those detailed here in relation to the Australian colonial period.

[49]Lloyd Ross, 'A New Social Order' quoted in Rowse, 133.

[50]Ian Turner, *Room for Manoeuvre: Writings on History, Politics, Ideas, and Play* (Richmond, Vic.: Drummond, 1982), 12.

[51]Clark, *History*, IV, 55.

[52]Clark, 54.

[53]Clark, 58.

[54]Clark, 56.

[55]Clark, *A History of Australia*, V, 1.

[56]Clark, *History*, IV, 406.

[57]It has been suggested that both Richardson and Clark consulted the same historical source, William Howitt's *Land, Labour and Gold* (Longman, Brown, Green and Longmans, 1855) which is a firsthand, detailed and authoritative text, as the basis for their accounts of the gold rush. This may be the case. Nonetheless, Howitt's account, although critical of the cupidity, crudity and rapacious instincts of some of the diggers, remains tied to a progressive ideology of British imperialism not shared by Richardson or Clark. The metaphoric references to the land as an enduring, maternal, punishing presence and the men who lusted after it with an unholy hunger are literary conventions adopted in Richarson's fiction and reiterated in Clark's history.

[58]Graeme Turner in *National Fictions* discusses the problem of mateship which he sees as an attack on difference and a deference to the values of the community rather than the self. Since he focuses on the construction of character within the Australian tradition, these connections are not pursued in his study. See 98-105.

[59]Teresa deLauretis, *Alice Doesn't: Feminism, Semiotics and Cinema*, 8.

[60]Henry Handel Richardson, *The Fortunes of Richard Mahony*, 13.

[61]Richardson, 16.

[62]Richardson, 928.

[63]H. M. Green, *A History of Australian Literature*, vol. I, 606.

[64]Heseltine, 'Review: "Images of Society and Nature",' *Meanjin*, 31, 1 (Mar. 1972), 18.

[65]See Katharine Susannah Prichard, *Coonardoo*, Eleanor Dark, *The Timeless Land* and Mary Durack, *Keep Him My Country*.

[66]Dark, *The Timeless Land* (Melbourne: Collins, 1980 rpt) 55, 112-13.

[67]Dark,195.

[68]Dark, 505.

[69]Prichard, *Coonardoo* (Sydney: Angus and Robertson,1973 rpt), 200.

[70]Susan Sheridan, 'Women Writers', in L. T. Hergenhan (ed.), *A New Literary History of Australia*.

[71]Durack, *Keep Him My Country*. (Adelaide: Rigby, 1975 rpt), foreword.

[72]See Hélène Cixous, 'Sorties', in Elaine Marks and Isabelle de Courtivron (eds), *New French Feminisms*, 96.

[73]David McKee Wright quoted on the dust jacket of Manning Clark, *In Search Of Henry Lawson*.

CHAPTER 5

[1]David McKee Wright, Preface to Henry Lawson's *Selected Poems* (Sydney, 1918) quoted in Denton Prout, *Henry Lawson: The Grey Dreamer*, 274.

[2]Vance Palmer, *The Legend of the Nineties*, 11.

[3]Manning Clark, *In Search of Henry Lawson* (South Melbourne: Macmillan, 1978), Preface.

[4]Colin Roderick, *The Real Henry Lawson*, 200 and fly leaf.

[5]Henry Lawson, quoted in Roderick, *The Real*, 179. For details on Lawson's deterioriation, see Prout, 274 ff.

[6]Clark, 66, 102.

[7]Henry Lawson in Colin Roderick (ed.), *Henry Lawson: Collected Verse*, vol. II, 269. Hereafter referred to as *C.V.* II.

[8]Henry Lawson in Colin Roderick (ed.), Henry Lawson *Collected Verse*, vol. I, 235. Hereafter referred to as *C.V.* I

[9]Lawson in Roderick (ed.), *C.V.* I, 'The Helpless Mothers', 15.

[10]David McKee Wright, quoted in Prout, 274. The three paragraphs of the Wright preface cited here are reprinted in full in Prout's biography of Lawson. Excerpts from these paragraphs also appear, their legendary views affirmed, in the critical studies of Lawson by Colin Roderick and Manning Clark.

[11]Wright in Prout, 274-75.

[12]See Richard White, *Inventing Australia: Images and Identity, 1688-1980*, 83, 103, 125 and chapters on 'The National Type', 'Bohemians and the Bush', and 'Diggers and Heroes', for a fuller discussion of these issues.

[13]Wright, in Prout, 275.

[14]Roderick, *The Real*, 176.

[15]Prout, 274.

[16]For a fuller discussion see Roderick, *The Real*, 176-7. Roderick, himself, is responsible for the reconstruction and editing of the unexpurgated Lawson.

[17]H. M. Green, *A History of Australian Literature*, vol. II, quoted in Prout, 275.

[18]See Roderick (ed.), *C.V.* I, 123, 129, 224, 54.

[19]Lawson in Roderick (ed.), *C.V.* I, 1.

[20]Lawson in Roderick (ed.), *C.V.* I, 361.

[21]Colin Roderick (ed.), *Henry Lawson: Short Stories and Sketches, 1888-1922*, 'Send Round the Hat', 480. Hereafter referred to as *S.S.S.*

[22]Lawson in Roderick (ed.), *S.S.S.*, 'In a Wet Season', 160-2.

[23]Lawson in Roderick (ed.), *S.S.S.*, 'The Selector's Daughter', 59-66. It is interesting to compare the early family interactions between the husband and wife in this story with those of 'A Child in the Dark, and a Foreign Father', 680-5. This tale, written in 1893, depicts the mother in a favorable light. The later tale,

written in 1902 and assumed to be an 'accurate' depiction of the Lawson household, does not. Yet, the construction of the family life is similar enough in the two stories for critics to assume that the same model was used to represent the two versions.

[24]Lawson in Roderick (ed.), *S.S.S.*, 'The Babies in the Bush', 403-15.

[25]Lawson in Roderick (ed.), *S.S.S.*, 'No Place for a Woman', 397-402.

[26] Lawson, in Roderick (ed.), *S.S.S.*, 'The Bush Undertaker', 57.

[27] Lawson, 57.

[28]H. P. Heseltine, 'Saint Henry: Our Apostle of Mateship', *Quadrant*, 5, 1 (Summer 1960-1), 8.

[29]Brian Matthews, *The Receding Wave: Henry Lawson's Prose*, 18-27.

[30]Lawson in Roderick (ed.), *S.S.S.*,'Water Them Geraniums', 569-86.

[31]Matthews, 27.

[32]Matthews, 182.

[33]Lawson in Roderick (ed.), *S.S.S.*, 'Water Them Geraniums', 572, 573.

[34]Lawson in Roderick (ed.), *S.S.S.*, 'Mitchell on the "Sex" and Other "Problems",' 303-64.

[35]Lawson in Roderick (ed.), *S.S.S.*, 'Mitchell . . .', 305.

[36]Lawson in Roderick (ed.), *S.S.S.*, 'Mitchell . . .', 306.

[37]Lawson in Roderick, *The Real*, 7.

[38]Clark, 61.

[39]Edward Garnett, 'Academy and Literature' (London, 8 March 1902) in Colin Roderick (ed.), *Henry Lawson Criticism, 1894-1971*, 124. Hereafter referred to as *H.L.C.*

[40]For a discussion see Brian Kiernan, 'From Mudgee Hills to London Town: A Critical Biography of Henry Lawson', in *The Essential Henry Lawson: The Best Works of Australia's Greatest Writer*, 12.

[41]White, 110.

[42]A. G. Stephens, 'Art in Australia', Sydney, Nov. 1922 in Roderick (ed.), *H.L.C.*, 235.

[43]White, 119.

[44]Fred Davison (1924), quoted in John Barnes, 'What has he Done for Our National Spirit?'—A Note on Lawson Criticism', *Australian Literary Studies*, 8, 4 (Oct. 1978), 486.

[45]For a discussion of the changing image of Australia after World War II see White, 'Young, White, Happy and Wholesome', 110-24.

[46]See R. L. Heathcote, 'Images of a Desert? Perceptions of Arid Australia', *Australian Geographical Studies*, 25 (April 1987), 7.

[47]Nettie Palmer, *Modern Australian Literature* (1924) excerpt in Roderick (ed.), *H.L.C.*, 235.

[48]Vance Palmer (1942), quoted in White, 153.

[49]Heseltine, 5.

[50]See, for example, articles by A. D. Hope, Vincent Buckley, Judith Wright and

Harry Heseltine in Grahame Johnston (ed.), *Australian Literary Criticism* and C. B. Christesen (ed.), *On Native Grounds*.

[51]H. P. Heseltine, 'The Literary Heritage', in Christesen, 15.

[52]Matthews, iii, 12.

[53]Roderick, quoted in Matthews, 15.

[54]Roderick, *The Real*, 33.

[55]Clark, 52. Compare these remarks with those made concerning the 'bush Mum' in C. M. H. Clark, *A History of Australia*, Vol. III, 272-3. Discussed in Chapter Three.

[56]Michael Roe, 'Challenges to Australian Identity and Esteem in Recent Historical Writing', *Tasmanian Historical Association: Papers and Proceedings* 25, 1 (Mar. 1978), 5.

[57]Lawson in Roderick (ed), *S.S.S.*, 'The Drover's Wife', 47-52. All quotations are taken from the source.

[58]Clark, *In Search of*, 52.

[59]Cited in Anne Summers, *Damned Whores and God's Police*, 38. Summers acknowledges Gilmore's reputation for being 'notoriously untruthful', however. This is a character trait which Roderick fails to mention when he credits Gilmore's veracity in asserting that Bertha Lawson provoked Henry's abusive behaviour. Gilmore, who is said to have had a crush on Lawson, blamed Bertha for the failure of their marriage.

[60]Roderick, *The Real*, 33.

[61]Prout, 51.

[62]Brian Matthews, 'Louisa and Henry and Gertie and the Drover's Wife', *Australian Literary Studies*, 9, 2 (May 1980), 286-97.

[63]See A. G. Stephens, 'A Poet's Mother', Red Page, *Bulletin*, 24 Oct. 1896 reprinted in Leon Cantrell (ed.), *A. G. Stephens: Selected Writings*, 268-71.

[64]E. J. Zinkhan, 'Louisa Lawson's "The Australian Bush-Woman"—A Source for "The Drover's Wife" and "Water them Geraniums"?', *Australian Literary Studies*, 10, 4 (Oct. 1982), 495-9.

[65]Zinkhan, 498.

[66]Louisa Lawson, 'The Australian Bush-Woman', Boston *Women's Journal* (27 July 1889), 233-4 and *Englishwoman's Review* (15 Aug. 1889), 383-4. The English version is reprinted in *Australian Literary Studies* 10, 4 (Oct. 1982), 500-3.

[67]See, for example, the Adelaide *Advertiser*, 'The Saturday Review', (4 Dec. 1982), 31, 34 and successive articles on 6-7 Dec. 1982.

[68]Prout, 17.

[69]Caroline Chisholm, 'Emigration and Transportation Relatively Considered', (1847), quoted in Summers, Prologue.

[70]Roderick disagrees. He claims that the story is part of the Lawson myth. See *The Real*, 7.

[71]Stephen Murray-Smith, *Henry Lawson*.

[72]Murray-Smith, 16.

[73]Murray-Smith, 15.

[74]Prout, 203.

[75]Murray-Smith, 10. A. G. Stephens' contemporary assessment supports this view. See his article, 'A Poet's Mother'.

[76]Roderick, *The Real*, 107.

[77]Clark, *In Search of*, 75, 113.

[78]Manning Clark, 'Henry Lawson' in Leonie Kramer, Russel Ward, Trevor Kennedy, Ray Martin and Richard Walsh (eds), *The Greats: The 50 Men and Women who Most Helped to Shape Modern Australia*, 74-9.

[79]Desmond O'Grady, 'Henry Lawson', in Chris Wallace-Crabbe (ed.) *The Australian Nationalists: Modern Critical Essays*, 73.

[80]Prout, 21.

[81]Prout, 16.

[82]Clark, *In Search of*, 9.

[83]See Prout, 139 and Roderick, *The Real*, 68.

[84]Prout claims that Bertha resisted the marriage, until Henry tricked her with a poem and a surprise visit to the registry where they were married without parental consent. But Roderick maintains that Bertha wanted the marriage and was not content until 'she had her way'.

[85]Prout, 138.

[86]Clark, *In Search of*, 70

[87]Roderick, 112.

[88]O'Grady, 80, 81.

[89]A. A. Phillips, 'The Craftsmanship of Lawson', in *The Australian Tradition*, 6. Compare this fulsome assessment of Lawson's craft with Phillips' critique of Barbara Baynton, 75-7, discussed in Chapter 6.

[90]Phillips, 16.

[91]Phillips, 'Lawson Revisited', 22.

[92]Phillips, 31.

[93]Phillips, 26.

CHAPTER 6

[1]A. A. Phillips, 'Barbara Baynton and the Dissidence of the Nineties', in *The Australian Tradition*,72.

[2]Phillips, 72.

[3]H. B. Gullett, 'Memoir of Barbara Baynton', in *Bush Studies*, 5.

[4]H. M. Green, *A History of Australian Literature*, Vol. I, 562.

[5]For details of Baynton's life see Sally Krimmer and Alan Lawson, 'Introduction', *Portable Australian Authors: Barbara Baynton*, ix-xxxi.

[6]See A. A. Phillips, 'Barbara Baynton's Stories', in *Bush Studies*, 29-42; Krimmer and Lawson, 'Introduction'; John McLaren, 'Loneliness and Vulnerability', *Australian Book Review*, 23 (Aug. 1980), 6; and Green, 561-2.

[7]Lucy Frost, interview on ABC Radio, 'Coming Out Show: Women and the Bush', 11 Oct. 1982. See also Lucy Frost, *No Place for a Nervous Lady: Voices from the Australian Bush*.

[8]Krimmer and Lawson, xxv.

[9]Krimmer and Lawson, xix.

[10]See 'Billy Skywonkie' in *Bush Studies*, 94. All references are taken from this text, 93-109.

[11]Krimmer and Lawson, xxiii.

[12]Green, 562.

[13]Barbara Baynton, 'The Chosen Vessel', *Bush Studies*, 132-40. For ease of reference to both Phillips' essay on Baynton and the text of the short story, this analysis will quote from both Phillips' essay, 'Barbara Baynton's Stories', which appears as a foreword to *Bush Studies*, and the version of the story 'The Chosen Vessel' which appears therein, unless otherwise indicated.

[14]A discussion of Stephens' review appears in A. A. Phillips, 'Barbara Baynton's Stories', *Bush Studies*, 36.

[15]See Krimmer and Lawson, 'Introduction', for details on correspondence between Baynton and Stephens and an analysis of Stephens' revisions to Baynton's texts.

[16]Phillips, 'Barbara Baynton's Stories', 36.

[17]Phillips first delivered a Commonwealth Literary Fund lecture in 1961 on Barbara Baynton which was published in *Overland* as 'Barbara Baynton and the Dissidence of the Nineties'. The article was included as a full new chapter in Phillips' 1966 edition of *The Australian Tradition* and reprinted in *The Australian Nationalists: Modern Critical Essays*, edited by Chris Wallace-Crabbe in 1971. A slightly revised version entitled 'Barbara Baynton's Stories', has introduced the 1965, 1971 and 1980 Angus and Robertson editions of *Bush Studies*.

[18]Phillips, 40.

[19] A brief but similar critique is offered by Vicki Steer in her article 'Australian National Identity, Rectifying an All-male Perspective', in *Women and Labour Papers*. I developed my analysis independently of Ms Steer's, although I would like to acknowledge her prior and similar work.

[20]Adrian Mitchell, 'Fiction' in Leonie Kramer (ed.), *The Oxford History of Australian Literature*, 75.

[21]Phillips, *The Australian Tradition*, 1-17.

[22]Krimmer and Lawson, xix.

[23]Krimmer and Lawson, xxiii.

[24]Krimmer and Lawson, xxv.

[25]Julia Kristeva, *Polylogues*, trans. by Josette Féral in 'The Powers of Difference', in Hester Eisenstein and Alice Jardine (eds), *The Future of Difference*, 92-3.

CHAPTER 7

[There are no notes for Chapter 7]

BIBLIOGRAPHY

Anon. 'Harry Butler. "I'm not a Turncoat" '; *News* (Adelaide), 29 Nov., 1986.

Auchmuty, Rosemary. 'The Truth about Sex', *Australian Popular Culture*, 169-189. Edited by Peter Spearitt and David Walker. Sydney: George Allen and Unwin, 1979.

Barrie, Lita. 'Further Toward a Deconstruction of Phallic Univocality Deferrals', in *Art Gallery & Museums Association of New Zealand Journal*, 17, 4 (Summer 1986-7), 3-12.

Barnes, John. 'Australian Fiction to 1920', *The Literature of Australia*, 134-80. Edited by Geoffrey Dutton. Ringwood, Vic.: Penguin, 1976.

_____. ' "What has he Done for Our National Spirit?" – A Note on Henry Lawson Criticism', *Australian Literary Studies* 8, 4 (Oct. 1978), 485-91.

Barthes, Roland. *Image, Music, Text*. New York: Hill and Wang, 1977.

_____. *Mythologies*. London: Jonathan Cape, 1972.

_____. *The Pleasure of the Text*. Trans. by Richard Millen. New York: Hill and Wang, 1975.

_____. *S/Z*. New York: Hill and Wang, 1977.

Baynton, Barbara. *Bush Studies*. Sydney: Angus and Robertson, 1965, rpt. 1980. Stories cited: 'A Dreamer', 45-53; 'Billy Skywonkie', 93-109; 'Bush Church', 110-31; 'Scrammy 'And', 72-92; 'Squeaker's Mate', 54-71; 'The Chosen Vessel', 132-40.

_____. *Human Toll*. In *Portable Australian Authors : Barbara Baynton*, 115-300. Edited by Sally Krimmer and Alan Lawson. St. Lucia, Qld: University of Queensland Press, 1980.

_____. 'The Tramp', *Bulletin*, 12 Dec. 1896, 32.

Bird, Delys. 'Australian Woman: A National Joke?', *Australian Journal of Cultural Studies* 1, 1 (May 1983), 111-14.

Bolton Geoffrey. *Spoils and Spoilers*. Sydney: George Allen and Unwin,1981.

Botsman, Peter. 'From Deserts Structuralists Come', *Foreign Bodies Papers*, 39-53. Edited by Peter Botsman, Chris Burns and Peter Hutchings. Leichhardt, N.S.W.: Local Consumption, 1981.

Brady, Veronica. 'Review of Graeme Turner's "National Fictions" ', 89-92. *Westerly*, 3 (Sept. 1987)

Brass, Ken and Peter Ward. 'Kakadu: Australia's Best Kept Secret'. *The Australian*, 24 May 1986.

Brown, Malcolm. 'Prisoner of Prejudice, Part Two: The Fight to Free Lindy', *National Times*, 22-26 Nov. 1985, 21-2.

Bryson, John. *Evil Angels*. Ringwood, Vic.: Penguin, 1985.

Buckley, Vincent. 'Foreword' to *The Receding Wave: Henry Lawson's Press* by Brian Matthews. Melbourne: Melbourne University Press, 1972.

_____. 'Utopianism and Vitalism', *Quadrant*, 3, 2 (1958-9) reprinted in *Australian*

Literary Criticism, 16-29. Edited by Grahame Johnston. Melbourne: Oxford University Press, 1962.

Burns, Graham. 'Bruce Pascoe: Writer with a Lawson Style', 33. *National Times on Sunday*, 10 Oct. 1986.

Butterfield, Herbert. *The Whig Interpretation of History*. Ringwood, Vic.: Penguin, 1973.

Callinan, Suzanne. 'Jury of her Peers,' 166-8, *Legal Services Bulletin*, 9, 4 (Aug. 1984).

Cantrell, Leon. *The 1980's: Stories, Verse, and Essays*. St Lucia, Qld: University of Queensland Press, 1977.

――――. ed. *A. G. Stephens: Selected Writings*. Sydney: Angus and Robertson, 1978.

――――. ed. *Bards, Bohemians, and Bookmen: Essays in Australian Literature*. St Lucia, Qld: University of Queensland Press, 1976.

Carroll, John, ed. *Intruders in the Bush: The Australian Quest for Identity*. Melbourne: Oxford University Press, 1982.

Carter, Paul. *The Road to Botany Bay: An Essay in Spatial History*. London: Faber and Faber, 1987.

Christesen, C.B., ed. *On Native Grounds: Australian Writing from 'Meanjin' Quarterly*. Sydney: Angus and Robertson, 1968.

Cixous, Hélène. 'Castration or Decapitation?' Trans. by Annette Kuhn. *Signs: A Journal of Women and Culture*, 7, 1 (Autumn 1981), 41-55.

――――. 'Demystifications: Sorties', *New French Feminisms: An Anthology*, 90-8. Edited by Elaine Marks and Isabelle de Courtivron. Amherst, Mass.: University of Massachusetts Press, 1980.

――――. 'La Jeune Née: An Excerpt,' Trans. by Meg Bortin. *Diacritics* (June 1977), 64-9.

――――. 'The Laugh of the Medusa', Trans. by Keith Cohen and Paula S. Cohen. *Signs : A Journal of Women and Culture*, 1, 4 (Summer 1976), 875-93.

――――. 'Poetry is/and (the) Political', *Bread and Roses*, 2, 1 (1980), 16-18.

Clark, C.M.H. *A History of Australia*. 5 vols. Melbourne: Melbourne University Press, 1973-81.

――――. 'Henry Lawson', *The Greats: The 50 Men and Women who Most Helped to Shape Modern Australia*, 74-9. Edited by Leonie Kramer, Russel Ward, Trevor Kennedy, Ray Martin and Richard Walsh. Sydney: Angus and Robertson, 1986.

――――. *In Search of Henry Lawson*. South Melbourne: Macmillan, 1978.

Clark, Manning, *see* Clark, C. M. H.

Clark, Roxanne. 'Turning Wild about Harry', *Advertiser* (Adelaide), 6 Dec. 1986.

Clarke, Marcus. 'The Australian Landscape: Comments on Two Paintings', *A Colonial City: High and Low Life—Selected Journalism of Marcus Clarke*, 363-47. Edited by L.T. Hergenhan. St. Lucia, Qld.: University of Queensland Press, 1972.

――――. 'Preface' to A. L. Gordon, *Sea Spray and Smoke Drift*. Melbourne: Clarson, Massina, 1876.

Collier, James. *The Pastoral Age in Australia*. London: Whitcombe and Tombs, 1911.

Coltheart, Lenore. 'Australian Misère: the Northern Territory in the Nineteenth Century', Ph.D. thesis, Griffith University, Brisbane, Queensland, 1982.

Connell, R. W. 'Images of Australia', *Quadrant*, 52 (March-April 1968), 9-19.

BIBLIOGRAPHY

Conway, Ronald. *The Great Australian Stupor*. Melbourne: Sun Books, 1971.
Coster, Peter. 'Riches Beneath an Ancient Land', *Advertiser* (Adelaide), 25 Sept. 1986, 23.
Coward, Rosalind. *Female Desire: Women's Sexuality Today*. London: Paladin, 1984.
_____ . 'Re-reading Freud: The Making of the Feminine', *Spare Rib* (May 1978), 43-6.
_____ and John Ellis. *Language and Materialism: Developments in Semiology and the Theory of the Subject*. London: Routledge and Kegan Paul, 1977.
Cowie, Elizabeth. 'Woman as Sign', *m/f*, 1 (1978), 49-63.
Craig, Carolyn. 'Colonial Women Writers: Barbara Baynton', *Refractory Girl*, 17 (1979), 33-4.
Craik, Jennifer. 'The Azaria Chamberlain Case and Questions of Infanticide', *Australian Journal of Cultural Studies*, 4, 2 (May 1987), 123-51.
Creed, Barbara. 'Horror and the Monstrous Feminine: An Imaginary Abjection', *Screen*, 27, 1 (Feb. 1986), 44-71.
Culler, Jonathan. *The Pursuit of Signs: Semiotics, Literature, Deconstruction*. London and Henley: Routledge and Kegan Paul, 1981.

Daniels, Kay, and Mary Murnane, eds. *Uphill all the Way: A Documentary History of Women in Australia*. St Lucia, Qld: University of Queensland Press, 1980.
_____ , Mary Murnane and Anne Picot, eds. *Women in Australia: An Annotated Guide to the Records*. 2 vols. Canberra: Australian Government Publishing Service, 1977.
Dark, Eleanor. *The Timeless Land*. London and Sydney: Collins, 1941, rpt 1973.
Davis, Robert Con. 'The Discourse of the Father', *The Fictional Father: Lacanian Readings of the text*, 1-26. Edited by Robert Con Davis. Amherst, Mass.: University of Massachusetts Press, 1981.
Davison, Graeme. 'Sydney and the Bush: An Urban Context for the Australian Legend', *Historical Studies*, 17, 71 (Oct. 1978), 191-209.
deLauretis, Teresa. *Alice Doesn't: Feminism, Semiotics, Cinema*. Bloomington, Indiana: Indiana University Press, 1982.
de Man, Paul. *Blindness and Insight*. New York: Oxford University Press, 1971.
_____ . 'Semiology and Rhetoric', *Diacritics* (Fall, 1971), 27-33.
Dermody, Susan, John Docker and Drusilla Modjeska, eds. *Nellie Melba, Ginger Meggs and Friends : Essays in Australian Cultural History*. Malmsbury, Victoria: Kibble Books, 1982.
Derrida, Jacques. *Dissemination*. Trans. with Introduction by Barbara Johnson. Chicago: University of Chicago Press, 1981.
_____ . *Of Grammatology*. Trans. with Introduction by Gayatra Spivak. Baltimore: Johns Hopkins Press, 1976.
_____ . 'The Purveyors of Truth', *Yale French Studies*, 52 (1976), 31-115.
_____ . *Spurs*. English trans. by Barbara Harlow. Introduction by Stefano Agosti. Chicago: University of Chicago Press, 1979.
_____ . *Writing and Difference*. Trans. with Introduction and Notes by Alan Bass. Chicago: University of Chicago Press, 1978.
Dixon, Robert. *The Course of Empire: Neo-Classical Culture in New South Wales, 1788-1860*. Melbourne: Oxford University Press, 1986.
Dixson, Miriam. *The Real Matilda*. Ringwood, Vic.: Penguin, 1976.

Docker, John. 'Australian Literature of the 1890's', *An Introduction to Australian Literature*, 7-22. Edited by C. D. Narasimhaiah. Brisbane: John Wiley & Sons, 1982.
———. *In a Critical Condition*. Ringwood, Vic.: Penguin, 1984.
Durack, Mary. *Keep Him My Country*. London: Constable, 1955, rpt Adelaide: Rigby, 1977.
Dutton, Geoffrey, ed. *The Literature of Australia*. Harmondsworth, Mddx: Penguin, 1964.

Eisenstein, Hester, and Alice Jardine, eds. *The Future of Difference*. Boston, Mass.: G.K. Hall & Co., 1980.
Elliott, Brian, and Adrian Mitchell, compilers. *Bards in the Wilderness: Australian Colonial Poetry to 1920*. Melbourne: Nelson, 1970.
Encel, Sol, Norman MacKenzie and Margaret Tebbutt. *Women and Society: An Australian Study*. Melbourne: Cheshire, 1974.

Felman, Soshana. 'Turning the Screw of Interpretation', *Yale French Studies*, 55-6 (1977), 94-208.
———. 'Women and Madness: The Critical Phallacy'. *Diacritics*, 5, 4 (Winter 1975), 2-10.
Féral, Josette. 'The Powers of Difference', *The Future of Difference*, 88-94. Edited by Hester Eisenstein and Alice Jardine. Boston, Mass.: G.K. Hall & Co., 1980.
Ferrier, Carole, ed. *Gender, Politics and Fiction: Twentieth Century Australian Women's Novels*. St Lucia, Qld: University of Queensland Press, 1985.
Fisher, Andrew. 'A Treasure Chest Buried Under a National Park'. *Advertiser* (Adelaide), 19 Sept. 1986.
Flanagan, Martin,'The Spectator at Play', *Advertiser*, Magazine section (11 Oct. 1986), 5.
Flood, Josephine. *Archaeology of the Dreamtime: The Story of Prehistoric Australia and Her People*. Sydney: Collins, 1983.
Foss, Paul. 'Theatrun Nondum Cognitorum', *The Foreign Bodies Papers*, 15-38. Edited by Peter Botsman, Chris Burns and Peter Hutchings, 1981.
Foucault, Michel. *The Archaeology of Knowledge*. Trans. by Alan Sheridan. London: Tavistock, 1976; New York: Pantheon, 1972.
———. 'The Discourse on Language'. Trans. by Rupert Swyer. In *The Archaeology of Knowledge*. Trans. by Alan Sheridan. New York: Pantheon, 1972, Appendix.
———. *The History of Sexuality, Vol. 1: An Introduction*. Trans. by Robert Hurley. London: Allen Lane, 1979.
———. *Language, Counter-Memory, Practice*. Trans. by Donald Bouchard and Sherry Simon. Ithaca, New York: Cornell University Press, 1977.
———. *The Order of Things: An Archaeology of the Human Sciences*. New York: Random House, 1971.
———. 'Politics and the Study of Discourse', *Ideology and Consciousness*, 3 (1978), 7-26.
———. *Power/Knowledge: Selected Interviews and Other Writings, 1972-77*. Edited by Colin Gordon. New York: Pantheon, 1980.
———. 'What is an Author'. Trans. from French by Donald Bouchard and Sherry Simon. In *Language, Counter-Memory, Practice*, 113-18. Edited by Donald Bouchard. Ithaca: New York: Cornell University Press, 1977.

BIBLIOGRAPHY

Frost, Lucy. Interview on ABC Radio, 'Coming Out Show: Women and the Bush', ABC Radio, 11 Oct. 1982.

_____. *No Place for a Nervous Lady: Voices from the Australian Bush*. Fitzroy and Ringwood , Vic.: McPhee Gribble and Penguin, 1984.

Gardner, Susan. 'My Brilliant Career: Portrait of the Artist as a Wild Colonial Girl', *Gender, Politics and Fiction*, 22-43. Edited by Carole Ferrier. St. Lucia, Qld: University of Queensland Press, 1985.

Garnett, Edward. 'Academy and Literature', *Henry Lawson Criticism, 1894-1971*, 124. Edited by Colin Roderick. Sydney: Angus and Robertson, 1972.

Gibson, Ross. *The Diminishing Paradise: Changing Literary Perceptions of Australia*. Sydney: Angus and Robertson, 1984.

Greason, David. 'Celebration of Worn-out Myths', Review of *Australia: Spirit of a Nation, National Times*, (11-17 Oct. 1985) 35.

Green, H. M. *A History of Australian Literature*. 2 vols. Sydney: Angus and Robertson, 1961.

Grieve, Norma, and Patricia Grimshaw, eds. *Australian Women: Feminist Perspectives*. Melbourne: Oxford University Press, 1981.

Grimshaw, Patricia. 'Women in History: Reconstructing the Past'. *Women, Social Science and Public Policy*, 32-55. Edited by Jacqueline Goodnow and Carole Pateman, Sydney: George Allen and Unwin, 1985.

Gullett, H. B. 'Memoir of Barbara Baynton', *Bush Studies*. Sydney: Angus and Robertson, 1980, 3-25.

Gunew, Sneja. 'Feminist Criticism: Positions and Questions', *Southern Review*, 16 (1983), 151-61.

_____. 'Framing Marginality: Distinguishing the Textual Politics of the Marginal Voice', *Southern Review*, 18, 2 (July 1985), 142-57.

_____. 'Migrant Women Writers: Who's on Whose Margins?', *Gender, Politics and Fiction*,163-78. Edited by Carole Ferrier. St Lucia, Qld: University of Queensland Press, 1985.

_____. 'What does Woman Mean?: Reading, Writing and Reproduction', *Hecate*, 9, 1 and 2 (1983), 111-22.

Hancock, W. K. *Australia*. London: Benn, 1930; rpt Brisbane: Jacaranda, 1961.

Hapnell, Charles. 'War Memorial Dog Fight'. *Advertiser* (Adelaide), 27 Nov. 1986, 17.

Haran, Peter, 'Missing Boys: The Mystery Deepens', *Sunday Mail* (Adelaide), 4 Jan. 1987, 3.

Harris, Max. *The Angry Eye*. Sydney: Pergamon Press, 1973.

Hartman, Geoffrey H., ed. *Psychoanalysis and the Question of the Text*. Selected Papers from the English Institute, 1976-77. New Series, No. 2. Baltimore and London: Johns Hopkins University Press, 1978.

Hawley, Janet. 'The Lost Works of Henry Lawson', *Advertiser* (Adelaide), 4, 6-7 Dec. 1982, 31, 34.

Heath, Stephen. 'Difference', *Screen*, 19, 3 (Autumn 1978), 51-112.

Heathcote, R. L. 'Images of a Desert? Perceptions of Arid Australia', *Australian Geographical Studies*, 25 April 1987, 3-25.

Hergenhan, L. T., ed. *A Colonial City: High and Low Life—Selected Journalism of Marcus Clarke*. St Lucia, Qld: University of Queensland Press, 1972.

Heseltine, H. P. 'The Literary Heritage', *On Native Grounds: Australian Writings from 'Meanjin' Quarterly*, 3-16. Edited by C. B. Christesen. Sydney: Angus and Robertson, 1968.

───── . 'Review: "Images of Society and Nature: Seven Essays on Australian Novels",' *Meanjin*, 31, 1 (Mar. 1972), 18.

───── . 'Saint Henry, Own Apostle of Mateship', *Quadrant*, 5, 1 (Summer 1960-1), 5-11.

Hirst, J. B. 'The Pioneering Legend', *Historical Studies*, vol. 18, 71 (Oct. 1978), 316-37.

Hope, A. D. 'Standards in Australian Literature', *Australian Literary Criticism*, 1-15. Edited by Grahame Johnston. Melbourne: Oxford University Press, 1961.

Houghton, Walter. *The Victorian Frame of Mind*. New York: Yale University Press, 1957, rpt. 1978.

Howitt, William. *Land, Labour and Gold*. Longman, Brown, Green and Longmans, 1855. Rpt Kilmore, Vic.: Lowden Press, 1972.

Inglis, K. S. 'The Anzac Tradition', *On Native Grounds*, 205-22. Edited by C. B. Christesen. Sydney: Angus and Robertson, 1968.

Irigaray, Luce, 'And the One Doesn't Stir without the Other'. Trans. by Helene Vivienne Wenzel. *Signs: A Journal of Women and Culture*, 1, 7 (Autumn 1981), 60-7.

───── . 'Demystifications: This Sex Which is not One'. Trans. by Claudia Reeder. In *New French Feminisms*, 99-106. Edited by Elaine Marks and Isabelle de Courtivron. Amherst, Mass.: University of Massachusetts Press, 1980.

───── . *Speculum of the Other Woman*. Trans. Gillian C. Gill. Ithaca, NY: Cornell University Press, 1985.

───── . 'The Power of Discourse and the Subordination of the Feminine'. *This Sex which is not One*. Trans. by Catherine Porter. Ithaca, NY: Cornell University Press, 1985.

───── . *This Sex which is not One*. Trans. by Gillian C. Gill. Ithaca, NY: Cornell Univeristy Press, 1985.

───── . 'When Our Lips Speak Together'. Trans. by Carolyn Burke. *Signs*, 6, 1 (Autumn 1980), 69-79.

Iseman, Kay. 'Barbara Baynton: Woman as "The Chosen Vessel",' *Australian Literary Studies*, 11, 1 (May 1983), 25-37.

───── . 'Dream, Disillusion and the Australian Tradition'. *Meanjin*, 38, 3 (1979) 275-85.

───── . 'Katharine Susannah Prichard, "Coonardoo" and the Aboriginal Presence in Australian Fiction'. *Women and Labour Conference Papers*, vol. 2, Melbourne, 1980, 540-50.

───── . 'Katharine Susannah Prichard: Of the (sic) End a New Beginning'. *Arena*, 54 (1979), 70-96.

Jameson, Frederic. 'Imaginary and Symbolic in Lacan: Marxism, Psychoanalytic Criticism, and the Problem of the Subject', *Yale French Studies*, 55-6 (1977), 338-95.

Johnson, Dianne. 'From Fairy to Witch: Imagery and Myth in the Azaria Case', *Australian Journal of Cultural Studies*, 2, 2 (Nov. 1984), 90-107.

Johnston, Grahame, ed. *Australian Literary Criticism*. Melbourne: Oxford University Press, 1962.

Jones, Ann Rosalind. 'Inscribing Femininity: French Theories of the Feminine' , *Making the Difference: Feminist Literary Criticism*. Edited by Gayle Green and Coppelia Kahn. New York: Macmillan, 1985, 80-112.

Kiernan, Brian. *Images of Society and Nature: Seven Essays on Australian Novels*. Melbourne: Oxford University Press, 1971.

_____ . 'Literature, History, and Literary History: Perspectives on the Nineteenth Century in Australia', *Bards, Bohemians and Bookmen*, 1-18. Edited by Leon Cantrell. St Lucia, Qld: University of Queensland Press, 1976.

_____ , ed. *The Essential Henry Lawson: The Best Works of Australia's Greatest Writer*. South Yarra, Vic.: Currey O'Neill, 1982.

Kingston, Beverley. *My Wife, My Daughter and Poor Mary Ann*. Melbourne: Nelson, 1975.

_____ , ed. *The World Moves Slowly: A Documentary History of Australian Women*. Stanmore, N.S.W.: Cassell Australia, 1977.

Kissane, Karen. 'A Prisoner of Prejudice?', *National Times*, 15-21 Nov. 1985, 8-10, 15, 17.

Kramer, Leonie, ed. *The Oxford History of Australian Literature*. Melbourne: Oxford University Press, 1981.

Krimmer, Sally. 'New Light on Barbara Baynton'. Notes and Documents, *Australian Literary Studies*, 7, 4 (Oct. 1976), 425-31.

_____ . and Alan Lawson (eds). *Barbara Baynton*. Portable Australian Author Series. St Lucia, Qld: University of Queensland Press, 1980.

Kristeva, Julia. 'Creations: Oscillation between Power and Denial'. Trans. by Marilyn A. August. In *New French Feminisms*, 165-71. Edited by Elaine Marks and Isabelle de Courtivron. Amherst, Mass.: University of Massachusetts Press, 1980.

_____ . *Desire in Language: A Semiotic Approach to Literature and Art*. Edited by Leon S. Roudiez. Trans. by Thomas Gora, Alice Jardine and Leon S. Roudiez. New York: Columbia University Press, 1980.

_____ . *Polylogues*. Paris: Editions du Seuil, 1977.

_____ . *Powers of Horror: An Essay on Abjection*. Trans. by Leon S. Roudiez. New York: Columbia University Press, 1982.

Lacan, Jacques. 'A Love Letter'. In *Jacques Lacan and the Ecole Freudienne: Feminine Sexuality*. Trans. by Jacqueline Rose. Edited by Juliet Mitchell and Jacqueline Rose. New York: Macmillan, 1982, 137-48.

_____ . *Ecrits: A Selection*. Trans. by Alan Sheridan. New York: Norton, 1977.

_____ . 'God and the Jouissance of The Woman'. *Jacques Lacan and the Ecole Freudienne: Feminine Sexuality*. Trans. by Jacqueline Rose. Edited by Juliet Mitchell and Jacqueline Rose. New York: Macmillan, 1982, 137-48.

_____ . 'The Insistence of the Letter in the Unconscious', *Yale French Studies*, 36-7 (1966), 112-47 . Edited by J. Ehrmann,

_____ . 'The Mirror Phase', *New Left Review*, 51 (1968), 71-7.

_____ . 'The Signification of the Phallus.' In *Ecrits: A Selection*. Trans. by Alan Sheridan, 281-91. New York: W.W. Norton, 1977.

Lake, Marilyn. ' "Building themselves up with Aspros": Pioneer Women Reassessed', *Hecate*, 7, 2 (1981), 7-19.

_____ . 'The Politics of Respectability: Identifying the Masculine Context', *Historical Studies*, 22 (April 1986), 116-31.

BIBLIOGRAPHY

—————. 'Socialism and Manhood: The Case of William Lane', *Labour History*, 50 (May 1986), 54-62.

Lansbury, Carol. *Arcady in Australia: The Evocation of Australia in English Literature*. Carlton: Melbourne University Press, 1970.

Laslett, Peter, ed. *Locke: Two Treatises on Government*. Cambridge: Cambridge University Press, 1960.

Lawson, Henry. *While the Billy Boils*. Sydney, 1901. Rpt Windsor, Vic.: Currey O'Neill, 1980.

—————. *Collected Prose*, Vol. 2: *Autobiographical and other Writings 1887-1922*. Edited by Colin Roderick. Sydney: Angus and Robertson, 1972. Essays cited: 'Crime in the Bush', 32-6; 'The Bush and the Ideal', 31-2; 'The City and the Bush', 28-1; 'The She Devil', 273-7.

—————. *Collected Verse*, 3 vols. Edited by Colin Roderick. Sydney: Angus and Robertson, 1967-9. Poems cited: 'A Song of the Republic', I, 1; 'Freedom on the Wallaby', I, 123; 'How the Land was Won', I, 361; 'One-Hundred-and-Three', II, 269; 'Roaring Days', I, 54; 'The Helpless Mothers', I, 15; 'The Southern Scout', I, 224; 'Triumph of the People', I, 129; 'Waving of the Red', I, 235.

—————. *Short Stories and Sketches 1888-1922*. Edited by Colin Roderick. Sydney: Angus and Robertson, 1972. Stories cited: 'A Child in the Dark, and a Foreign Father', 680-5; 'A Double-Buggy at Lahey's Creek', 586-99; 'A Sketch of Mateship', 466-7; 'Brighten's Sister-in-Law', 555-68; 'Drifting Apart', 603-9; 'His Adopted Daughter', 178-81; 'His Country—After All', 201-3; 'His Mother's Mate', 42; 'Hungerford', 105-7; 'In a Wet Season', 160-2; 'Joe Wilson's Courtship', 537-55; 'Jones's Alley', 35-42; 'Mitchell on Matrimony', 287-90; 'Mitchell on the "Sex" and Other "Problems"', 303-6; 'Mitchell on Women', 290-3; 'No Place for a Woman', 397-402; 'Rats', 57-8; 'Send Round the Hat', 469-80; 'She Wouldn't Speak', 114-16; 'Telling Mrs. Baker', 415-24; 'That Pretty Girl in the Army', 481-92; 'The Babies in the Bush', 403-15; 'The Bush Undertaker', 52-7; 'The Drover's Wife', 47-52; 'The Hero of Red Clay', 293-303; 'The Iron Bark Chip', 329-32; 'The Loaded Dog', 332-6; 'The Romance of the Swag', 499-502; 'The Selector's Daughter', 59-66; 'The Shanty-Keeper's Wife', 263-7; 'The Shearing of the Cook's Dog', 94-6; 'Water Them Geraniums', 569-86.

Lawson, Louisa. 'The Australian Bush-Woman', *Englishwoman's Review*, 15 Aug. 1889, 383-4, and 15 Oct. 1889, 469-74. Originally printed in Boston *Women's Journal* (27 July 1889), 233-4. Reprinted in *Australian Literary Studies*, 10, 4 (Oct. 1982), 500-3.

Lawson, Sylvia. *The Archibald Paradox: A Strange Case of Authorship*. Ringwood, Vic.: Penguin, 1983.

—————. 'Please Don't Put The Boot Into Henry Lawson's Mum'. *National Times*, 15-21 Nov. 1986, 35.

Lee, S. E. '*The Bulletin*: J. F. Archibald and A. G. Stephens,' *The Literature of Australia*, 273-88. Edited by G. Dutton. Harmondsworth, Mddx: Penguin, 1964.

Levy, Bronwen. 'Constructing the Woman Writer: The Reviewing Reception of Hazzard's *The Transit of Venus*', *Gender, Politics and Fiction*, 179-99. Edited by Carole Ferrier. St Lucia, Qld: University of Queensland Press, 1985.

216

BIBLIOGRAPHY

Lindsay, Jack. 'Barbara Baynton: A Master of Naturalism'. *Decay and Renewal*. Sydney: Wild and Woolley Press, 1976, 262-6.

McGregor, Craig. *Profile of Australia*. Ringwood, Vic.: Penguin, 1968.

MacKenzie, Norman. *Women in Australia*. Melbourne: Cheshire, 1962.

McLaren, John. 'Loneliness and Vulnerability', *Australian Book Review*, 23 (August 1980), 6.

McQueen, Humphrey. *A New Britannia?*. Ringwood, Vic.: Penguin, 1970.

Maiden, A. N. 'Witch Hunt: Lindy and the Australian Psyche', *Time (Australia)*, 24 (15 June 1987), 32-35.

Mares, F. H. '*The Fortunes of Richard Mahony*: A Reconsideration', *On Native Grounds: Australian Writing from 'Meanjin' Quarterly*, 87-94. Edited by C. B. Christesen. Sydney: Angus and Robertson, 1968.

Marks, Elaine, and Isabelle de Courtivron, eds. *New French Feminisms: An Anthology*. Amherst, Mass.: University of Massachusetts Press, 1980.

Matthews, Brian. 'Henry Lawson's Fictional World', *Bards, Bohemians, and Bookmen: Essays in Australian Literature*, 170-200. Edited by L. Cantrell. St Lucia, Qld: University of Queensland Press, 1976.

_____. 'Introduction', *Henry Lawson: Selected Stories*. Adelaide: Rigby, 1971, i-xii.

_____. 'Lawson Scholars: The Sparks Fly'. *Advertiser* (Adelaide), 5 March 1983, 21.

_____. *Louisa*. Fitzroy, Vic.: McPhee-Gribble, 1987.

_____. 'Louisa and Henry and Gertie and the Drover's Wife', *Australian Literary Studies*, 9 (May 1980), 286-97.

_____. *The Receding Wave: Henry Lawson's Prose*. Melbourne: Melbourne University Press, 1972.

Matthews, Jill Julius. *Good and Mad Women: The Historical Construction of Femininity in Twentieth Century Australia*. Sydney: George Allen and Unwin, 1984.

Meek, Robert. *Social Science and the Ignoble Savage*. Cambridge: Cambridge University Press, 1976.

Metz, Christian. *Film Language: A Semiotics of the Cinema*. Trans. by Michael Taylor. New York: Oxford University Press, 1974.

Mitchell, Adrian. 'Fiction', *The Oxford History of Australian Literature*, 75. Edited by Leonie Kramer. Melbourne: Oxford University Press, 1981.

Mitchell, Juliet and Jacqueline Rose (eds). *Jacques Lacan and the École Freudienne: Feminine Sexuality*. London: Macmillan, 1982.

Moi, Toril. *Sexual/Textual Politics: Feminist Literary Theory*. London: Metheun, 1985.

Moore, T. Inglis. 'The Meanings of Mateship', *On Native Grounds: Australian Writing from 'Meanjin' Quarterly*. Edited by C. B. Christesen. Sydney: Angus and Robertson, 1968, 223-34.

_____. *Social Patterns in Australian Literature*. Sydney: Angus and Robertson, 1971.

Morris, Meaghan. 'Aspects of French Feminist Literary Criticism', *Hecate*, 5, 2 (1979), 63-72.

_____. 'The Pirate's Fiancee'. In *Michel Foucault: Power, Truth, Strategy*, 148-68. Edited by Paul Patton and Meaghan Morris. Sydney: Feral Publications, 1979.

_____. 'Two Types of Photographic Criticism Located in Relation to Lynne Silvermann's Series', *Art and Text*, 6 (1982), 61-73.

BIBLIOGRAPHY

Mulvey, Laura. 'Afterthoughts on "Visual Pleasure and Narrative Cinema", inspired by *Duel in the Sun* ', *Framework* 15-17 (1981), 12-15.
————. 'Visual Pleasure and Narrative Cinema', *Screen*, 16, 3 (Autumn 1975), 206-15.
Murray-Smith, Stephen. *Henry Lawson*. Melbourne: Oxford University Press, 1972.

O'Grady, Desmond. 'Henry Lawson', *The Australian Nationalists: Modern Critical Essays*, 69-84. Edited by Chris Wallace-Crabbe. Melbourne: Oxford University Press, 1971.
O'Hearn, D. J. 'Weeds grow Over a Culture's Hopes', *National Times on Sunday*, 11 Oct. 1986, 35.
Oliver, H. J. 'Lawson and Furphy', *The Literature of Australia*, 288-305. Edited by G. Dutton. Harmondsworth, Mddx: Penguin, 1964.
Ollif, Lorna. *Louisa Lawson: Henry Lawson's Crusading Mother*. Adelaide: Rigby, 1978.
Oxley, Harry. 'Ockerism: The Cultural Rabbit', *Australian Popular Culture*, 190-209. Edited by Peter Spearitt and David Walker. Sydney: George Allen and Unwin, 1979.

Palmer, Nettie. *Modern Australian Literature*. Melbourne and Sydney: Lothian, 1924.
Palmer, Vance. *Legend of the Nineties*. Melbourne: Melbourne University Press, 1954.
Phillips, A. A. *The Australian Tradition: Studies in a Colonial Culture*. Melbourne: Cheshire-Lansdowne, 1958; second edn. 1966.
————. 'Barbara Baynton and the Dissidence of the Nineties', *Overland*, 22 (Dec. 1961), 15-20, rpt in *The Australian Nationalists*, 149-58. Edited by Chris Wallace-Crabbe. Melbourne: Oxford University Press, 1971.
————. 'Barbara Baynton's Stories'. *Bush Studies*. Sydney: Angus and Robertson, 1965; rpt 1980, 29-42.
————. 'The Craftsmanship of Lawson', *The Australian Tradition*. Melbourne: Cheshire-Lansdowne, 1958, rev. edn, 1966, 1-16.
————. 'The Cross Eyed Clio: McQueen and the Australian Tradition', *Meanjin*, 30 (Jan. 1971), 108-13.
————. 'Henry Lawson as Craftsman' and 'The Literary Heritage Reassessed'. In *On Native Grounds: Australian Writing from 'Meanjin' Quarterly*, 63-74, and 17-26. Edited by C. B. Christesen. Sydney: Angus and Robertson, 1968.
————. 'Lawson Revisited', *The Australian Nationalists*, 85-99. Edited by Chris Wallace-Crabbe. Melbourne: Oxford University Press, 1971.
Pike, Andrew, and Ross Cooper. *Australian Film: 1900-1977: A Guide to Feature Film Production*. Melbourne: Oxford University Press, 1980.
Pons, Xavier. *Henry Lawson, Out of Eden: A Psychoanalytic View*. Sydney: Angus and Robertson, 1984.
Powell, J. M. *Mirrors of the New World: Images and Image Makers in the Settlement Process*. Canberra: Australian National University Press, 1978.
Prichard, Katharine Susannah. *Coonardoo*. London: Jonathan Cape, 1929; rpt Sydney: Angus and Robertson, 1973.
Prout, Denton. *Henry Lawson: The Grey Dreamer*. Adelaide: Rigby, 1963.

Reed, Janet and Kathleen Oates. *Women in Australian Society 1901-1945: A Guide to the Holdings of Australian Archives.* Canberra: Australian Government Publishing Service, 1977.

Reiger, Kereen. *The Disenchantment of the Home: Modernizing the Australian Family 1880-1940.* Melbourne: Oxford University Press, 1985.

Reynolds, Henry. *The Other Side of the Frontier.* Townsville: James Cook University of North Queensland, 1981.

Richardson, Henry Handel. *The Fortunes of Richard Mahony* comprising vol. 1: *Australia Felix* (1917), vol. 2: *The Way Home* (1925) and vol. 3: *Ultima Thule* (1929). First published under one title London: Oxford University Press, 1930: rpt Melbourne: William Heinemann, 1948.

Roderick, Colin. *Henry Lawson: Poet and Short Story Writer.* Sydney: Angus and Robertson, 1966.

———. 'Lawson the Poet', *Bards, Bohemians, and Bookmen: Essays in Australian Literature,* 203-17. Edited by Leon Cantrell. St Lucia, Qld: University of Queensland Press, 1976.

———. *The Real Henry Lawson.* Adelaide: Rigby, 1982.

———. ed. *Henry Lawson: Autobiographical and Other Writings 1887-1922.* Sydney: Angus and Robertson, 1972.

———, ed. *Henry Lawson Collected Prose,* vol. 1: *Short Stories and Sketches, 1888-1922;* vol. 2: *Autobiographical and other Writings 1887-1922.* Sydney: Angus and Robertson, Memorial Edition, 1972.

———, ed. *Henry Lawson: Collected Verse,* vol. 1: *1885-1900* (1967); vol. 2: *1901-1909* (1968); vol. 3: *1910-1922* (1969). Sydney: Angus and Robertson, 1967-9.

———, ed. *Henry Lawson Criticism.* Sydney: Angus and Robertson, 1972.

———, ed. *Henry Lawson: Short Stories and Sketches 1888-1922.* Sydney: Angus and Robertson, 1972.

Rowse, Tim. *Australian Liberalism and National Character.* Melbourne: Kibble, 1978.

Said, Edward. *Orientalism.* New York: Pantheon, 1978.

———. 'The Problem of Textuality', *Critical Inquiry,* 4 (1978), 673-714.

Schaffer, Kathryn Lois. 'The "Place" of Woman in the Australian Tradition: An Analysis of the Discourse.' Ph.D. thesis. University of Pittsburgh, Pa., USA. May 1984.

———. 'Landscape Representation and National Identity', *Australian Journal of Cultural Studies,* 4, 2 (1987), 47–60.

Sheridan, Alan. *Michel Foucault: The Will to Truth.* London: Tavistock, 1980.

Sheridan, Susan. ' Review of *Who is She?: Images of Women in Australian Fiction',* *Australian Literary Studies,* 11, 9 (1984), 546-52.

———. ' "Temper Romantic: Bias, Offensively Feminine": Australian Women Writers and Literary Nationalism', *Kunapipi,* 7, 2 and 3 (1985), 49-58.

———. 'Women Writers', *A New Literary History of Australia.* Edited by L. T. Hergenhan. Ringwood, Vic.: Penguin, forthcoming (1988).

Silverman, Kaja. *The Subject of Semiotics.* Oxford: Oxford University Press, 1983.

Slemon, Stephen. 'Cultural Alterity and Colonial Discourse', *Southern Review,* 20 (Mar. 1987), 102-7.

Smith, Bernard. *The Antipodean Manifesto: Essays in Art and History.* Melbourne: Oxford University Press, 1976.

BIBLIOGRAPHY

———— . *European Vision and the South Pacific: 1768-1850: A Study in the History of Art and Ideas.* Oxford: Clarendon Press, 1969.

Stanton, Domna. 'Language and Revolution: the Franco-American Dis-Connection', *The Future of Difference*, 73-87. Edited by Hester Eisenstein and Alice Jardine. Boston: G.K. Hall, 1980.

Steer, Vicki. 'Australian National Identity: Rectifying an All-Male Perspective', 518-31. *Second Women and Labour Conference Papers*, Melbourne, 1980.

Stephens, A. G. 'A Poet's Mother', Red Page, *Bulletin*, 24 Oct. 1896. Rpt in *Selected Writings*, 68-271. Edited by Leon Cantrell. Sydney: Angus and Robertson, 1978.

———— . 'Art in Australia', *Henry Lawson Criticism*, 217. Edited by Colin Roderick. Sydney: Angus and Robertson, 1972.

———— . 'Lawson's Prose', *Bulletin*, 29 Aug. 1896. Rpt in *Henry Lawson Criticism*, 51-3. Edited by Colin Roderick. Sydney: Angus and Robertson, 1972.

Stokes, John Lort. *Discoveries in Australia: with an account of the coasts and rivers explored and surveyed during the voyage of H.M.S. Beagle, in the years 1837-1843.* 2 vols. London: T. & W. Boone, 1946. Rpt Adelaide: S.A. Libraries Board, 1969.

Summers, Anne. *Damned Whores and God's Police.* Ringwood, Vic.: Penguin, 1975.

———— . 'The Self Denied: Australian Women Writers—their Image of Women', *Refractory Girl*, 2 (Autumn 1973), 4-11.

———— , and Margaret Bettison. *Her Story: Australian Women in Print, 1788-1975.* Sydney: Hale and Iremonger, 1980.

Taylor, Paul. 'A Culture of Temporary Culture', *Art and Text*, 16 (1984-5), 94-108.

Teale, Ruth, ed. *Colonial Eve: Sources on Women in Australia, 1788-1914.* Melbourne: Melbourne University Press, 1978.

Todd, F. M. 'Henry Lawson', *Australian Literary Criticism*, 128-38. Edited by Grahame Johnston. Melbourne: Oxford University Press, 1962.

Turner, Graeme. *National Fictions: Literature, Film and the Construction of Australian Narrative.* Sydney: Allen and Unwin, 1986.

Turner, Ian. *Room for Manoeuvre: Writings on History, Politics, Ideas and Play.* Richmond, Vic: Drummond, 1982.

Walker, David. *Dream and Disillusion: A Search for Australian Cultural Identity.* Canberra: Australian National University Press, 1976.

———— . 'The Getting of Manhood', *Australian Popular Culture*, 121-144. Edited by Peter Spearitt and David Walker. Sydney: George Unwin and Allen, 1979.

Wallace-Crabbe, Chris, ed. *The Australian Nationalists: Modern Critical Essays.* Melbourne: Oxford University Press, 1971.

Ward, Russel. *The Australian Legend.* Melbourne: Oxford University Press, 1958, 2nd edn, 1965.

Webby, Elizabeth, 'Parents rather than Critics: Some Early Reviews of Australian Literature', *Bards, Bohemians, and Bookmen*, 19-38. Edited by Leon Cantrell. St Lucia, Qld: University of Queensland Press, 1976.

White, Haydon. *Metahistory: The Historical Imagination in Nineteenth Century Europe.* Baltimore: Johns Hopkins, 1973.

BIBLIOGRAPHY

White, Richard. 'The Importance of Being "Man",' *Australian Popular Culture*, 145-68. Edited by Peter Spearitt and David Walker. Sydney: George Allen and Unwin, 1979.

———. *Inventing Australia: Images and Identity, 1688-1980*. Sydney: George Allen and Unwin, 1983.

Wilkes, G. A. 'The Eighteen Nineties', *The Australian Nationalists: Modern Critical Essays*, 30-40. Edited by Chris Wallace-Crabbe. Melbourne: Oxford University Press, 1971.

———. *The Stockyard and the Croquet Lawn: Literary Evidence for Australia's Cultural Development*. Port Melbourne: Edward Arnold, 1981.

Williams, Raymond. *Culture*. London: Fontana, 1981.

Williamson, Kristin. 'Setting a Redback on our Psyche', *National Times on Sunday* (19 Oct. 1986), 28.

Windschuttle, Elizabeth, ed. *Women, Class and History: Feminist Perspectives on Australia, 1788-1978*. Sydney: Fontana, 1980.

Windsor, Gerard. 'Art or Antiques: A Review of "Portable Australian Authors: Barbara Baynton",' *Quadrant*, 25, 3 (Mar. 1981), 69.

Yong, C. F. *The New Gold Mountain: The Chinese in Australia 1901-1921*. Richmond, S.A.: Raphael Arts, 1977.

Zinkhan, E. J. 'Notes and Documents: Louisa Lawson's "The Australian Bush-Woman"—A Source for "The Drover's Wife" and "Water them Geraniums",' *Australian Literary Studies*, 10, 4 (Oct. 1982), 495-9.

INDEX

Aboriginal culture, 1-2, 58, 59, 189
Aborigines, xi, 2, 11, 67, 102, 172, 187
  as other, 23, 27, 102
  colonial perceptions of, 59, 99, 187
  exclusion from discourse, 49, 94, 95,
    96, 97, 195n
Adams, Arthur, 148
Adams, Frances, 44, 52
  on the bush, 57, 88
Advertiser, 43
Allen, Judith, 75
Australia:
  as body of woman, 61, 77-9
  as locus of desire, xi, 1, 3, 84
  cultural studies of, 16-18, 28, 29-34,
    65-70, 73-7, 85-91, 155, 179-81
  early historical descriptions of, 1, 59-60
  in relation to England, 16, 21, 38, 59,
    86, 180, 182
  see also bush; landscape
Australian character, 4, 8, 18-20, 42, 52,
  95-8, 176, 179-83
  as constituted by discourse, 10-11, 15-
    16, 80-1, 98, 117, 132
  as masculine construction, 4, 21, 42,
    118, 149, 172
Australian nationalism, 30, 32-3, 41, 46,
  76, 132, 148
  as construct of discourse, 16-18, 25-7,
    129-30
  as jealous mistress, 85-6
Australian tradition, 4, 29, 44
  A.A. Phillips as spokesman for, 14, 16,
    155-6
  as constituted by texual discourse, 15,
    18, 80-1, 105-6
  as construction of nation's idea of self, 15
  Lawson in, 20, 36, 39-40, 81, 113-18
Australian type:
  as Anzac soldier, 20, 115, 129, 182
  as bushman, 12, 20, 28, 116

  as bush Mum, 14, 132
  as cultural construction, 4, 8-9, 19-21
  as gold rush digger, 20, 97
  as Gough Whitlam, 21, 179, 182
  as Henry Lawson, 112-18
  as normative, 12-13
  as Paul Hogan, 11, 13, 20, 26
Aveling, Marian:
  on women in Australia history, 6

Barthes, Roland, 80
  on cultural myths, 18
Barrie, Lita, 144
Bates, Daisy, 63, 174
Baynton, Barbara, xiv, xv, 44
  as dissident within Australian tradition,
    xiv, 148, 155, 157, 159
  as a radically dissident writer, 27, 147,
    169
  biographical accounts of, 150-1, 155
  Bush Studies, 150, 154
  Christian imagery in, 167-8
  criticism of short stories, 150-2
  in relation to A.A. Phillips, 155-62
  in relation to Australian tradition, 148,
    150, 155, 169
  irony in, 149, 150-1, 163
  theme of the maternal in, 165-8
  woman as effect of discourse in, 155
  see also 'The Chosen Vessel'
Bicentenary:
  as focus for national identity, xi, 3, 172
Bicentennial Authority, xi, 2, 3
binary opposition:
  in A.A. Phillips' critique of Baynton, 157
  in discourse, 13-14
  in Lawson's prose, 125-6
  in myth of typical Australian, 19
  woman within, 69
Bird, Delys, 8

222